BASEBALL'S RESERVE SYSTEM

The Case and Trial of Curt Flood v. Major League Baseball

By Neil F. Flynn

Published by Walnut Park Group, Inc.
Springfield, Illinois
2006

BASEBALL'S RESERVE SYSTEM: THE CASE AND TRIAL OF CURT FLOOD V. MAJOR LEAGUE BASEBALL

Copyright© 2005 by Neil F. Flynn
All rights reserved.
Printed in the United States of America
Edited by James M. Morphew
Cover and book design by Charles J. Copley Graphics

Published by Walnut Park Group, Inc.
1035 South Second Street
Springfield, Illinois 62704
www.walnutparkgroup.com

Flynn, Neil F.
  Baseball's reserve system : the case and trial of
 Curt Flood v. Major League Baseball / Neil F. Flynn.
  p. cm.
  Includes bibliographical references.
  LCCN 2005937635
  ISBN 0-9776578-0-9

  1. Flood, Curt, 1938- 2. Baseball players--Salaries, etc.--United States--History. 3. Major League Baseball (Organization)--Trials, litigation, etc. 4. Free agents (Sports)--United States--History. 5. Baseball--Economic aspects--United States--History. 6. Industrial relations--United States--History. 7. Collective bargaining--Baseball--United States--History. I. Title

GV880.F55 2006   331.2'81796357'0973
                      QBI05-600215

  The material quoted on pages 39-44, 287, 294, 323-325 is copyright© 1991 by Marvin Miller. A Birch Lane Press Book by Carol Publishing Corp. All rights reserved. Reprinted by arrangement with Kensington Publishing Corp.
  Permission to reprint the quote on page 46 was granted by the rights holder of *Hardball: The Education of a Baseball Commissioner*, copyright 1987, Times Books.
  The quote on page 294 is from *The Brethren*, by Bob Woodward and Scott Armstrong (New York: Simon and Schuster Adult Publishing Group, copyright 1979). Reprinted by permission.
  The quote on page 184 is from *Memoirs of Bing Devine* (Sports Publishing L.L.C.; Champaign, Illinois, copyright 2004). Reprinted by permission.

To my parents,
Estelle and Francis Flynn

BASEBALL'S RESERVE SYSTEM: THE CASE AND TRIAL OF CURT FLOOD V. MAJOR LEAGUE BASEBALL

TABLE OF CONTENTS

Chapter 1 — Introduction 1

Chapter 2 — The 1967-68 Seasons 7

Chapter 3 — The Trade 11

Chapter 4 — Baseball's "Reserve System" 18

Chapter 5 — The Decision To Challenge 37

Chapter 6 — The Suit 48

Chapter 7 — Pre-Trial (January 16, 1970—May 18, 1970) 61

Chapter 8 — The Trial—Day One—May 19, 1970 68
  Testimony of Curt Flood
  Testimony of Marvin J. Miller

Chapter 9 — Day Two—Thursday, May 21, 1970 95
  Testimony of Jack R. (Jackie) Robinson
  Testimony of Henry (Hank) Greenberg
  Testimony of Marvin Miller (recalled)
  Testimony of James P. Brosnan

TABLE OF CONTENTS

Chapter 10 — Day Three—Friday, May 22, 1970 107
    Testimony of Robert R. Nathan

Chapter 11 — Day Four—Monday, May 25, 1970 112
    Testimony of Alvin R. (Pete) Rozelle

Chapter 12 — Day Five—Tuesday, May 26, 1970........................120
    Testimony of Walter J. Kennedy
    Testimony of Robert Alan Eagleson
    Testimony of Clarence Sutherland Campbell

Chapter 13 — Day Six—Wednesday, May 27, 1970.....................133
    Testimony of Bowie K. Kuhn

Chapter 14 — Day Seven—Thursday, May 28, 1970 157
    Testimony of Bowie K. Kuhn (continued)

Chapter 15 — Day Eight—Monday, June 1, 1970........................167
    Testimony of Charles S. ("Chub") Feeney

Chapter 16 — Day Nine—Tuesday, June 2, 1970 176
    Testimony of Charles S. ("Chub") Feeney (continued)
    Testimony of Vaughn P. ("Bing") Devine
    Testimony of Joseph Henry Garagiola
    Testimony of Joseph E. Cronin

Chapter 17 — Day Ten—Wednesday, June 3, 1970.....................190
    Testimony of Francis L. Dale
    Testimony of John J. McHale
    Testimony of Robert A. Reynolds

Chapter 18 — Day Eleven—Thursday, June 4, 1970 205
    Testimony of Robert A. Reynolds (continued)
    Testimony of Ewing F. Kauffman

Chapter 19 — Day Twelve—Friday, June 5, 1970 216
    Testimony of John J. Gaherin

Chapter 20 — Day Thirteen—Monday, June 8, 1970..................228
    Testimony of John Clark, Jr.

Chapter 21 — Day Fourteen—Tuesday, June 9, 1970 235
    Testimony of John Clark, Jr. (continued)
    Testimony of Marvin Miller (rebuttal)

Chapter 22 — Day Fifteen—Wednesday, June 10, 1970 249
    Testimony of Bill Veeck
    Testimony of John J. Gaherin (surrebuttal)

Chapter 23 — Post Trial...261

Chapter 24 — The Decision..274

Chapter 25 — The Appeal...286

Chapter 26 — The United States Supreme Court.......................293

Chapter 27 — The Aftermath of *Flood v. Kuhn* and the Era
    of Free Agency..310

Chapter 28 — Conclusions and Observations............................319

References and Sources 328

Cases..329

Answers to Trivia Questions 330

FOREWORD

Sometime back, during the Summer of 2001, I had occasion to converse with some old friends about St. Louis, Missouri (where I grew up), the neighborhood (Walnut Park), our childhood, the umpteen-hundred schoolyard and sandlot baseball, soccer, and football games in which we participated and, of course, to embellish on our accomplishments and successes in those games.

During that conversation, the subject of the St. Louis Cardinal baseball team came into focus. For those who did not grow up in St. Louis, or for those who are not baseball fans, the decade of the 1960s was an incredibly exciting time to be a Cardinal fan. For instance, in the 60s, the Cardinals won the World Championship in 1964 by beating Mickey Mantle, Whitey Ford, Elston Howard and the New York Yankees in a seven game series; won the World Championship in 1967 by defeating Carl Yastrzemski, Reggie Smith, Jim Lonborg and the Boston Red Sox in a seven game series; and lost the 1968 World Series to Denny McClain, Mickey Lolich, Al Kaline and the Detroit Tigers. In the 1960s, Cardinal fans had the great fortune to watch the likes of Bob Gibson, Tim McCarver, Bill White, Julian Javier, Dick Groat, Dal Maxvill, Ken Boyer, Mike Shannon, Lou Brock, Curt Flood, Roger Maris, Orlando Cepeda, Steve Carlton, Joe Torre and many others.

Baseball's Reserve System: The Case and Trial of Curt Flood v. Major League Baseball

As we discussed old times, someone recalled the lawsuit filed by Curt Flood against the major league baseball club owners and the Commissioner of Baseball following Curt Flood's trade to the Philadelphia Phillies after the 1969 season. What followed this recollection, however, was a somewhat puzzling discussion of the Curt Flood suit, its outcome and its significance.

One of the participants in this conversation described the event as Curt Flood's successful challenge of major league baseball's reserve system thereby ushering in the age of "free agency". Another participant described the event as Flood having lost the suit, but that his legal setback became the impetus for the start of the Major League Baseball Players' Association to be headed later by Marvin Miller. Other participants recalled that the United States Supreme Court had actually ruled in favor of the owners and the Commissioner of Baseball and against Curt Flood—but that the case was later settled out of court.

While the participants in the conversation certainly could not agree upon the details—much less the outcome or importance of the Flood case—the conversation then shifted to Curt Flood the individual, his motives, his arguments and what had become of the star center-fielder after the case. These points were discussed with at least as much, if not more, imprecision than the lawsuit itself.

A few months later, I decided to research this topic. During that time, I read a great deal about the Flood case and some of its background. For instance, I read Curt Flood's *The Way It Is*, a book which was written during the time of the trial in the summer of 1970. I also read Bowie Kuhn's *Hardball, The Education of a Baseball Commissioner*. Bowie Kuhn was the Commissioner of Major League Baseball and was also a named party-defendant in the Curt Flood suit. My background reading also included Marvin Miller's *A Whole Different Ball Game*. Marvin Miller was the Executive Director of the Major League Baseball Players' Association at and during the time of the Curt Flood lawsuit. Finally, I have read numerous law journal articles and commentary, some staunchly supportive and others highly critical of the U.S. Supreme Court's rationale and decision in *Flood v. Kuhn*. While there exists a substantial body of articles and commentary regarding the court's decision in *Flood v. Kuhn*, I was surprised how little I was able to find and read about the trial itself, including the parties, the lawyers, the judges, the witnesses, the issues, the strategy of the litigants, and the presentation of the arguments, testimony, and other evidence.

In the late Spring of 2002, and only after obtaining the invaluable assistance of several individuals, I was able to ascertain the location of the actual transcript of the 1970 trial of *Flood v. Kuhn*. Shortly thereafter, my good fortune continued and I was on my way to New York City where I procured a complete copy (over 2,000 pages) of the trial transcript and numerous other trial court documents. On the return flight home, I recall thinking that I had just rediscovered the "Rosetta stone". Needless to say, I was quite excited and could hardly wait to read it.

My interest and fascination with this story are reflected in the following pages. I sincerely hope that you enjoy it.

Acknowledgments

I need to acknowledge and thank so many individuals for their assistance, support, patience, encouragement and inspiration during the writing of this book. I want to acknowledge and to thank my good friends, Neil Houtsma, Bob Hall, Jerry Donovan, Rich Sullivan, Tom Londrigan, Alec Messina and my brother Dan for their review of various drafts and for their insightful and invaluable comments and suggestions; to Mark Edwards, Mike Barnstead and Mike Badger for their encouragement and for providing photos, trading cards and articles on the career of Curt Flood; to Jordan Call, Tom Murphy, Rich Prendergast, Jim Houlihan, Tom Walsh, Jon Ellis and Patrick, Kevin, Moira, Maggie and Suzanne Morphew, and to my sister Mary Frances and my brothers Mark, Tim and Dan for their continuing interest and unwavering encouragement; to my mother in law, Jean Schwab, for proofreading each and every draft and redraft from the beginning of this project; to Judge Harlington Wood and to U. S. Senator Richard Durbin and his staff, especially Bill Houlihan, for their efforts, guidance and assistance in obtaining copies of pertinent documents, transcripts and other public records; to Gene Callahan for his enthusiasm and for his assistance in obtain-

ACKNOWLEDGMENTS

ing various permissions from Major League Baseball; to Taylor Penseneau and Rick Davis for their kindness, their advice and generous assistance in the preparation and publication of this book; to the staff at the National Archives in New York City for their help in the preparation and retrieval of the trial transcript and other court documents.

Many thanks to Marvin Miller, Allan Zerman and Jay Topkis for taking the time to talk with me and for their recollections and helpful insight; and to the publishers, authors, and rights holders, including Simon and Schuster, Sports Publications, Topps Cards, Inc. and Marty Appel, who graciously granted me permission to use certain materials and to reprint and include various passages from their works.

A special thanks to my good friend Jim Morphew for his outstanding work and for generously giving of his time and talents to edit this book; and to my assistant and dear friend, Carole Bax, but for whose outstanding efforts, tireless work and commitment this book would not have been accomplished.

Finally, I want to acknowledge and to express my deepest gratitude and appreciation to my wife, Susan, my sons Daniel and Sean, and my daughter Mallory for their loving patience and for listening (sometimes repeatedly) to me describe each and every one of my "latest discoveries" during and throughout the writing of this book. More importantly, I thank my family for their constant source of love, devotion, support, encouragement and inspiration.

CHAPTER 1
INTRODUCTION

The date was Friday, January 16, 1970. Five days earlier, the underdog Kansas City Chiefs defeated the Minnesota Vikings 23-7 in New Orleans in Super Bowl IV; three months earlier, the "Miracle Mets" shocked the baseball world and defeated the Baltimore Orioles in five games to win the World Series; six months earlier, Bill Russell and the Boston Celtics defeated Wilt Chamberlain and the Los Angeles Lakers to win the NBA title (this was the Celtics eleventh title in thirteen seasons); six months earlier, the Montreal Canadians won their second consecutive Stanley Cup Championship by defeating the second year expansion St. Louis Blues—four games to none; St. Louis University had just defeated the University of San Francisco 4-0 to win its seventh NCAA Men's Soccer Championship in eleven years; six months earlier, the St. Philip Neri Soccer Club won its second consecutive (under-19) national championship; Joe Frazier was the heavyweight boxing champion of the world (Muhammad Ali's title was taken away in 1967); the year before, *Midnight Cowboy* won the Oscar for the Best Picture; President Richard Nixon had not yet completed his first year in office; war was continuing to rage in Southeast Asia; five months earlier, members of the Charles

Baseball's Reserve System: The Case and Trial of Curt Flood v. Major League Baseball

Manson cult brutally murdered eight people in Los Angeles, including actress Sharon Tate; six months earlier, 500,000 people attended the Woodstock Rock Festival at Max Yasgar's Farm; *Jesus Christ Superstar* had hit Broadway and was denounced by the Catholic Church; just months earlier, the American press discovered the U.S. military's coverup involving Lieutenant William Calley and the killing of Vietnamese civilians in what became known as the "My Lai Massacre"; the previous summer, Mary Jo Kopeckne, an aide to Senator Ted Kennedy drowned at Chappaquidick; less than six months earlier, astronaut Neil Armstrong uttered "That's one small step for man, one giant leap for mankind" from the surface of the moon during the Apollo 11 Mission; only days earlier, USC beat Michigan in the Rose Bowl 10-3; Penn State beat Missouri in the Orange Bowl 10-3; and Texas beat Notre Dame 21-17 to win the 1970 Cotton Bowl; Steve Owens from Oklahoma had just won the Heisman Trophy; and political and antiwar protests were not just limited to college campuses.

Three months earlier, Curtis Charles Flood had just finished what would turn out to be his last season with the St. Louis Cardinals. On October 8, 1969, following the Cardinals disappointing fourth place finish in the National League, the St. Louis Cardinals traded center fielder Curt Flood to the Philadelphia Phillies in a seven player deal. At the time of the trade, Flood was thirty-one years old, at the top of his game, and in the prime of his life.

Flood had been the starting center fielder for the St. Louis Cardinals since 1961. He played on the Cardinals 1964 World Series Championship team that beat the New York Yankees in what turned out to be the last World Series for the likes of Mickey Mantle, Whitey Ford, Elston Howard and Tony Kubek. In 1965, Flood became one of the team's co-captains and remained such until the 1969 season. Flood was also a key component of the 1967 Cardinals World

CHAPTER 1: INTRODUCTION

Series Championship team that defeated Carl Yastrzemski and the Boston Red Sox in a seven game series (in which Cardinal pitcher Bob Gibson pitched and won three complete games and gave up only 3 runs). During the 1967 season, Flood had a batting average of .335.

In 1968, Flood again led the Cardinals in winning their second consecutive National League pennant—their third in five seasons. In 1968, however, the Cardinals lost a heartbreaking seventh game to the Detroit Tigers (including 31 game winner Denny McClain, Mickey Lolich, Al Kaline, Willie Horton, Norm Cash and Bill Freehan). During his twelve seasons with the Cardinals, Flood won seven Gold Glove awards, had a 255 errorless game streak (a record), played in three All-Star Games, and was regarded by many as the best defensive center fielder in major league baseball.

In professional baseball, as well as in other professional sports, trades are not an uncommon occurrence. What was different, and indeed extraordinary about this trade, however, was that Curtis Charles Flood refused to recognize the "right" of the Cardinals to assign his contract or to "trade" him to the Philadelphia Phillies (or any other team for that matter) without his approval. In doing so, Flood challenged a practice which was invented, designed, implemented and rigorously enforced by the club owners for over 80 years—a practice frequently referred to and better known as "the reserve system".

While Curt Flood was not the first person or major league player to challenge baseball's reserve system, the timing of Flood's lawsuit must be placed in its proper perspective. It was the late 1960s—a decade of great racial tension and unrest; the Vietnam War was dividing the country; and now Curt Flood, a black man, was going to challenge the lily-white major league baseball establishment, and in the process, Flood would argue that despite being paid

Baseball's Reserve System: The Case and Trial of Curt Flood v. Major League Baseball

$90,000 annually, baseball's reserve system was tantamount to slavery and peonage.

It was on January 16, 1970 that Curtis Charles Flood filed suit challenging major league baseball's "reserve system". His challenge manifested itself in a landmark case tried in the Federal District Court in New York City during the spring of 1970, and ultimately decided by the U.S. Supreme Court in June 1972. Flood's case was simple. He argued that under the reserve system, a player was prohibited from exercising certain rights guaranteed to all citizens under the United States Constitution, and that consequently, under baseball's reserve system, a player was reduced to a mere piece of property. Flood further argued that once he signed a contract (in his case, when he was eighteen years old with the Cincinnati Reds in 1957), he was "owned" by that team for life. His "owner" could, without the consent or without consulting the player, trade, sell, assign any and all rights of the player to any other team. Further, under the "reserve system", if a player and owner could not agree on the terms of a contract for any given year, the player could not lawfully negotiate or talk to any other team or seek employment with any other team; and no team could lawfully seek to hire or enter into any negotiations with the player. Moreover, and as long as the owner tendered a contract to the player by March 1st of the playing season (even if that contract reduced the player's salary by as much as 20% from the level of the previous year's salary), the player's options were as follows: sign the contract or retire from professional baseball. In other words, even if the player refused to sign a contract for any playing season, the "reserve system" prohibited the player from negotiating his services to any other team, and no team could offer employment or otherwise negotiate with that player.

Again, Flood's case was simple. He maintained that the "reserve system", irrespective of its origins, its "benefits" to

Chapter 1: Introduction

the game and to the "integrity of the sport", was a system of collusion among the owners which operated to unlawfully restrict his right to make a living and make his services available to a willing employer. He maintained that the "reserve system" violated the federal antitrust laws (most notably the Sherman Act and the Clayton Act); violated a variety of state antitrust laws (both statutory and common law); that the reserve system was tantamount to slavery in violation of the Thirteenth Amendment of the United States Constitution; and that the "reserve system" was the equivalent of "peonage" and, as such, was in violation of federal law.

In June of 1972, after a two and a half year legal battle, the U.S. Supreme Court denied Flood any relief from the "reserve system". Although many law journal articles have analyzed the Supreme Court's decision, relatively little has been written about the trial itself and the testimony and other evidence actually presented by Plaintiff Curt Flood and by the defendants.

In its analysis and decision in *Flood v. Kuhn*, the U.S. Supreme Court relied upon two prior U.S. Supreme Court decisions—*Federal Baseball Club of Baltimore v. National League of Professional Baseball Clubs* (1922) and *Toolson v. New York Yankees* (1953). Very generally, these cases held that professional baseball was not "interstate commerce", and accordingly, major league baseball was not subject to the federal antitrust statutes. It must be emphasized that this "baseball exemption" was not created by Congress and is mentioned nowhere in the Sherman Act or the Clayton Act—but rather, the exemption was created by the Supreme Court itself in its 1922 decision in *Federal Baseball*. It is also crucial to note that between 1953 (the year of the *Toolson* decision) and 1972 (the year of the Supreme Court's decision in *Flood v. Kuhn*), the federal courts held that professional football, professional basketball, professional boxing and the professional theatrical arts industry were indeed subject to the federal antitrust statutes and regulation. In other words, the Supreme Court of the United States ruled that professional baseball, separate and distinct from *all other professional sports* and entertainment, was exempt from federal antitrust regulation—a result which the Supreme Court itself concluded was "irrational" and "inconsistent".

Flood was thirty-one years old after the 1969 season and thirty-two when the trial began in May of 1970. He was still in the prime of his playing career. Although Flood made a short comeback with the Washington Senators during the 1971 season, Flood's decision to challenge organized baseball cost him his baseball career, and much more. Despite the U.S. Supreme Court's denial of Flood's claims and holding that baseball was exempt from antitrust regulation, professional baseball players had "free agency" by 1975—without the passage of an Act of Congress and without the reversal of the Supreme Court's decision in *Flood v. Kuhn.*

CHAPTER 2
THE 1967-68 SEASONS

In 1970, Flood wrote that the 1967-68 St. Louis Cardinals team "must have been the most remarkable team in the history of baseball." Interestingly, Flood emphasized the team's social achievements, without which the team's on-the-field victories and accomplishments would have been less triumphant, and far less important. In his 1970 book, *The Way It Is*, Flood also made some remarkable observations about a number of his Cardinal teammates. One need not be a history professor to recall the many explosive racial incidents and incendiary political and social events of the 1960s. In sharp contrast, Flood wrote that the individual Cardinal players were as free of bigotry and "racist poison" as any group of twentieth-century Americans could possibly have been. It was Flood's view that not many of his teammates had been that way before joining the Cardinals, but that they had changed.

Flood credits fellow black teammate Bob Gibson as the person most responsible for building the spirit of that team and for knocking down the traditional barriers to establish communications with the "palefaces". Actual friendships developed. Flood described a young, white Tim McCarver as a rugged kid and as a "peckerwood" from Tennessee, "and we were the black, black cats." The barriers began to topple—and in 1965, Flood and McCarver were named the team's co-captains.

Flood reflected that the 1967-68 Cardinal team's unique unity was solidified by several players with unpromising reputations. Before the 1967 season, the Cardinals acquired Orlando Cepeda (affectionately nicknamed "Cha Cha") in a trade with the San Francisco Giants. (For you serious baseball fans, who did the Cardinals trade for Orlando Cepeda?) Flood recalls that Cepeda had been traded after being described as having "too much Latin temperament" and being a "prima donna" by some sports media and baseball writers. Flood's version was that Cepeda was "out of his tree" with frustration over the intellectual and spiritual meanness of the Giants' management. Upon arriving in St. Louis, Cepeda was welcomed into a genuinely civilized atmosphere where, according to Flood, Cepeda responded with high energy, enthusiasm and tremendous batting power.

The 1967 Cardinals also included the likes of Roger Maris. Many of the Cardinal players were apprehensive about Maris joining the 1967 squad. The press in New York had characterized the Yankee star as an egocentric grouch. Would he fit in? Flood wrote that Maris was "a great guy" and a veteran player who loved the Cardinals' atmosphere. Although Maris was a "hard used 33 years old" and was hampered by the effects of many injuries, Flood unequivocally asserted that Maris was as instrumental as anyone in the Cardinal successes of 1967 and 1968.

If you believed what the sportswriters were saying at the time, another "human porcupine" was ace pitcher Bob Gibson. Not only was Gibson accused of being a super-militant black, he supposedly enjoyed making people feel uncomfortable about it. The truth, according to Flood, was that Gibson tolerated no "racist garbage", and he was more interested in ending racial estrangement than accentuating it.

CHAPTER 2: THE 1967-68 SEASONS

By the summer of 1970, Flood had filed and lost his suit against major league baseball in the United States District Court (the trial court); he had experienced a long and painful trial which was not attended by a single active major league baseball player; he was experiencing serious financial difficulty with his painting and portrait businesses; and the likelihood of winning his lawsuit on appeal was uncertain. Perhaps most importantly, Flood was unsure whether, at age 32, he would ever play professional baseball again.

Despite these setbacks, Flood's 1970 recollections of the 1967-68 Cardinals and their accomplishments were anything but bitter or resentful. Flood credited the "volatile" Cepeda, the "impossible" Maris and the "impenetrable" Gibson as three of the most important ingredients of the Cardinal success. He referred to the Cardinal squad as an amalgamation of Latins, blacks, liberal whites and "redeemed peckerwoods"—victorious on and off the baseball diamond. Flood also recalled that the Cardinals of 1967 and 1968 loved what they had accomplished, and that they believed the Cardinal team consisted of the "greatest bunch of human beings on earth". Based upon conversations with players on other teams, Flood wrote that the Cardinals of 1967-68 were the envy of the league not only because of their playing ability and winning seasons, but also because of their camaraderie and team unity.

In 1967, Curt Flood had a batting average of .335 and, in 1964, Flood tied with Roberto Clemente for the most hits (211) in the National League. Many regarded Curt Flood as the best defensive centerfielder in professional baseball. Led by the incredible pitching of Bob Gibson and Steve Carlton; the infield of Mike Shannon (3rd), Dal Maxvill (SS), Julian Javier (2nd), Orlando Cepeda (1st), and the outfield of Roger Maris (RF), Lou Brock (LF) and Curt Flood (CF), the Cardinals dominated the National League, won the pennant by ten games, and went on to defeat the Boston Red Sox in seven games to win the World Series.

In 1968, Flood's batting average was .301 and finished the season with 186 hits. Again. the Cardinals (nicknamed "El Birdos" by then Cardinal radio announcer, Harry Caray) dominated the National League, won the pennant, and went on to play the Detroit Tigers in the 1968 World Series. Undoubtedly, the 1968 Cardinals were the most exciting team in baseball that year. Despite the awesome talent and the team's unparalleled camaraderie, the Cardinals lost a gut wrenching (assuming you were a Cardinal fan) seven game World Series. Ironically, some commentators branded Curt Flood the Series "goat" for misjudging Jim Northrup's fly ball in the top of the seventh inning of Game Seven. Despite the successes of 1967 and 1968, the 1969 Cardinals' season would soon prove to be a very different story.

Chapter 3
The Trade

Following the 1968 season, the players' pension negotiations between the Major League Baseball Players' Association and the owners became contentious and divisive. In short, the owners attempted to sever the link between the players' pension fund and baseball's radio and television revenues. The Players' Association maintained that these revenues should be shared between the league and the players' pension and retirement plan. To apply some pressure, many players refused to sign their individual salary contracts for the 1969 season until the owners agreed to improvements in the players' retirement plan.

After these negotiations concluded in an acceptable compromise, several of the Cardinals' key players "added insult to injury" by demanding substantial salary increases. Flood had been offered, but rejected a salary of $77,500 for the 1969 season. Flood "held out" and did not sign his 1969 contract until March 3, 1969—for $90,000. Bob Gibson, Lou Brock, Tim McCarver and several other Cardinal players had also negotiated substantial salary increases for the 1969 season. As a result, August A. Busch, Jr., beer magnate and owner of the Cardinals, became the owner of the highest player payroll in major league baseball.

Baseball's Reserve System: The Case and Trial of Curt Flood v. Major League Baseball

For the 1969 Cardinals, change was in the air. After the 1968 season, Roger Maris retired from baseball. More was about to change-and rapidly! Flood recalled that the Cardinal owner commenced the 1969 season with a "spectacular tantrum" during which Mr. Busch distorted the team's attitudes toward the game of baseball, Cardinal fans and toward the team's owner himself.

On March 22, 1969, during spring training, August A. Busch, Jr. set the stage by ordering all of the Cardinal players to a special meeting in St. Petersburg, Florida—the site of the Cardinals' training camp. This event was not intended to be an ordinary meeting among the owner, players and coaching staff. For this meeting, Mr. Busch summoned the corporate directors and officers, the players and coaching staff, and he invited the press.

According to Flood, August Busch delivered "the speech" during which he questioned the integrity of the players' attitudes; accused the players of upstaging and disrespecting devoted Cardinal fans; questioned the players' commitment to their professional baseball efforts; deplored the tactics and methods of the players' union; and depicted the players as a rabble of ingrates. After totally humiliating the entire Cardinal squad, Mr. Busch did manage to exhort his team to go win another pennant in 1969. Despite winning two successive pennants, to the Cardinal owner, the players were still "livestock". Flood wrote that the players had been put in their place, that the team was demoralized, and that the 1969 season was lost before it ever started.

Just a few days after "the speech", the Cardinals' front office announced the trade of one of the team's most popular players, first baseman, Orlando Cepeda. (Another trivia question. For whom did the Cardinals trade Orlando Cepeda?) To Flood, Cepeda had symbolized the cohesiveness of the 1967-68 Cardinals, and with this trade, "the glue was gone" and "the great Cardinals were all washed up."

Chapter 3: The Trade

Flood wrote that the 1969 Cardinals became a "morose and touchy team", whose concentration suffered as did the remarkable spirit of fraternity that had helped the Cardinals dominate the National League for the last two seasons. The players no longer believed that they played for the best organization in baseball. To the players, the front office seemed intent on reinstating conventional relations with the players, a condition that Flood said finds the players "in a constant state of terrified insecurity." So the 1969 Cardinals began to behave like conventional baseball players, they grumbled and they groused.

As the 1969 season progressed, Flood began to realize that his departure became a foregone conclusion. Flood recalled that he had long been known throughout the league as an "agitator" in that he spoke out against the doubleheader, the 162-game season as well as against the inequities and outrageousness of baseball's reserve system. During the 1969 season, Flood's outspokenness was even more vigorous and even ended up in newspaper articles—and sometimes not too anonymously. Especially at $90,000 a year, this behavior did not sit well with the Cardinals' management.

In furtherance of Mr. Busch's assertion that some of the "high priced" players were not "sufficiently dedicated" to their baseball professions, Flood recollected that Cardinal management complained about Lou Brock's auto dealership and flower shop; nagged Cardinal pitcher Nelson Briles about his electronics dealership; pitcher Bob Gibson about his business interests in Omaha, Nebraska; and catcher Tim McCarver about his restaurant business in Memphis. Now that Flood's name was associated with a photography business along with his painting of oil portraits, how could Flood ever keep his mind on baseball?

When Flood later attempted to invoke a provision in his (as well as every player's) contract to avoid what Flood believed to be commercial exploitation by businessmen and advertisers seeking product and service endorsements, the Cardinals' management reacted harshly, and pointed out that those "player endorsements" were "interviews" and "promotional undertakings" for "the betterment of the game". In the eyes of the Cardinal ownership, he had indeed committed another "mortal sin" against "the good of the game".

Flood wrote about what he referred to as the "tensest episode " of the 1969 season. Late in the 1969 season, while the Cardinals still had a mathematical chance of winning the Eastern Division, Flood suspected that the front office had given up on the 1969 season and that the management had decided to "build for the future". Flood believed that the Cardinal front office had ordered Cardinal manager Red Schoendienst to begin playing a couple of young players regularly in the lineup, first baseman Joe Hague and catcher Ted Simmons. An angry Flood surmised that the front office was intentionally sabotaging the team's pennant chances; was intentionally preventing Flood and other veteran players from having good seasons; and concluded that the Cardinal management would "rub it in" during next year's contract negotiations. After confronting manager Red Schoendienst, Flood was convinced beyond doubt that the batting order and lineup changes had been ordered by the front office.

More angered than before, Flood relayed his feelings to a reporter for the *St. Louis Globe-Democrat*. The next day, reporter Jack Herman published Flood's views that the top management had "tossed in the towel" for 1969. Although Herman attributed Flood's remarks to "an unnamed veteran", Cardinal General Manager Bing Devine's response had an ominous tone. Devine was quoted as saying that the only reason the regulars and veterans were complaining was that they were fearful of losing their jobs.

Chapter 3: The Trade

The 1969 Cardinals finished fourth in the National League's Eastern Division, thirteen games behind the New York Mets. Despite the fourth place finish, Flood had hit safely 173 times—eleventh in the National League. Although his .285 batting average was lower than his usual, only 19 full-time players in the National League had higher averages that year. But the 1969 season was now over and none of that mattered. What followed was a phone call on the morning of October 8, 1969—a call that would change Flood's life—and perhaps change baseball.

That morning, Flood was in his St. Louis apartment preparing to leave on a trip to Copenhagen, Denmark—one of his favorite places. The phone rang. It was Jim Toomey, who Flood described as a "middle-echelon coffee drinker" in the front office of the St. Louis Cardinals. Flood recalled the conversation as cold, succinct, and painfully to the point. Toomey told Flood that he and teammates Tim McCarver, Joe Hoerner and Byron Browne had been traded to the Phillies for Richie Allen, Cookie Rojas and Jerry Johnson. Toomey's only other commentary was "Good luck, Curt", and "Thanks a lot". Flood wrote that he, a "hard boiled realist", was "a weeping child" by the time he hung up the phone; and that he spent the remainder of that day in his apartment and answered none of the continuously incoming phone calls.

St. Louis National Baseball Club, Inc.

October 8, 1969

Mr. Curtis C. Flood
4466 West Pine
St. Louis, Missouri 63108

Dear Curt:

Enclosed herewith is Player Report Notice #614 covering the OUTRIGHT assignment of your contract to the Philadelphia Club of the National League, October 8, 1969.

Best of luck.

Sincerely yours,

Bing Devine
General Manager

BD:maq
enc.

AUGUST A. BUSCH, JR., PRESIDENT / BUSCH MEMORIAL STADIUM / ST. LOUIS, MISSOURI 63102 / 314-421-3060

General Manager Bing Devine's "trade letter" to Curt Flood dated October 8, 1969.

Chapter 3: The Trade

> **NOTICE TO PLAYER** No. 614
>
> **NOTICE TO PLAYER OF RELEASE OR TRANSFER**
> NATIONAL LEAGUE
>
> *October 8*, 19*69*
>
> To Mr. *Curtis Charles Flood*
>
> You are hereby notified as follows:
> 1. ~~That you are unconditionally released.~~
> 2. That your contract has been assigned to the *Philadelphia*
> Club of *National* League. ~~(a) Without right of recall.~~
>   ~~(b) With right of recall.~~
>
> (Cross out parts not applicable. In case of optional agreement, specify all conditions affecting player.)
>
> ST. LOUIS NATIONAL BASEBALL CLUB, INC.
>   Corporate Name of Club.
>   President
>
> ☞ Copy must be delivered to player; also forwarded to President of League of which Club is a member, and to the Commissioner.

The "postcard notice" of the Assignment of Flood's contract to the Philadelphia Phillies dated October 8, 1969.

Chapter 4
Baseball's Reserve System

While a comprehensive analysis of the origins of the "reserve system" is beyond the scope of this work, it is nonetheless important to have some understanding of its origin and the historical context in which the reserve system commenced. On February 2, 1876, the National League, the oldest league in professional sports, adopted its constitution and thereby came into legal existence. The new league had only eight teams. Each of these teams, however, enjoyed certain exclusive rights and a territorial monopoly. The League founders believed that by limiting the number of teams, this would reduce the demand for players and drive down player salaries, and consequently, increase the owners' profits.

By the 1879 season, the National League was in serious financial trouble and struggling to maintain it existence. In an effort to address these economic difficulties, the owners decided to curtail (secretly) the unrestrained competition for the services of baseball players. Under this approach to limit competition, each team was allowed to "reserve" five players on its roster. Once a player was "reserved" by his team, no other team could attempt to negotiate or "tamper" with that "reserved player".

Chapter 4: Baseball's Reserve System

By 1883, the "reserve system" was expanded to cover and bind every player on every team's roster. As a result of this practice, team owners were no longer required to compete financially for the services of the players. As the owners expected, salaries of the players fell dramatically. As evidence of this impact, players' salaries fell from approximately sixty (60) percent of total team revenues to below fifteen (15) percent on average.[1]

The next step in the progression of the "reserve system" dealt with the National Leagues's rival—the American League. The reserve system was no longer an intra-league issue and matter, its application was now expanded to inter-league competition for players. In 1903, the National League signed an agreement with a rival league, the American League, in which the leagues agreed to respect each other's player reservation rights and effectively divided the market for players. The league structure as embodied in that 1903 agreement has remained virtually unchanged for about 100 years.[2]

Anti-trust Challenges to Baseball's Reserve System

By 1911, game attendance throughout both leagues was strong and on the rise. The average player's annual salary was under $2500. Beginning in 1913, baseball's reserve system would be impacted by yet another major development— the formation of a new league- the Federal League. Interestingly, the new Federal League owners did not utilize a "reserve system" to attract and maintain quality players. Rather, Federal League owners attempted to attract major league players with the incentive of long term contracts.

---

[1] Roger Abrams, *Legal Bases: Baseball and the Law*, 46-47.

[2] Gerald W. Scully, *The Business of Major League Baseball*, p. 14.

Baseball's Reserve System: The Case and Trial of Curt Flood v. Major League Baseball

From 1913-1915, approximately 240 major league baseball players "defected from" the National and American Leagues (Major League Baseball) to the Federal League. By 1915, the two rival leagues continued to bid for the services of quality players and, as a result, the profitability of both leagues was negatively and significantly impacted.

In November 1915, Major League Baseball and the Federal League entered into an agreement pursuant to which the Federal League would dissolve. This agreement also provided that the Federal League owners (except one) would be compensated in the amount of $600,000.

The one team excluded from this settlement agreement was the Baltimore Terrapins. The worlds of major league baseball and antitrust regulation were on a collision course.

Federal Baseball Club of Baltimore, Inc. v. National League of Professional Baseball Clubs (Federal Baseball)

In 1916, the Federal Baseball Club of Baltimore filed a suit against major league baseball alleging various antitrust violations of the Sherman Act and the Clayton Act. The suit was filed in the Supreme Court of the District of Columbia. Despite obtaining a favorable judgment at the trial court level, that decision was overturned by the Court of Appeals for the District of Columbia. The Court of Appeals held that baseball was neither *interstate* activity, nor an activity of *commerce*. (In order for the Sherman Act to apply, the plaintiff had to establish that the activity complained of was commerce, and that this commerce was interstate in nature.)

In 1922, the U.S. Supreme Court affirmed the Appellate Court's decision. Justice Oliver Wendell Holmes authored this Supreme Court decision in which major league baseball's antitrust exemption was first created. In pertinent part, Holmes wrote:

"...The business is giving exhibitions of base ball [sic],

CHAPTER 4: BASEBALL'S RESERVE SYSTEM

which are purely state affairs. It is true that, in order to attain for these exhibitions the great popularity that they have achieved, competitions must be arranged between clubs from different cities and States. But the fact that in order to give the exhibitions the Leagues must induce free persons to cross state lines and must arrange and pay for their doing so is not enough to change the character of the business..."

It is upon this passage and the Court's holding in *Federal Baseball* that baseball's longstanding exemption from federal antitrust law was based.

There is little doubt that if *Federal Baseball* had been litigated in the year 2000, the decision would have been quite different. Baseball is today—and has been for many years—unquestionably a business that is interstate in nature. While the Supreme Court's opinion in *Federal Baseball* can be (and has been) criticized, it is important to recall that in 1922, the Supreme Court had also held that product manufacturing was a purely state-regulated activity and therefore outside the scope of the Sherman Act. If, in 1922, product manufacturing was not deemed to be "interstate commerce", then it may not be completely inconsistent to also conclude that baseball games, which are *played* entirely within a state's boundaries, are not interstate commerce. Finally, Holmes' opinion in *Federal Baseball* was not limited to the determination that baseball was purely an intrastate activity. Holmes' opinion also concluded that "exhibitions" of baseball were not commerce at all. The next significant court challenge would not occur until 27 years later.

Gardella v. Chandler

In 1945-46, immediately after World War II, several major league players were offered more lucrative contracts to play professional baseball in the Mexican League. Three St.

Louis Cardinal star players, Max Lanier, Lou Klein and Fred Martin, Dodger catcher Mickey Owen, and St. Louis Browns shortstop Vern Stephens were among the Mexican League's first major acquisitions. For a while there was panic among the National and American League owners that the Mexican League would emerge as a legitimate league and a competitor for the top players. By the end of 1946, it became clear that the Mexican League did not have the financial resources to sustain a competitive challenge to professional baseball in the United States.

In June of 1946, then Commissioner of Baseball, Albert "Happy" Chandler, decreed that the U.S. players who "jumped" to the Mexican League would be *banned* from major league baseball *for five years*. (It is noteworthy that the players in question denied that they had "jumped" or otherwise "breached" their contracts, but rather had signed to play in the Mexican League only *after* their existing contracts had *expired*.) One of the players banned for playing professional baseball in the Mexican League was New York Giants' Danny Gardella. By every account, Gardella was a journeyman player who made the most of the opportunity to play major league ball while so many other players were off fighting during the War. Gardella's "sin" was that he agreed to play in 1946 for the Vera Cruz team of the Mexican League-a team not officially recognized by major league baseball.

In October of 1947, Danny Gardella filed a suit against the Commissioner and all of major league baseball to recover treble damages for certain antitrust violations of the Sherman Act and the Clayton Act. In his case, Gardella argued that the "reserve clause" of the standard player contract deprived Gardella of his means of livelihood; and that organized baseball's enforcement of the "reserve clause" constituted a monopoly and unlawful restraint of trade in violation of the these federal antitrust statutes. On July 13,

CHAPTER 4: BASEBALL'S RESERVE SYSTEM

1948, the U.S. District Court for the Southern District of New York dismissed the *Gardella* suit for lack of jurisdiction, citing the U.S. Supreme Court's decision in *Federal Baseball* as authority for its ruling. The District Court concluded that the U.S. Supreme Court's decision in *Federal Baseball* had exempted all of baseball—including baseball's reserve system—from antitrust regulation.

It is interesting to note that in *Gardella v. Chandler*, the Commissioner and other defendants raised an argument which would again be at the heart of the Major League Baseball's defense twenty years later in *Flood v. Kuhn*. Chandler and the other defendants argued that "organized baseball", which supplies millions of Americans with desirable diversion, would be unable to exist without the "reserve clause".

On February 9, 1949, the Appellate Court in *Gardella v. Chandler* reversed the trial court and remanded the case for a trial on the issue of whether the "reserve clause" violated the antitrust Acts. Not coincidentally, on June 5, 1949, Commissioner Chandler offered an "amnesty" to all of the players—except Gardella—who had "defected" to the Mexican League. Thereafter, on October 8, 1949, prior to the commencement of the trial, the *Gardella v. Chandler* "reserve clause" litigation was settled out of court. The settlement included a cash payment to Gardella in the amount of $60,000.

For the time being, Major League Baseball had successfully defused the *Gardella* case with an amnesty and an out of court settlement. Commissioner Chandler was quoted in the press as saying "I'm so relieved, if I were a drinking man, I'd get drunk." Incidentally, Danny Gardella returned to the major leagues and played in one game and had one at bat in what would be his last season in 1950—with the St. Louis Cardinals!

The significance of the Appellate Court's (2nd Circuit) decision in *Gardella* cannot be underestimated. For the first time in American jurisprudence, a federal court specifically held that the *business of baseball* was *interstate commerce*; that federal court's do have jurisdiction over the business of baseball; and that the business of baseball, including baseball's reserve system, was indeed subject to—and not exempt from—the federal antitrust Acts. (It was the same 2nd Circuit Appellate Court that would hear Curt Flood's appeal twenty-two years later.)

Toolson v. New York Yankees, Inc.

Just four years after *Gardella* was decided, baseball's antitrust exemption would again reach the U.S. Supreme Court in *Toolson v. New York Yankees, Inc.* George Earl Toolson was a minor league baseball player in the New York Yankee organization. The Yankees assigned Toolson's contract to the Binghamton club, another minor league team. As a result of Toolson's refusal to report to the Binghamton club pursuant to the standard player contract and the regulations of "organized baseball", Toolson was placed on the "ineligible list" by Commissioner Chandler and thereby prohibited from playing professional baseball.

Toolson filed suit in the United States District Court for the Southern District of California. Toolson claimed that baseball's reserve system pursuant to which he was "owned" by the Yankees, violated the federal antitrust Acts and that he was thereby deprived of his livelihood. The District Court, relying upon *Federal Baseball*, dismissed Toolson's suit and upheld baseball's antitrust exemption. On December 12, 1952, the U.S. Court of Appeals for the Ninth Circuit affirmed the District Court's decision.

Toolson's suit reached the U.S. Supreme Court in 1953. The significance of *Toolson* was that for the first time, the issue before the U. S. Supreme Court was the legality of baseball's *reserve system* itself. In a short *per curium* opinion,[3] and without reexamining the underlying issues, the Supreme Court affirmed baseball's antitrust exemption on the authority and precedent of *Federal Baseball*.

In *Toolson*, the U.S. Supreme Court 1) specifically decided *not* to reexamine the underlying facts of the *Toolson* case *nor* reexamine the bases for the Court's decision in *Federal Baseball*; 2) reasoned that the business of baseball and the major league baseball club owners had relied upon (and apparently had a right to rely upon) the Court's 1922 decision in *Federal Baseball*; 3) determined that Congress had not intended to bring baseball "within the scope of the federal antitrust laws"; and 4) concluded that if there are "evils in this field which now warrant application to it of the antitrust laws", those "evils" must be addressed by legislation passed by the Congress, and not by Supreme Court decision.

In 1952, after extended hearings, a Subcommittee of the House of Representatives Judiciary Committee on the Study of Monopoly Power issued its report dealing with organized baseball in relation to the Sherman Act. Clarifying its position with respect to four bills then pending before Congress, the Subcommittee did *not* take the position that organized baseball and other professional sports were already exempt from the broad coverage of the Sherman Act. To the contrary, the Subcommittee stated as follows:

"Four bills have been introduced in the Congress, three in the House, one in the Senate, *intending to give baseball and all other professional sports a complete and unlimited immunity from the antitrust laws*. The requested exemption would extend to all professional sports enterprises and to all acts in the conduct of such enterprises. The law would no longer require competition in any facet of business activity of any

---

[3] *per curiam* means "by the court". A per curium decision means the opinion was issued as an opinion of the whole court as distinguished from an opinion written by any one judge or judges.

sport enterprise. ...*Such a broad exemption could not be granted without substantially repealing the antitrust laws."*

The House Subcommittee was chaired by Congressman Emmanuel Celler of New York. The Subcommittee heard testimony from many baseball players, club owners and industry representatives. In fact, Chairman Celler would be heard to complain of the level and intensity of the lobbying effort saying, "I want to say...that I have never known, in my 35 years of experience, of as great a lobby as that descended upon the House than the organized baseball lobby. ...They came upon Washington like locusts."[4]

It is important to note that the House Subcommittee actually suspended its consideration of legislation which would have specifically exempted baseball and other professional sports from the federal antitrust Acts *in anticipation of the U.S. Supreme's Court's decision* in the *Toolson* case. Ironically, in *Toolson,* the Supreme Court affirmed baseball's antitrust exemption in anticipation that Congress would definitively address the issue by legislation.

The Court in *Toolson* reasoned that, for over 30 years, the Congress was aware and continued to be aware of the U.S. Supreme Court's decision in *Federal Baseball.* Since during that thirty year period, Congress failed to pass legislation which would clarify, limit or "overturn" baseball's antitust exemption established by *Federal Baseball,* the Supreme Court apparently concluded that by this Congressional "inaction" or "acquiesence", Congress was expressing its intent to continue baseball's antitrust exemption.

A careful review of the record and chronology of relevant events calls this judicial analysis and reasoning into serious question. It is critical to note that all of the bills then pending before Congress would have continued baseball's antitrust exemption by specifically adding appropriate amendatory

---

[4] Abrams, *supra.*

language to the Sherman Act and the Clayton Act. If, as the Supreme Court held, it was Congress's intent to leave baseball's antitrust exemption intact, it must be emphasized that *none of those bills (which would have expressly set forth baseball's antitrust exemption in statute) were passed by the Congress*. It could have just as easily and accurately been argued that by Congress's *failure* to pass legislation to "codify" the Supreme Court's decision in *Federal Baseball*, Congress was expressing its intent that the business of baseball was *not* entitled to an antitrust exemption.

At the time of Curt Flood's trade to the Phillies in 1969, and with respect to baseball's antitrust exemption and the legality of baseball's reseve system, the *Federal Baseball—Gardella—Toolson* trilogy would be the "law of the land".

Antitrust Regulation and Other Professional Sports

In 1890, pursuant to its constitutional authority to regulate interstate commerce, Congress enacted the Sherman Act. The origin of the Sherman Act and the history of its passage are lengthy and complex. However, the fundamental purpose of the Sherman Act was to prevent industrial monopolies from using their market power to disrupt and influence the national economy. The first section of the Sherman Act prohibits contracts, combinations, and conspiracies that restrain trade. Section 2 of the Sherman Act prohibits monopolization as well as attempts and conspiracies to monopolize.[5]

While Congress intended that the passage of the Sherman Act would ensure free-market competition, only those trade practices and agreements that *unreasonably* restrain trade and competition violate the Sherman Act. More specifically, certain trade practices and agreements are so

---

[5] 15 U.S.C. § 1,2.

egregious, restrictive and anticompetitive, that courts apply the "per se" test. For example, in an antitrust case, if the plaintiff can prove that the defendants (two or more companies or businesses) engaged in price setting or price fixing in the same relevant market area, the defendants' conduct violates the Sherman Act "per se", or by itself, and without the need to prove additional facts. On the other hand, business practices which are less egregious and do not rise to the "per se" level, are reviewed by the courts under the "rule of reason" standard. Under this standard of review, courts will consider "the totality of the circumstances" and allow the defendants to justify the restriction or practice as a reasonable restraint necessary to differentiate a product or to permit a particular industry to exist.

Following the U.S. Supreme Court's decisions in *Federal Baseball* and *Toolson*, the federal courts would hear and decide antitrust cases relating to professional sports *other than baseball*. These other professional sports team owners and organizations maintained that they deserved to be exempted from the federal antitrust laws. That legal position and argument was rational, logical and consistent. Yet, between 1953 (the year of the *Toolson* decision) and 1970 (the year that Curt Flood filed his suit) the federal courts would conclude otherwise.

United States v. International Boxing Club (1955)

In *U.S. v. International Boxing Club*, the United States government filed a civil antitrust action against the International Boxing Club of New York, Madison Square Garden and two individual defendants. The defendants were engaged in the business of promoting professional boxing contests. The Justice Department's complaint charged that the defendants, in the course of engaging in this interstate commerce and business, entered into various agreements, boycotts and conspiracies in violation of the Sherman Act. The defendants argued that under *Federal Baseball* and *Toolson, all businesses involving exhibitions of an athletic nature* were exempt from the federal antitrust laws.

In rejecting the boxing industry's position, Chief Justice Earl Warren, speaking for the U.S. Supreme Court's majority stated:

"...[C]ontrary to their [defendants] argument, *Federal Baseball* did not hold that all businesses based on professional sports were outside the scope of the antitrust laws. The issue confronting us is, therefore, not whether a previously granted exemption should continue, but whether an exemption should be granted in the first instance. And that issue is for Congress to resolve, not this Court."

United States v. Shubert (1955)

On the same day that the U.S. Supreme Court ruled in *U.S. v. International Boxing Club* (January 31, 1955), the Supreme Court also decided *U.S. v. Shubert*. In *Shubert*, like the *International Boxing Club* case, it was the federal government that commenced the action. The Justice Department filed a civil antitrust action against a number of corporations and individuals engaged in the business of producing legitimate theatrical attractions; booking those theatrical attractions throughout the United States; and operating theatres in eight states for the presentation of those theatrical attractions.

The Justice Department alleged that the defendants, while engaging in this business, violated the Sherman Act. The defendants argued that their business, based upon the U.S. Supreme Court's ruling in *Toolson,* was already exempt from federal antitrust regulation. In rejecting the defendants' argument, Chief Justice Earl Warren, again writing for the Court's majority, wrote the following:

"...The defendants would have us convert this narrow application of the [*Toolson*] rule into a sweeping grant of [antitrust] immunity to every business based on the live presentation of local exhibitions, regardless of how extensive its interstate phases may be. We cannot do so. If the *Toolson* holding is to be expanded- or contracted- the appropriate remedy lies with Congress."

Radovich v. National Football League (1957)

In 1957, in *Radovich v. National Football League,* the U.S. Supreme Court would clarify the application of the *Toolson* doctrine and determine whether the business of professional football was within the scope of the Sherman Act.

The plaintiff, Bill Radovich, began his professional football career in 1938 when he signed a contract to play with the Detroit Lions of the National Football League. After four seasons of play with the Lions, Radovich entered the Navy and, after World War II, returned to play for the Lions in the 1945 season. In 1946, because of the illness of his father, Radovich requested that he be transferred to a National Football League club in Los Angeles. The Lions refused to trade or transfer Radovich as he requested. Radovich then signed with and played the 1946 and 1947 seasons for the Los Angeles Dons, a member team of the All American Conference.[6]

In 1948, the San Francisco Clippers, a member of the Pacific Coast League which was affiliated with but not a competitor of the National Football League, offered to employ Radovich as a player-coach. However, the National Football League advised the Clippers that Radovich was "blacklisted" and, as a result, any affiliated club signing Radovich would be subject to significant penalties. There-

---

[6] This professional football league began operations in 1946 and disbanded after the 1949 season.

CHAPTER 4: BASEBALL'S RESERVE SYSTEM

after, the Clippers refused to sign Radovich.

In his suit, Radovich alleged 1) that this "blacklisting" by the National Football League (NFL) effectively prevented his employment in organized professioinal football in the United States; 2) that this "blacklisting" was a result of a conspiracy among the NFL and its teams to monopolize commerce in professional football in the United States; 3) that the purpose of the conspiracy was to control, regulate and dictate the terms upon which organized professional football would be played throughout the United States in violation of the Sherman Act; 4) that part of the conspiracy was to boycott the All-Amercan Conference and its players with a view to its destruction and thus strengthen the monopolistic position of the NFL; and 5) that under the Clayton Act, Radovich was "injured in his business or property by reason of [antitrust] law violations, and as such was entitled to sue the violators and seek treble damages".

The defense asserted by the NFL and its teams was straight forward and simple. Boiled down to its core, the NFL asserted that its agreements and practices were no different than those in organized professional baseball, and which the Supreme Court held in *Federal Baseball* and *Toolson* to be outside the scope of federal antitrust regulation.

In a 6-3 decision, the Supreme Court ruled that the business of professional football was interstate commerce and therefore subject to antitrust regulation under the Sherman Act. The Court expressly acknowledged the inconsistency of its ruling as well as the Court's inexplicable distinction between the business of professional football and that of professional baseball. Moreover, the nation's highest court concluded that the "orderly way to eliminate error or discrimination if there be, is by legislation and not by court decision."

In *Toolson* (1953), and again in *Radovich* (1957), the U.S. Supreme Court expressly stated that it was up to Congress and not the federal courts to correct the "error or discrimination". To put the Supreme Court's rationale in proper perspective, it must be noted that in the instance of professional baseball and the antitrust exemption, it was the *Supreme Court itself* that created the "error or discrimination" with its ruling in *Federal Baseball.* In 1954, just three years before the Court's decision in *Radovich,* the U.S. Supreme Court eliminated the "error or discrimination"created by the Supreme Court's own decision in *Plessey v. Ferguson* (1896). In *Plessey v. Ferguson,* the Supreme Court upheld racially segregated public schools, and ruled that "separate but equal" schools did not violate the Equal Protection Clause of the U.S. Constitution. Between 1896 and 1954, Congress did *not* pass legislation to correct this "error or discrimination", but rather it was the Supreme Court itself that corrected its own "error or discrimination" by its decision in *Brown v. Board of Education (1954).* It must be emphasized that in *Brown v. Board of Education,* the Supreme Court did not acquiese, defer to or wait for Congress to correct the "error or discrimination" of racially segregated public schools; the Court reversed its ruling in *Plessey v. Ferguson,* and held that "separate but equal" schools violated the Equal Protection Clause of the United States Constitution. Similarly, the Supreme Court did not defer to or wait for Congress to pass legislation to "correct" a previous Court decision in the area of legislative reapportionment *(Baker v. Carr, 1962);* in the area of legislative redistricting *(Reynolds v. Simms,* 1963); in the areas of criminal procedure and the rights of the accused *(Miranda v. Arizona,* 1963) and in a host of other areas of law and regulation—particularly in the years of the "Warren Court" (1954-69).

Under the Supreme Court's *Toolson-Radovich* rationale, once the Supreme Court makes a ruling or decision—regardless of when the decision was made—and unless

Chapter 4: Baseball's Reserve System

Congress takes "positive action" (i.e., passes legislation to "overrule" or clarify that particular court decision), the Supreme Court is bound (as well as all of the lower federal courts) by the doctrine of "stare decisis" (rule of precedent) to reaffirm that earlier Supreme Court decision. This Supreme Court rationale was preposterous.

Salerno v. American League of Professional Baseball Clubs (1970)

In *Salerno v. American League of Professional Baseball Clubs*, plaintiffs were former umpires in the American League who had been discharged from employment by then American League President, Joseph E. Cronin. The discharged umpires filed a complaint against the American League and the Commissioner of Baseball alleging, among other things, that major league baseball was in violation of the federal antitrust laws. Predictably, the defendants moved to dismiss the suit and, on the basis of *Federal Baseball* and *Toolson*, argued that the U.S. District Court had no jurisdiction. The District Court dismissed the suit.

On appeal, the U S. Court of Appeals for the Second Circuit affirmed the lower court's ruling and wrote in pertinent part:

" We freely acknowledge our belief that *Federal Baseball* was not one of Mr. Justice Holmes' happiest days, that the rationale of *Toolson* is extremely dubious and that, to use the Supreme Court's own adjectives, the distinction between baseball and other professional sports is 'unrealistic,' 'inconsistent' and 'illogical.'...[P]utting aside instances where factual premises have all but vanished and a different principle might thus obtain, we continue to believe that the Supreme Court should retain the exclusive privilege of overruling its own decisions....While we should not fall out of our chairs with surprise at the news that *Federal Baseball* and *Toolson* had been overruled, we are not at all certain the Court is ready to give them a happy despatch."

Haywood v. National Basketball Association (1971)

In March 1971, the U.S. Supreme Court considered the applicability of federal antitrust regulation to the business of professional basketball. More specifically, at issue in *Haywood* was the legality (under the Sherman Act) of the professional basketball college player draft.

The plaintiff, Spencer Haywood, played with the 1968 U.S. Olympic team and then went on to attend college. Under then existing National Basketball Association (NBA) rules, a college player could not be drafted until four years after he graduated from high school. Prior to college graduation, Haywood signed a contract to play professional basketball with the NBA's rival, the American Basketball Association. Thereafter, upon turning twenty-one years of age, Haywood repudiated the contract alleging fraud, and signed another contract with the Seattle club of the NBA. Haywood's signing with the Seattle club was less than four years after his high school class had graduated (thus leaving Haywood ineligible to be drafted under the NBA's rules). The NBA threatened to disallow the contract and also threatened the Seattle club with various sanctions.

Haywood then filed an antitrust action against the NBA alleging that the NBA's conduct was tantamount to a group boycott; and that the NBA's boycott was a "per se" violation of the Sherman Act. The U. S. District Court issued an injunction prohibiting the NBA from enforcing its rules against Haywood, and from imposing sanctions against the Seattle team. The U.S. Court of Appeals affirmed the District Court's issuance of the injunction.

In sustaining the injunction issued by the U.S. District Court, Supreme Court Justice Douglas wrote that

CHAPTER 4: BASEBALL'S RESERVE SYSTEM

"...[b]asketball...does not enjoy exemption from the antitrust laws."

* * * * * * * * * * *

It was during the Fall of 1969 that Curt Flood decided not to accept the "trade" from the St. Louis Cardinals to the Philadelphia Phillies, and instead, to file a suit in federal court challenging the legality of baseball's reserve system. While Flood was advised and clearly understood that the challenge was anything but a "sure bet winner", it was also fair to conclude that his lawsuit was not necessarily a hopeless case. Among other things, Flood and his legal advisors would carefully consider the following facts and chronology:

1. The U.S. Supreme Court's 1922 decision in *Federal Baseball* construed the exhibition of baseball to be outside the definition of interstate commerce—a legal conclusion that had been heavily criticized and continually scrutinized.

2. Twenty-seven years later in *Gardella v Chandler* (1949), the U.S. Court of Appeals for the Second Circuit specifically held that the business of baseball was indeed subject to and not exempt from the Sherman Act. Prior to the *Gardella* case being heard on appeal, major league baseball and Gardella entered into an out of court settlement. Consequently, the *Gardella* decision was never reviewed by the U.S. Supreme Court. As it would turn out, the same U. S. Court of Appeals for the Second Circuit would eventually review the U.S. District (trial) Court's decision in *Flood v. Kuhn.*

3. While the U.S. Supreme Court's 1953 decision in *Toolson* reaffirmed baseball's antitrust exemption, the Court's decision was "split". The majority's (per curium) decision was made expressly "without reexamination of the underlying issues" and in reliance upon the Court's holding in *Fed-*

35

eral Baseball—a ruling that was frequently and heavily criticized by the the Supreme Court itself!

4. After *Toolson* (1953), the U.S. Supreme Court would consider the applicability of the federal antitrust laws and the business of *other professional sports*. From a legal and antitrust perspective, were these other sports different than baseball? If so, how and why? The result?

Between 1955 and 1971, the U.S. Supreme Court ruled that the business of professional boxing, the business of theatrical attractions, the business of professional football, and the business of professional basketball were all subject to and not exempt from federal antitrust regulation.

It would not be until 1970 in *Flood v. Kuhn* that the federal courts (and eventually the U.S. Supreme Court in 1972) would again be specifically confronted with baseball's reserve system and the federal antitrust laws.

CHAPTER 5
THE DECISION TO CHALLENGE

On October 9, 1969, the day after the call from Jim Toomey, the "hard evidence" arrived in the mail. A preprinted form with hand written insertions officially advised Flood that his contract had been assigned to the Philadelphia Club of the National League. The notice was signed by the Cardinals' General Manager, Bing Devine. Flood later phoned Devine and told him that he would not report to Philadelphia and that Flood planned to retire. Devine advised Flood that retirement was his decision and then wished Flood the "Best of Luck".

In *The Way It Is*, Flood wrote that he took the "trade" to Philadelphia personally; that he had become an expert on major league baseball's "spurious paternalism" and a connoisseur of its ugliness. Flood acknowledged that he had fallen from grace in the eyes of Cardinal management, and that he would likely be traded. Nevertheless, Flood admitted that he was deeply hurt and that he felt unjustly cast out.

To avoid the media and to think more clearly about his future, Flood then took his trip to Copenhagen. While in Denmark, Flood met with a couple of potential business associates in contemplation of opening what Flood described as "an American-style cocktail lounge." When

Baseball's Reserve System: The Case and Trial of Curt Flood v. Major League Baseball

Flood returned to St. Louis in late October, he was met by John Quinn, General Manager of the Philadelphia Phillies. Upon meeting Quinn for the first time, Flood reportedly told Mr. Quinn that he was "wasting his time" because Flood had "already made up his mind". What wasn't clear was what Flood had purportedly decided.

During this first meeting at a St. Louis hotel, Flood was impressed with Mr. Quinn. Flood described Quinn as having a warm personality and who was understanding of Flood's feelings and the reasons for his hesitancy. Quinn told Flood that the Phillies were genuinely excited about Flood becoming a Phillie; that a new ball park was under construction in Philadelphia; that the Philadelphia club and organization were being overhauled; and that more positive changes and developments were underway in Philadelphia and within the Philadelphia organization. Quinn was more than confident that the Phillies would negotiate a salary that was satisfactory to Flood for the 1970 season. After the meeting, Flood wrote that he was no longer bothered about relocating to the City of Philadelphia, but that he continued to be offended by the vice grip of baseball's reserve system which "afflicted" all professional baseball players. Flood agreed to meet again with John Quinn.

For his next session of advice, Flood called upon a young St. Louis lawyer who had done legal work for the operators of Flood's photography business. His name was Allan Zerman. Flood confided in Zerman and expressed his frustration with his current circumstances and, in particular, with the reserve system. In essence, Zerman advised Flood that the only way to avoid the trade to Philadelphia was to challenge the reserve system on antitrust grounds. It was during this meeting that Zerman asked if Flood ever considered bringing a suit against major league baseball to challenge the reserve system. Flood wrote that at the time of his conversation with Zerman, Flood had already given

Chapter 5: The Decision to Challenge

serious thought for several weeks about bringing such a lawsuit. Moreover, Flood believed that someone would eventually challenge major league baseball's "right" under the reserve system to treat players like commodities.

Flood's next step was to call Marvin Miller, Executive Director of the Major League Baseball Players' Association, to ask for an appointment. Flood arrived in New York in early November 1969 for his meeting with Miller. At this meeting, Flood told Miller that he wanted to file a suit to challenge the reserve system. Flood recalled that Miller responded with an abundance of caution. Miller noted that such a suit could take two to three years; that the cost of litigation would be enormous; that Flood would be giving up several years of playing and salary; and that he could lose the suit. As an additional consequence, Miller warned Flood that he could forget about ever becoming a major league baseball scout, coach or manager after his playing career. At the conclusion of the meeting, Miller insisted and Flood agreed to return to St. Louis and think the situation over more thoroughly.

Before leaving New York, Flood met for dinner and drinks with John Quinn. That same evening, Quinn offered Flood a contract and additional reimbursements that would raise Flood's 1970 compensation to over $100,000. Flood told Quinn that he would get back to him and let him know. Following the advice of Miller, Flood returned to St. Louis where he remained virtually secluded in his apartment for a couple of weeks.

Sometime around the middle of November, Flood telephoned Miller and told him that he wanted to proceed with a legal challenge to baseball's reserve system. In his 1991 book, *A Whole Different Ball Game,* Miller recalled this conversation with Flood:

"My feelings were mixed at that moment. Realistically, we had little chance of overthrowing a reserve clause that had a half a century of court precedents on its side, but at least in Curt Flood, we had the right man and the right situation with which to mount the challenge. Since this could turn out to be a landmark case, it was absolutely essential that the man at the center of it be someone with great personal integrity. As to Flood's personal qualities there could be no doubt. But I would still have to convince the players that Flood would not back out on us once the Association committed its resources to his case. If Flood turned out to have feet of clay, the players' chances of ever modifying the reserve rules through legal action would be damaged. But I was persuaded that Flood meant what he said and that he was in the case to the end..."

The first troublesome issues were whether and to what extent the Association would support the Flood challenge. Miller and Flood discussed the possibility of the Players' Association paying some of Flood's expenses in relation to this legal challenge. Miller told Flood that he did not feel that it was appropriate to seek the Association's support for his living expenses, but did suggest that Flood may wish to seek the Association's support for his legal expenses. Flood agreed to do so and planned to go to New York to discuss the next steps.

When Flood arrived in New York (sometime in the third week of November), Miller suggested that Flood make his presentation personally to the Executive Board of the Players' Association. The Executive Board was scheduled to meet on December 13th in San Juan, Puerto Rico. As Miller advised, Flood traveled to San Juan to meet with the Board.

In San Juan, Miller assembled the Executive Board and apprized the members of Flood's intentions. After a long discussion among the Board's members outside the presence of Flood, it was now Curt's turn. As anticipated, some of the questions centered on whether Flood had considered whether taking this step may insure that his baseball playing career would come to an abrupt halt. Flood assured the group that he had indeed taken that possibility into consideration. Moreover, he assured the Association that if he filed the suit, he would not settle the case out of court—regardless of the amount of any settlement offer. Miller recalls that Flood fielded the [Board's] questions "as cleanly as he fielded sinking line drives".

What followed, however, was a question from Board member and San Francisco Giant catcher Tom Haller—a question that was perhaps on the minds of many Board members, but was difficult to raise. Haller first mentioned the civil rights struggles of the 1960s, the black power movement, and cited examples of racial discrimination in America. Haller's question was short and direct: "Are you doing this simply because you're black and you feel that baseball has been discriminatory?"

According to Miller, all eyes were on Flood as he prepared to respond.

"All the things you say are true," Flood replied, looking directly at Haller, "and I'd be lying if I told you that as a black man in baseball I hadn't gone through worse times than my white teammates. ...I'll also say that, yes, I think the change in black consciousness in recent years has made me more sensitive to injustice in every area of my life. But I want you to know that what I'm doing here I'm doing as a ballplayer, a major league ballplayer, and I think it's absolutely terrible that we have stood by and watched this situation go on for so many years and never pulled together to do anything about it. It's improper, it shouldn't be allowed to go any further, and the circumstances are such that, well, I guess this is the time to do something about it."

The Board then excused Flood and continued its deliberations. After considerable discussion, the Board members decided to grant Flood's request for financial support by agreeing to pay Flood's attorney fees (but not his living expenses). However, the Board proposed that if Flood won the suit and was awarded monetary damages, the Association would be reimbursed for the expenses advanced on behalf of Flood's challenge. Without hesitation, Flood agreed. The Executive Board voted 25-0 to support Flood's case. The focus now quickly shifted. Who would Flood retain as his attorney?

The first day back from the meeting in Puerto Rico, Miller telephoned his first choice of counsel for the Flood case. His name was Arthur Goldberg. When Miller began working for the Steelworkers Union in 1950, Arthur Goldberg was general counsel for that union. Miller had worked closely with Goldberg through the 1950s in all major labor negotiations for the Steelworkers Union. On Goldberg's lawyering skills and his ability to persuade, Miller wrote the following:

"...I didn't always agree with him [Goldberg] on policy matters, but I respected his ability; his oral arguments in...court...in opposition to the government's imposition of an eight-day Taft-Hartley injunction against the 1959 steel strike were models of clarity and logic. He could be brilliant on his feet. I had seen him present a case in the circuit court for well over two hours with just a couple of notes to fall back on."

In 1961, President John F. Kennedy appointed Goldberg Secretary of the Department of Labor. Later, President Kennedy appointed and Goldberg served as a Justice of the U.S. Supreme Court. While on the Supreme Court, Goldberg wrote the majority opinion in several major antitrust cases. In 1964, President Lyndon Johnson asked Goldberg to resign from the Supreme Court and to accept an appointment as United States Ambassador to the United Nations. When President Nixon took office in 1969, Goldberg returned to private practice as a partner in a New York law firm. Miller also knew that Goldberg was a life long baseball

Chapter 5: The Decision to Challenge

fan. From Miller's perspective, "it would have been impossible to imagine anyone better suited to lead the fight against the reserve clause."

During their phone conversation, Goldberg seemed intrigued by the notion of representing Curt Flood. Goldberg agreed to meet at a New York hotel for breakfast the next morning with Marvin Miller and Dick Moss, General Counsel for the Players' Association. Miller could not have been more pleased with the conversation with Goldberg and Goldberg's apparent willingness to accept the case. But Miller remained worried. That same morning, Miller had read a headline in the *New York Times* which announced that the New York Democratic Party was seeking Goldberg to be its candidate in the 1970 election for Governor against Nelson Rockefeller. Miller wrote of his worry:

"After we had made our pitch and Goldberg seemed receptive, I produced the paper and asked him what his intentions were. Arthur, I said 'I'm not trying to get any inside information, but our situation is that Flood's case is not going to be decided in just a few months, as you know. In fact, it's probably going to go all the way to the United States Supreme Court, and if you have to drop out to become a candidate, it could really cripple things for us. And if you *win*, I *know* you're not going to have time.' We *all* laughed about that; I probably should have said "when you win." Goldberg replied that he had absolutely no intention of running for governor. I haven't informed them yet, he told me, but I'm going to withdraw. I'm flattered that they want to nominate me, but I really don't want to be governor. At this point I had no option but to accept his word or find a new lawyer, and since it didn't seem possible that we could get a better lawyer than Arthur Goldberg, I decided to trust him."

Miller continued to discuss the case with Goldberg and how much he would charge for his services. After some back and forth, Goldberg expressed his deep interest in the case and told Miller that he [Goldberg] "would regard it as *pro bono* work, a public service to upset a series of unconscionable rulings that should have been overturned by the courts a long time ago. Goldberg finally proposed to have his associates be paid for their services on an hourly basis, but that Goldberg would be reimbursed for his expenses only. Miller couldn't have been more thrilled. Miller wrote, "...Arthur Goldberg for expenses! That was like Sandy Koufax pitching for pass-the-hat." Miller agreed to schedule a meeting between Goldberg and Flood as soon as possible.

Sometime prior to Goldberg's first meeting with Flood, Miller briefed Goldberg on the relevant background and status of the players-owners negotiations regarding baseball's reserve system. Miller informed Goldberg that the first Basic Agreement negotiated between the players' union and the owners covered the 1968-69 seasons. Miller also highlighted the fact that during these players-owners negotiations in 1968, the players demanded an end to a team's "iron clad" control of a player for that player's entire playing career. This demand by the players was rejected by the owners. It was Miller's assessment that obtaining concessions from the owners on this issue through collective bargaining was hopeless. As a result, the 1968 Agreement called for the players and owners to study alternatives and modifications to the reserve system.

In addition, Dick Moss briefed Goldberg on the facts and the court's holdings in three prior cases in which baseball's reserve system was litigated: *Federal Baseball* (1922); *Toolson v. New York Yankees* (1953); and *Gardella v. Chandler* (1949). Goldberg then informed Miller and Moss that Goldberg would be assisted in his preparation of the case by two associates: Jay Topkis and Max Gitter. It was on December 15, 1969 that Flood met with Goldberg at his law office in

Chapter 5: The Decision to Challenge

New York. Flood was nervous about meeting Goldberg. After all, it was not everyday that someone—particularly a major league baseball player—attends a conference in the private office of a former U.S. Supreme Court justice. Moreover, Flood believed that his future may depend on the impression he would leave with Goldberg. Flood wrote that Goldberg put him at ease and again reviewed all of the dire possibilities that could result from this lawsuit.

Flood had a marquee lawyer and a good case; Goldberg had a quality client and high profile litigation; and Miller had made the marriage.

It was only nine days later, on Christmas Eve 1969, that the first shot was fired—Flood's famous "I'm not a piece of property" letter to Baseball Commissioner Bowie Kuhn:

"Dear Mr. Kuhn:

After twelve years in the major leagues, I do not feel that I am a piece of property to be bought and sold irrespective of my wishes. I believe that any system which produces that result violates my basic rights as a citizen and is inconsistent with the laws of the United States and of the several States.

It is my desire to play baseball in 1970, and I am capable of playing. I have received a contract offer from the Philadelphia Club, but I believe I have the right to consider offers from other clubs before making any decisions. I, therefore, request that you make known to all Major League Clubs my feelings in this matter, and advise them of my availability for the 1970 season.

                              Sincerely yours,

                              Curt Flood."

Commissioner Kuhn's response would follow just six days later-on December 30,1969:

" Dear Curt[7]

This will acknowledge your letter of December 24, which I found on returning to my office yesterday.

I certainly agree with you that you, as a human being, are not a piece of property to be bought and sold. That is fundamental in our society and I think obvious. However, I cannot see its applicability to the situation at hand.

You have entered into a current playing contract with the St Louis club which has the same assignment provision as those in your annual Major League contracts since 1956. Your present contract has been assigned in accordance with its provisions by the St Louis club to the Philadelphia club. The provisions of the playing contract have been negotiated over the years between the clubs and the players, most recently when the present Basic Agreement was negotiated two years ago between the clubs and the Players' Association.

If you have any specific objection to the propriety of the assignment, I would appreciate your specifying the objection. Under the circumstances, and pending any further information from you, I do not see what action I can take and cannot comply with the request contained in the second paragraph of your letter.

---

[7] The Players' Association took issue with this salutation. Bowie Kuhn wrote the following: "...the Players' Association did not like any part of my letter, beginning with "Dear Curt," which was categorized as a symbol of the same old "plantation mentality" that they found so patronizing. Since I did not know Flood personally, I was supposed to call him Mr. Flood."

CHAPTER 5: THE DECISION TO CHALLENGE

I am pleased to see your statement that you desire to play baseball in 1970. I take it this puts to rest any thought, as reported earlier in the press, that you were considering retirement.

Sincerely yours,

Bowie Kuhn"

The war had just started.

CHAPTER 6
THE SUIT

It was now one hundred days since receiving the October 8, 1969 "postcard notice" of his trade to the Phillies. In this one hundred day period, Curt Flood had been a busy man. During that time, Flood had traveled to Copenhagen; met with and entertained offers from Phillies' General Manager, John Quinn; discussed his circumstances and desire to challenge major league baseball's reserve system with Marvin Miller and Dick Moss; traveled to San Juan Puerto Rico to meet with the Major League Players' Association in December; and retained a former U.S. Supreme Court Justice as his legal counsel. It was on Friday, January 16, 1970 that Curtis Charles Flood filed his suit in the U.S. District Court for the Southern District of New York.

Curtis C. Flood v. Bowie Kuhn, et al. (70 Civ. 202)

In *Flood v. Kuhn, et al*, Plaintiff Curtis Charles Flood filed a five part (what lawyers call "counts") complaint alleging that the organization and operation of major league baseball violated the the federal antitrust statutes, violated the antitrust statutes of a number of States, violated the common law, and subjected Flood to peonage and involuntary

Chapter 6: The Suit

servitude in violation of the Thirteenth Amendment of the U.S. Constitution.

The Parties

Plaintiff: Curtis Charles Flood

Defendants:
Bowie Kuhn, Individually and as Commissioner of Baseball;
Charles S. Feeney, Individually and as President of the National League of Professional Baseball Clubs;
Joseph E. Cronin, Individually and as President of the American League of Professional Baseball Clubs;
Atlanta Braves, Inc.;
Chicago National League Ball Club; (Chicago Cubs)
The Cincinnati Reds, Inc.;
The Houston Sports Association; (Houston Astros)
Los Angeles Dodgers, Inc.;
Montreal Baseball Club Ltd.; (Montreal Expos)
Metropolitan Baseball Club Inc.; (New York Mets)
Philadelphia National League Club; (Philadelphia Phillies)
Pittsburgh Athletic Co., Inc.; (Pittsburgh Pirates)
St. Louis National Baseball Club, Inc.; (St. Louis Cardinals)
San Diego Padres;
San Francisco Giants' Baseball Club;
Baltimore Baseball Club, Inc.; (Baltimore Orioles)
Boston Red Sox;
Cleveland Indians, Inc.;
Detroit Baseball Club; (Detroit Tigers)
New York Yankees, Inc.;
The Washington Senators, Inc.;
Golden West Baseball Co.; (California Angels)
Chicago White Sox;
Kansas City Royals Baseball Club;
Minnesota Twins, Inc.;

Baseball's Reserve System: The Case and Trial of Curt Flood v. Major League Baseball

Oakland Athletics;
Pacific Northwest Sports, Inc. (Seattle Pilots)

Defendants' Involvement in Interstate Commerce

Flood's first count alleged that he was a major league baseball player "widely regarded as a skilled and outstanding centerfielder"; that from 1958-1969, he played with the St. Louis National Baseball Club, Inc. (the St. Louis Cardinals); that the defendants were the major figures and entities comprising major league professional baseball; that the defendants (other than Commissioner Kuhn, President Cronin and President Feeney) were the major league baseball clubs comprising the National and American Leagues; that these baseball clubs "were engaged in the business of staging baseball games, transporting players and equipment, purchasing equipment, contracting with television and radio stations, purchasing and selling refreshments and novelties through concessions at baseball stadiums, and other business activities"; that consequently, defendants were engaged in and their activities had a substantial impact on interstate commerce and trade; and that defendants' involvement in interstate commerce had increased markedly since 1950. (Paragraph 6 of Count One alleged that in 1950, box office receipts from baseball exhibitions were almost six times the receipts from national radio and television contracts. By 1969, however, radio and television receipts had increased to ten times their 1950 levels and exceeded box office revenues).

Organized Baseball

In the next portion of the Complaint, Flood described how the defendants collectively comprised "organized baseball". More specifically, Flood alleged that the defendants, together with more than 125 minor league clubs, comprised an industry and structure commonly called "Organized Baseball"; that this structure existed by virtue of various agreements among defendants; that Commissioner Bowie Kuhn was the central figure in and the "chief executive officer of the industry"; that the Commissioner had sweeping powers and duties, including the power to make binding decisions in relation to disputes between clubs, the power to impose fines and discipline upon the clubs and leagues, and the power to discipline or remove any club officer or employee; that Defendants Feeney and Cronin, as Presidents of the Major Leagues, had the power to discipline clubs, players, and umpires, the power and duty to review each player-club contract, and that no such player-club contract was effective or legally binding until approved by the appropriate league President; that no player, club, organization, league or other entity could enter Organized Baseball without recognizing the Commissioner and submitting to the Commissioner's jurisdiction; that all minor league clubs recognized and submitted themselves to the jurisdiction of the Commissioner; and that the defendants were also tied to the minor league clubs in that each club defendant owned, or had a working arrangement with a number of minor league clubs; and that anyone that desired to play professional baseball in the United States had to play on defendants' terms or not at all.

The Reserve System

Flood's first count then described those elements of professional baseball's reserve system which caused him "irreparable injury". Flood alleged that by virtue of the reserve system, organized baseball had a *lifetime grip* on a player; and that "from the moment a player leaves the amateur ranks of high school, college, or sandlot baseball, the

```
                    6A
       UNITED STATES DISTRICT COURT
       SOUTHERN DISTRICT OF NEW YORK
       - - - - - - - - - - - - - - - - - - x
       CURTIS C. FLOOD,                     :
                      Plaintiff,            :
             -against-                      :
       BOWIE K. KUHN, Individually and as   :
       Commissioner of Baseball, CHARLES S.
       FEENEY, Individually and as President :   70 Civ. 202
       of the National League of Professional
       Baseball Clubs, JOSEPH E. CRONIN,    :
       Individually and as President of the
       American League of Professional Base- :    COMPLAINT
       ball Clubs, ATLANTA BRAVES, INC.,
       CHICAGO NATIONAL LEAGUE BALL CLUB,   :
       THE CINCINNATI REDS, INC., THE
       HOUSTON SPORTS ASSOCIATION, LOS      :
       ANGELES DODGERS, INC., MONTREAL BASE-
       BALL CLUB LTD., METROPOLITAN BASEBALL :
       CLUB, INC., PHILADELPHIA NATIONAL
       LEAGUE CLUB, PITTSBURGH ATHLETIC CO., :
       INC., ST. LOUIS NATIONAL BASEBALL
       CLUB, INC., SAN DIEGO PADRES, SAN    :
       FRANCISCO GIANTS' BASEBALL CLUB,
       BALTIMORE BASEBALL CLUB, INC.,       :
       BOSTON RED SOX, CLEVELAND INDIANS,
       INC., DETROIT BASEBALL CLUB, NEW YORK :
       YANKEES INC., THE WASHINGTON SENATORS,
       INC., GOLDEN WEST BASEBALL CO.,      :
       CHICAGO WHITE SOX, KANSAS CITY
       ROYALS BASEBALL CLUB, MINNESOTA      :
       TWINS, INC., OAKLAND ATHLETICS, and
       PACIFIC NORTHWEST SPORTS, INC.       :
                      Defendants.           :
       - - - - - - - - - - - - - - - - - - x
```

Plaintiff, CURTIS C. FLOOD, by his attorneys Paul, Weiss, Goldberg, Rifkind, Wharton & Garrison, alleges:

FIRST CAUSE OF ACTION, AGAINST ALL DEFENDANTS

Jurisdiction

1. This claim arises under the Sherman Anti-Trust Act and the Clayton Anti-Trust Act. Jurisdiction is conferred upon this Court by 28 U.S.C. § 1337.

First page of Flood's Complaint commencing his lawsuit on January 16, 1970.

Chapter 6: The Suit

```
                            31A
         UNITED STATES DISTRICT COURT
         SOUTHERN DISTRICT OF NEW YORK
         - - - - - - - - - - - - - - - - x
         CURTIS C. FLOOD,                :
                         Plaintiff,      :    Civil Action
                                              70 Civ. 202
                         -against-       :
         BOWIE K. KUHN, et al.,          :    ANSWER
                         Defendants.     :
         - - - - - - - - - - - - - - - - x
```

       The defendant Bowie K. Kuhn, by his attorneys, Donovan Leisure, Newton & Irvine, and Arnold & Porter, answers the Complaint as follows:

<u>First Defense</u>

       The defendant says as follows with respect to the paragraphs of the Complaint:

       1. Defendant admits that the action purports to arise under the Sherman Act and the Clayton Act as alleged in paragraph 1 and that the plaintiff seeks to invoke the jurisdiction of this Court under Section 1337 of the Judicial Code, but denies that the action is well founded thereunder or that the Court has jurisdiction thereunder.

       2. The allegations of paragraph 2 are admitted.

       3. The allegations of the first sentence of paragraph 3 are denied. The allegations of the second, third, fourth and fifth sentences of paragraph 3 are admitted. The allegations of the sixth sentence of paragraph 3 are denied, except that defendant Kuhn admits the defendant clubs are engaged in the business of exhibiting baseball games.

       4. With respect to the allegations of paragraph 4, defendant admits that under present concepts of interstate commerce

First page of Commissioner Kuhn's Answer to the Complaint.

player must play for the team which first 'acquires' him or its 'assignee'."

Flood's characterization of the reserve system continued in more detail:

1) The player contract was required by defendants' rules to be uniform throughout the Major Leagues, and was not subject to variation (except for the amount of compensation) at the instance of any player; that the club had the 'option' to renew the contract for an additional year after its termination; that each player was required to sign a new contract containing that option every year; and that if the player failed to sign a contract, the club may unilaterally renew the contract containing the 'option clause' and so on indefinitely. Thus, the so-called 'option' was, in effect, a contract for perpetual service.

2) The uniform contract also provided that the club may 'assign' the player, regardless of the player's wishes, to another club, and once so assigned, the player was required to sign a new uniform contract containing the 'option clause'.

3) Each year, each club "reserved" forty players. If a player was "reserved", or under contract to a club, or on a "negotiation list" of a club, no other club could negotiate with or contract with the player, nor may the player negotiate with any other club. Even after his retirement as an active player, the player could not become a coach or manager unless the club which had 'rights' to him as a player released him unconditionally. Defendants disguised this practice of binding a player to one team for life under rules prohibiting 'tampering'. These practices were enforced by the disciplinary powers of the Commissioner and the concerted actions of the clubs.

Flood then alleged that he "was ready and eager to play baseball in 1970"; that "by letter dated December 24, 1969", Flood informed the Commissioner and the teams that he wished to play; that Flood had also asked the Commissioner and the teams that he be declared a 'free agent' and that he wanted to conduct negotiations with the various teams for a contract for the 1970 playing season; and that by letter December 30, 1969, the Commissioner denied his request.

Pursuant to the reserve system, Flood alleged that defendants were engaging in a conspiracy and boycott to prevent him from playing baseball in the 1970 season, or ever, "for any professional baseball club other then [sic] the Philadelphia Phillies;" that this conspiracy and boycott violated the Sherman Act; and that unless equitable relief was granted, these violations would continue and succeed in causing irreparable damage to Flood.

In Count Two, Flood's Complaint reasserted all of the allegations of Count One regarding the defendants' involvement in interstate commerce; the structure and control of the Commissioner and organized baseball; and baseball's reserve system. However, in Count Two, Flood alleged that the defendants' "arrangements, agreements and conspiracy...restrained...plaintiff's free exercise of playing professional baseball in New York, California, and other states and...in violation of other anti-trust and anti-blacklisting...and civil rights statutes of the several states in which they stage baseball games."

In his third count, Flood alleged that the defendants' "arrangements, agreements and conspiracy" restrained trade and Flood's free exercise of playing professional baseball *in violation of the common law. Black's Law Dictionary* defines "common law" as that body of law and juristic theory which was originated, developed and formulated in England, and was adopted by most States. As distinguished from law created by the enactments of legislatures, the common law comprises the body of those principles and rules of action "which derive their authority solely from the usages and customs of immemorial antiquity, or from the judgments and decrees of the courts recognizing, affirming and enforcing such usages and customs; and in this sense, particularly the ancient unwritten law of England."

In Count Four, Flood alleged that the defendants were engaged in a conspiracy to force him to play solely for one professional baseball club to the exclusion of all other professional baseball clubs; to subject him to "peonage and involuntary servitude" in violation of the Thirteenth Amendment of the United States Constitution; and to deprive Flood of his freedom of labor in violation of the Norris-LaGuardia Act.

In Count Five, Flood's claim again alleged violations of the Sherman Antitrust Act and the Clayton Antitrust Act. However, Count Five named only two clubs as defendants—the St. Louis Cardinals and the New York Yankees. Specifically, Count Five alleged that defendant St. Louis Baseball Club. Inc. "limited the sale of beer in the stadium...to the beer produced by [its] affiliated company [i.e., Anheuser Busch, Inc.], and excluded all other beer companies from selling or attempting to sell beer through concession sales in the stadium" in violation of the Sherman and Clayton Antitrust Acts; and that the "effect of this violation had been...to increase the revenues of the beer company and diminish the revenues of defendant St. Louis National Baseball Club, Inc. available for player salaries, including that of plaintiff."

Similarly, Count Five alleged that the Defendant New York Yankees, Inc., was owned by the Columbia Broadcasting System (CBS), "one of the three national radio and television networks which might bid on the right to broadcast professional baseball games"; that as a result of its ownership of the New York Yankees, Columbia Broadcasting System had refrained from bidding on such broadcast rights "with consequent injury to competition..." in violation of the Sherman and Clayton Antitrust Acts; and that the consequence of this antitrust violation "reduce[d] the revenues of Organized Baseball from the sale of broadcast rights, in which revenues players such as plaintiff would share."

Request for Relief

Finally, Flood asked the Court:
    1. to declare the "reserve system" and "defendants' conspiracy against plaintiff" unlawful under the Sherman Antitrust Act;
    2. to declare the "reserve system and defendants' conspiracy against plaintiff to be unlawful" under California, New York, and under other statutes of the several states, and under the common law;
    3. to declare the "reserve system and defendants' conspiracy against plaintiff to be unlawful under the Thirteenth Amendment of the United States Constitution" and under federal statutes;
    4. to "preliminarily and permanently" enjoin the defendants "from enforcing the reserve system against plaintiff and from conspiring not to allow any baseball club other than the Philadelphia Phillies to negotiate with plaintiff"; and
    5. to order defendants to pay plaintiff for his non-baseball business interests in the amount of $25,000 trebled, and for effectively terminating plaintiff's baseball career in the amount of $1,000,000 trebled, plus the costs of litigation and reasonable attorneys fees.

The Complaint was filed by Flood's attorneys, Arthur J. Goldberg, a member of the New York firm of Paul, Weiss, Goldberg, Rifkind, Wharton & Garrison; and by Allan H. Zerman of Clayton, Missouri. In support of his Complaint, Flood submitted to the Court an affidavit also dated January 16, 1970. The affidavit sets forth Flood's allegations, but in a far less legalistic fashion. The affidavit provides important insight into Flood's assessment of his stance against major league baseball.

A few of the more significant excerpts from Flood's affidavit are noted below:

- "....I face two alternatives. Under either of them I will suffer irreparable damage to my career or to my dignity as a human being and my non-baseball life....

 (a) I can refuse to report to Philadelphia, in which case I will not be able to play baseball in the coming season, which begins about March 1, 1970. The loss of this playing season will, since I like other players am getting older, constitute an irreparable loss in my career as a professional baseball player; and indeed a year's layoff may cause my abilities to deteriorate much more than the mere aging process would.

 (b) I can play baseball for the Philadelphia Phillies, a course which defendants are trying to force upon me by their conspiracy. If I do so, however, I will lose the very rights which I am asserting in this lawsuit; to be free from a state of involuntary servitude, to be free to contract, and to be a free man. Therefore, I shall not play for Philadelphia under these conditions..."

- "Unless I can obtain injunctive relief immediately,...I shall be unable to negotiate a contract for the 1970 season in time to commence spring training and prepare for the season."

- "I have played professional...baseball for 14 years. Between 1958 and 1969 I played for the St. Louis Cardinals.... During that time, I state with all humility, I have become proficient in my position and have been recognized in the profession as a skilled and outstanding ballplayer, as is apparent from the salaries I have received, the most recent being $90,000 for the 1969 season. I have played in numerous World Series and All Star games."

- "On October 9, 1969, I received an index card sized notice of my 'sale' to the Philadelphia Phillies. I also

CHAPTER 6: THE SUIT

received a four-line covering letter from the General Manager of the Cardinals and a phone call from a club official. After my 12 years of service to the Cardinals these were the only communications I received from the club upon my 'sale' to the Phillies."

- "I do not believe that I am a chattel to be bought and sold irrespective of my wishes. Consequently, on December 24, 1969, I wrote to the Commissioner of Baseball advising him that I am ready and willing to play baseball in 1970 and asking him to make known to all of the Major League clubs, including St. Louis, that I am available to play for the 1970 season and I would like to consider contract offers from the clubs other than Philadelphia before making my decision. By letter dated December 30, 1969 the Commissioner denied my request."

- "The purported assignment to the Philadelphia Phillies came at the time in my life and career when I had already developed substantial business and social ties in the City of St. Louis...I have established in St. Louis two photographic studios and one portrait studio called 'Curt Flood studios'...I believe this business may fail if I am forced to leave St. Louis. In addition, for the past two years I have been chairman of a local organization called 'Aunts and Uncles', an organization which helps orphan children. I make this reference only to show that baseball players, like anyone else, develop community ties which the existing baseball system frustrates."

- "...Had my wishes and situation been considered, I would not have been traded by the Cardinals to another club. In this litigation I seek to have declared unlawful the system by which defendants are able to bind a baseball player to one club or it's 'assignee' for a lifetime and...allow a team to completely ignore a player's wishes."

- "As a consequence of this 'reserve system,' I am now the 'property' of the Philadelphia Phillies. No other ball club, including St. Louis, will negotiate with me or make me an offer to play for the 1970 season."

- "I believe that, were it not for the concerted action now being taken by defendants to enforce that 'reserve system,' numerous clubs would negotiate with me for the coming season. I base this belief on what I believe to be and what others have told me are my substantial skills in playing baseball."

- "Accordingly, and since the continuance of the defendants' conspiracy will cause me irreparable harm, I urgently request this Court to grant a preliminary injunction to prevent the defendants from preventing my employment by any team other than the Philadelphia Phillies in furtherance of their conspiracy."

In order to play major league baseball in the 1970 season (for any team other than the Phillies), it was imperative that Flood obtain the court order enjoining enforcement of his "trade" to the Phillies—and essentially baseball's "reserve system" as it applied to him—and to obtain that judicial relief in a big hurry. Time was not on the side of Curtis Charles Flood, and his lawyers knew it!

Chapter 7
Pre-Trial (January 16–May 18, 1970)

With the beginning of spring training just weeks away, Flood and his lawyers knew that they needed an early court hearing date—and a favorable court ruling. An early hearing date would be difficult—particularly in light of the fact that Flood had sued twenty-seven defendants residing or domiciled in more than fourteen states, the District of Columbia and Canada—all of which were entitled to retain legal counsel, and defend against Flood's suit.

The case would be heard by Federal District Court Judge Irving Ben Cooper. Judge Cooper was appointed to the federal bench in 1962 by President John F. Kennedy. At the time of the trial, the London, England born Caucasian jurist was just shy of his sixty-eighth birthday. In 1925, Cooper graduated from Washington University School of Law in St. Louis, Missouri; had engaged in the private practice of law in New York City from 1927-1938; served as special counsel in the New York City Department of Investigations; served as a New York City magistrate; and beginning in 1939, served as an Associate Justice and as the Chief Justice of the New York Court of Special Sessions.

On February 3, 1970, less than three weeks after the suit was filed, the parties first appeared in the New York courtroom of Judge Cooper to argue Flood's emergency motion for an injunction. The twenty-seven defendants decided to consolidate their legal representation and have two sets of lawyers. Defendant Commissioner Bowie Kuhn was represented by the firm of Donovan, Leisure, Newtown & Irvine, and the firm of Arnold & Porter, while all of the other defendants were represented by the firm of Wilkie, Farr & Gallagher and the firm of Baker, Hostetler & Patterson.

Flood's request for an injunction was of critical importance. Flood's lawyers argued that the reserve system clearly violated the Sherman Antitrust Act; that Flood would certainly prevail on the merits at trial; that Flood was entitled to relief from his purported trade and from the reserve system; and that the court should declare Flood a free agent, and permit Flood to negotiate a contract with any team of his choice. The defense, on the other hand, argued that Flood's transfer to the Phillies was a lawful transaction pursuant to a legally valid contract; that Flood would not prevail on the merits of his suit at trial; that Flood was not entitled to be declared a free agent; and perhaps more fatal at this point in the litigation, that the court, on the basis of the *Federal Baseball* and *Toolson* cases, should dismiss Flood's suit.

The parties argued their respective positions in the chambers of Judge Cooper. At the conclusion of the hearing, Judge Cooper took the case "under advisement", and informed counsel that he would issue a written order. In the meantime, baseball's spring training was in full swing — without Curt Flood.

Four weeks later, on Wednesday, March 4, 1970, Judge Cooper issued his ruling. Flood and his lawyers would not have to read far into the fifteen page order to learn Flood's fate — at least for the 1970 playing season.

..."Baseball has been the national pastime for over one hundred years and enjoys a unique place in our American

CHAPTER 7: PRE-TRIAL (JANUARY 16–MAY 18, 1970)

heritage. Major league professional baseball is avidly followed by millions of fans, looked upon with fervor and pride and provides a special source of inspiration and competitive team spirit especially for the young."

The sermon of Preacher Cooper continued:

"Baseball's status in the life of the nation is so pervasive *that it would not strain credulity to say the Court can take judicial notice that baseball is everybody's business.* To put it mildly and with restraint, *it would be unfortunate indeed if a fine sport and profession, which brings surcease from daily travail and an escape from the ordinary to most inhabitants of this land,* were to suffer in the least because of the undue concentration by any one or any group on commercial and profit considerations. *The game is on higher ground; it behooves everyone to keep it there.*

From what the papers before us reflect, we are certain that plaintiff and defendants each believe they have the best interests of the game at heart. In general, defendants contend that the reserve system is essential to prevent a relapse into the instability of those early years of professional baseball when players were free to change teams. Plaintiff, and apparently the Major League Baseball Players' Association, too, concede the need for some form of reserve on players, but argue that these objectives can be met by a less restrictive system.

The grip may well be far too tight and it may be best to loosen the bonds without permitting the slightest sag to the body of the game. However, courts do not sit as arbitrators. We have no power to devise and enforce alternatives to the present reserve system that may accommodate the interest of both parties.

The sole question before us is whether plaintiff has made the necessary showing to entitle him to a preliminary injunction restraining the operation of the reserve system and making plaintiff a free agent pending a final resolution upon a trial of the substantial issues of fact and law presented by this lawsuit. Under recognized principles, applicable to motions for preliminary injunctive relief, the Court is constrained to deny the motion. *This however is the first inning.* We are simply deciding that at this initial stage of the lawsuit, plaintiff is not entitled to the substance of the ultimate relief he seeks."

Although the Court's decision denied Flood any chance of reporting to spring training on time, and, for all practical purposes, any chance to play in the 1970 season for any team other than the Phillies, Judge Cooper did order the trial to commence on May 19, 1970. It is virtually unheard of for *any* federal trial to actually begin within four months of the date the suit is filed. It is also nothing short of amazing that this case was tried without any party taking the deposition of any witness or serving interrogatories on the other parties or otherwise undertaking what lawyers refer to as "discovery".

The federal rules of trial practice allow and encourage the parties to undertake extensive *pretrial* discovery. The policy of discovery is to allow the parties to better evaluate their cases, and to avoid "surprise" evidence at trial. In *Flood v. Kuhn,* no discovery was undertaken. Why? When asked this question thirty-three years later, Jay Topkis, one of Flood's trial lawyers, said he "honestly didn't recall", but thought that it "might have had to do with Flood's desire to get to trial as soon as was possible".

The pretrial motions and legal wrangling, however, were not over. Following the Court's denial of Flood's request for an injunction, the defendants asked the Court to dismiss the suit. Counts I-IV of Flood's complaint attacked the legality of major league baseball's reserve system. (Count V alleged certain *unrelated* antitrust violations on the part of only two of the defendants—the St. Louis Cardinals and the New York Yankees). The basis for the defendants' motion to

CHAPTER 7: PRE-TRIAL (JANUARY 16-MAY 18, 1970)

dismiss Counts I-IV was that under *Toolson,* professional baseball was exempt from antitrust regulation. Therefore, as lawyers say, these four counts must be dismissed in that they "fail to state a claim upon which relief can be granted."

Regarding Count V, defendants filed affidavits which, in the words of Judge Cooper, "fatally undercut" Flood's claims. In the case of the St. Louis Cardinals, the defense presented the affidavit of Cardinal General Manager Bing Devine. In pertinent part, Devine's affidavit stated that

"the beers sold at the St. Louis ballpark are not limited to beers produced by Anheuser-Busch. Rather, two of the four beers sold at the ballpark are produced by companies in which neither the St. Louis Club nor Anheuser-Busch has any ownership or other interest whatsoever".

In the case of the New York Yankees, the defense submitted the affidavit of William C. McPhail, Vice President of Sports for CBS Television Network, a division of Columbia Broadcasting Systems, Inc. (CBS). Flood's claim was that CBS refrained from bidding on broadcast rights to professional baseball games, thereby reducing the competition for and the revenues received by Organized Baseball from the sale of those broadcast rights, in which revenues the players, including Flood, would share. In his affidavit, McPhail detailed his personal involvement in and his submission of bids for the broadcast rights of the World Series and the All Star Games for the years 1967 and 1968, as well as for the national television rights to the Saturday Game of the Week for the years 1966, 1967 and 1968. However, these CBS bids were not accepted.

Curiously (and without explanation), Flood's lawyers did not dispute the facts presented in the defendants' affidavits. On April 3, 1970, Judge Cooper entered an order in favor of the defense and dismissed Count V. Regarding Counts I-IV, however, Judge Cooper deferred his ruling on any of the defense's motions until the trial—*and ordered the*

Baseball's Reserve System: The Case and Trial of Curt Flood v. Major League Baseball

trial to begin on May 19, 1970, in just over six weeks. Judge Cooper reasoned as follows:

"...we believe the trial must encompass the factual issues raised respecting the reserve system—hailed as a blessing by proponents; condemned as destructive by antagonists. We have ordered an early trial herein; the considerations which impelled that decision likewise weigh heavily in favor of developing all of the facts at one trial so as to avoid the possibility of piecemeal determinations and consequent delay. Additionally, exploration of the operation and effect of the reserve system is vital to any determination respecting plaintiff's fourth cause of action based on involuntary servitude. Potentially, it may also illuminate the question of the continued vitality of baseball's judicially-derived antitrust exemption."

The parties, lawyers, sports writers, general public and especially Judge Cooper all knew that the trial court's decision would be appealed all the way to the United States Supreme Court.

While the defense suffered a setback at being ordered to proceed to trial, the Flood camp faced significant problems of its own. At this early stage of the case, the lawyers for Flood had to make a critically important strategic decision. Flood's lawyers had to decide if they should present at trial only those facts which pertained directly to Curt Flood—his contract and his "trade" to the Phillies—and argue that baseball's reserve system, *as it applied to Flood,* was so egregious that baseball's reserve system constituted a "per se" violation of federal antitrust law. Alternatively, Flood's lawyers could, in addition, present evidence essentially "comparing" the operation of baseball's reserve system to the operation of the "reserve systems" which existed in other professional sports such as football, hockey and basketball. Under this "comparative approach", Flood's lawyers would later argue that the court should apply a so-

Chapter 7: Pre-Trial (January 16-May 18, 1970)

called "rule of reason" test (rather than the "per se" test) to determine whether baseball's reserve system constituted an "unreasonable" restraint of trade in violation of federal antitrust law. In terms of time, the more limited and focused evidentiary presentation (the "per se" approach) would certainly require fewer witnesses and significantly less time to present, but at the same time, must meet a more stringent burden of proof. While the more expansive evidentiary presentation (the "rule of reason" approach) would be required to meet a less stringent burden of proof, it would most certainly lengthen the trial, complicate the arguments, and allow the defense to divert attention from Curt Flood's basic and fundamental arguments.

For Curt Flood, waiting six weeks for the start of his trial seemed like an eternity.

Chapter 8
The Trial—Day One—May 19, 1970

It was Tuesday, May 19, 1970, and the hour was 10:00 a.m. The setting was the Federal District Court for the Southern District of New York. Just seven months earlier, Curt Flood received the phone call and postcard notice of his "assignment" to the Philadelphia Phillies. Four months earlier, he filed his suit. The courtroom was packed with sports writers, journalists, and baseball enthusiasts. It was the day that Curtis Charles Flood would finally get his chance to take the stand.

Shortly after 10:00 a.m., Judge Cooper brought the court to order. After the usual formalities and introductions, Judge Cooper asked whether the parties were ready to proceed. In response, defense counsel Mark Hughes stated that "the defendants are not ready, your Honor, but we have been directed to be here at this time and proceed with the trial, so we are here". Despite Hughes' jagged edged comment, Judge Cooper launched into a pretrial oration complimenting all of the attorneys for their "splendid show of cooperation", and oddly referring to Flood's counsel as "Justice" Goldberg.

The defense would have liked nothing better than to delay the trial and embark on a lengthy and expensive pre-

Chapter 8: The Trial—Day One—May 19, 1970

trial discovery process, including interrogatories, depositions and requests for documents and other relevant information. After all, following the Court's denial of Flood's request for the injunction that would have allowed him to play in the 1970 season, the defense did not care if the case ever got tried. Both the race against time and the burden of proof rested squarely in the camp of Curt Flood and his lawyers. When Judge Cooper, however, expedited the trial, the defense had to prepare for war and the baseball generals were angry.

At the outset of the trial, as expected, defense counsel renewed their motions to dismiss Flood's suit on the grounds that the court lacked subject matter jurisdiction. Again, as expected, Judge Cooper denied those motions. Next, the plaintiff and all of the defendants waived their opportunities to make an opening statement to the Court—an opportunity which would not have been waived had this case been tried before a jury. It was 10:20 a.m., and it was time for Curtis Charles Flood to take the witness stand.

Testimony of Curt Flood

Under questioning by Goldberg, Flood testified that he started playing baseball at the age of nine in the little league and sandlot; and played American Legion baseball and in high school. Upon graduating from high school in 1956, Flood testified that he signed a major league contract with the Cincinnati Reds; that he did not read the contract nor did he consult with a lawyer prior to signing; and that he was not familiar with baseball's so-called "reserve system" when he signed the contract. Flood's first contract was for $4,000 a year.

During his first season with the Reds, he was assigned to play in the Carolina League in High Point, North Carolina. Flood testified that "it was particularly bad being a black ballplayer in Carolina.... We lived separately...were housed...and ate separately. Despite the segregation and horrific treatment, Flood had an extraordinarily good playing year—he hit .340, hit 30 home runs, and "led the league in everything except home runs that year".

In 1957, Flood spent spring training with the Reds, but played the 1957 season with the Reds' farm team in Savannah, Georgia in the South Atlantic League—a Class A team. For that season, Flood was paid $4,000. Except for the last few weeks, Flood played the entire 1957 season with the Savannah team. Flood had a .300 average, drove in 80 runs, and made the League's All-Star team. At the end of the 1957 season, the Reds' management suggested that Flood play in Venezuela during the winter and learn to play infield. (At this time, the Reds had Frank Robinson and Vada Pinson in the outfield.) Flood testified that he was a "terrible" infielder, and that his Venezuelan experience confirmed "that I was an outfielder". While in Venezuela, Flood was notified by telegram that he had been traded to the St. Louis Cardinals. He was "shocked". Flood also noted that the telegram was the only communication he received from the Reds regarding the trade.

In March 1958, Flood reported to the St. Louis Cardinals training camp. After Spring training, Flood was sent to Cardinals AAA farm club in Omaha, Nebraska. Fifteen games into the season, Flood was recalled to St. Louis—and never returned to the minors. He played the remainder of the 1958 season in the majors, hit .255 in 1959, and .287 in 1960. In 1961, Curt Flood became the starting center fielder for the Cardinals—and was paid $15,000 annually. Flood testified that in those days, there were no genuine contract negotiations between a player and management. "I would go into the general manager's office knowing full well that I couldn't play any place else in the world and negotiate for a better contract."

Chapter 8: The Trial—Day One—May 19, 1970

Early in Flood's testimony, in response to a routine objection voiced by defense counsel, Judge Cooper admonished the witness for being unresponsive to the question. The tone of Judge Cooper's commentary was insulting. At one point, Cooper told Flood that defense counsel were "unhappy" and that they "have a right to be unhappy" with Flood's testimony. In an almost taunting manner, Judge Cooper inquired "Mr. Flood, I presume you are not finding this as easy as getting up at bat, is that right?"

Goldberg then directed Flood to his professional baseball accomplishments.

Batting averages:
1962—.296	1965—.310	1968—.301
1963—.302	1966—.267	1969—.285
1964—.311	1967—.335	Career Average—.293

Although disappointed with his performance in 1969, Flood's .285 average was the second highest on the team.

Flood played twelve consecutive seasons for the St. Louis Cardinals. During those twelve seasons, the Cardinals were in the World Series three times: 1964, 1967 and 1968, and won the World Series in 1964 and 1967. Flood was appointed co-captain from 1965-1969, won seven Golden Glove awards, was selected for the National League All-Star team three times; and set a record of 223 consecutive errorless games.

Flood's base salary beginning in 1961:
1961—$12,500	1964—$23,000	1967—$50,000
1962—$16,000	1965—$35,000	1968—$72,500
1963—$17,500	1966—$45,000	1969—$90,000

Goldberg then directed his witness to 1969 and the circumstances leading up to the trade.

Baseball's Reserve System: The Case and Trial of Curt Flood v. Major League Baseball

UNIFORM PLAYER'S CONTRACT

National League of Professional Baseball Clubs

Parties Between ST. LOUIS NATIONAL BASEBALL CLUB, INC.
herein called the Club, and CURTIS CHARLES FLOOD
of 4466 West Pine, St. Louis, Missouri, herein called the Player.

Recital The Club is a member of the National League of Professional Baseball Clubs, a voluntary association of twelve member Clubs which has subscribed to the Major League Rules with the American League of Professional Baseball Clubs and its constituent Clubs and to the Professional Baseball Rules with that League and the National Association of Baseball Leagues. The purpose of those rules is to insure the public wholesome and high-class professional baseball by defining the relations between Club and Player, between Club and Club, between League and League, and by vesting in a designated Commissioner broad powers of control and discipline, and of decision in case of disputes.

In consideration of the facts above recited and of the promises of each to the other, the parties agree as follows:

Agreement
Employment 1. The Club hereby employs the Player to render, and the Player agrees to render, skilled services as a baseball player during the year 1969 including the Club's training season, the Club's exhibition games, the Club's playing season, and the World Series (or any other official series in which the Club may participate and in any receipts of which the player may be entitled to share).

Payment 2. For performance of the Player's services and promises hereunder the Club will pay the Player the sum of $90,000, in semi-monthly installments after the commencement of the playing season covered by this contract. Payment shall be made on the day the amount becomes due, regardless of whether the Club is "home" or "abroad".
If a monthly rate of payment is stipulated above, it shall begin with the commencement of the Club's playing season (or such subsequent date as the Player's services may commence) and end with the termination of the Club's scheduled playing season and shall be payable in semi-monthly installments as above provided.
Nothing herein shall interfere with the right of the Club and the Player by special covenant herein to mutually agree upon a method of payment whereby part of the Player's salary for the above year can be deferred to subsequent years.
If the Player is in the service of the Club for part of the playing season only, he shall receive such proportion of the sum above mentioned, as the number of days of his actual employment in the Club's playing season bears to the number of days in said season.
Notwithstanding the rate of payment stipulated above, the minimum rate of payment to the Player for each day of service on a Major League Club shall be at the rate of $10,000 per year; except, if a Player physically joins a Major League Club on or after September 1, he shall be paid during September at the rate of $8,500 per year for each day of service until he has accumulated a total of 60 days of Major League service, after which he shall be paid at the rate of $10,000 per year for each day of service with such Major League Club.
Payment to the Player at the rate stipulated above shall be continued throughout any period in which a Player is required to attend a regularly scheduled military encampment of the Reserve of the Armed Forces or of the National Guard during the Club's playing season.

Loyalty 3. (a) The Player agrees to perform his services hereunder diligently and faithfully, to keep himself in first-class physical condition and to obey the Club's training rules, and pledges himself to the American public and to the Club to conform to high standards of personal conduct, fair play and good sportsmanship.

Baseball Promotion (b) In addition to his services in connection with the actual playing of baseball, the Player agrees to cooperate with the Club and participate in any and all promotional activities of the Club and its League, which, in the opinion of the Club, will promote the welfare of the Club or professional baseball, and to observe and comply with all requirements of the Club respecting conduct and service of its team and its players, at all times whether on or off the field.

Pictures and Public Appearances (c) The Player agrees that his picture may be taken for still photographs, motion pictures or television at such times as the Club may designate and agrees that all rights in such pictures shall belong to the Club and may be used by the Club for publicity purposes in any manner it desires. The Player further agrees that during the playing season he will not make public appearances, participate in radio or television programs or permit his picture to be taken or write or sponsor newspaper or magazine articles or sponsor commercial products without the written consent of the Club, which shall not be withheld except in the reasonable interests of the Club or professional baseball.

Player Representations
Ability 4. (a) The Player represents and agrees that he has exceptional and unique skill and ability as a baseball player; that his services to be rendered hereunder are of a special, unusual and extraordinary character which gives them peculiar value which cannot be reasonably or adequately compensated for in damages at law, and that the Player's breach of this contract will cause the Club great and irreparable injury and damage. The Player agrees that, in addition to other remedies, the Club shall be entitled to injunctive and other equitable relief to prevent a breach of this contract by the Player, including, among others, the right to enjoin the Player from playing baseball for any other person or organization during the term of this contract.

Condition (b) The Player represents that he has no physical or mental defects known to him, which would prevent or impair performance of his services.

Interest in Club (c) The Player represents that he does not, directly or indirectly, own stock or have any financial interest in the ownership or earnings of any Major League Club, except as hereinafter expressly set forth, and covenants that he will not hereafter, while connected with any Major League Club, acquire or hold any such stock or interest except in accordance with Major League Rule 20(e).

Service 5. (a) The Player agrees that, while under contract, and prior to expiration of the Club's right to renew this contract, he will not play baseball otherwise than for the Club, except that the Player may participate in post-season games under the conditions prescribed in the Major League Rules. Major League Rule 18(b) is set forth on page 4 hereof.

Other Sports (b) The Player and the Club recognize and agree that the Player's participation in other sports may impair or destroy his ability and skill as a baseball player. Accordingly the Player agrees that he will not engage in professional boxing or wrestling; and that, except with the written consent of the Club, he will not engage in any game or exhibition of football, basketball, hockey or other athletic sport.

Flood's contract with the St. Louis Cardinals for the 1969 season.

Chapter 8: The Trial—Day One—May 19, 1970

Assignment

No Salary Reduction

Reporting

Obligations of Assignor and Assignee Clubs

6. (a) The Player agrees that this contract may be assigned by the Club (and reassigned by any assignee Club) to any other Club in accordance with the Major League Rules and the Professional Baseball Rules.
   (b) The amount stated in paragraph 2 hereof which is payable to the Player for the period stated in paragraph 1 hereof shall not be diminished by any such assignment, except for failure to report as provided in the next sub-paragraph (c).
   (c) The Player shall report to assignee Club promptly (as provided in the Regulations) upon receipt of written notice from the Club of the assignment of this contract. If the Player fails so to report, he shall not be entitled to any payment for the period from the date he receives written notice of assignment until he reports to the assignee Club.
   (d) Upon and after such assignment, all rights and obligations of the assignor Club hereunder shall become the rights and obligations of the assignee Club; provided, however, that
      (1) The assignee Club shall be liable to the Player for payments accruing only from the date of assignment and shall not be liable (but the assignor Club shall remain liable) for payments accrued prior to that date.
      (2) If at any time the assignee is a Major League Club, it shall be liable to pay the Player at the full rate stipulated in paragraph 2 hereof for the remainder of the period stated in paragraph 1 hereof and all prior assignors and assignees shall be relieved of liability for any payment for such period.
      (3) Unless the assignor and assignee Clubs agree otherwise, if the assignee Club is a National Association Club, the assignee Club shall be liable only to pay the Player at the rate usually paid by said assignee Club to other players of similar skill and ability in its classification and the assignor Club shall be liable to pay the difference for the remainder of the period stated in paragraph 1 hereof between an amount computed at the rate stipulated in paragraph 2 hereof and the amount so payable by the assignee Club.

Moving Expense

(e) If this contract is assigned by a Major League Club to another Major League Club during the playing season, the assignor Club shall pay the Player, for all moving and other expenses resulting from such assignment, the sum of $300 if the contract is assigned between Clubs in the same zone; the sum of $600 if the contract is assigned between a Club in the Eastern Zone and a Club in the Central Zone; the sum of $900 if the contract is assigned between a Club in the Central Zone and a Club in the Western Zone; and the sum of $1,200 if the contract is assigned between a Club in the Eastern Zone and a Club in the Western Zone. The Eastern Zone shall include the Philadelphia, New York and Pittsburgh Clubs in the National League and the Baltimore, Boston, New York and Washington Clubs in the American League; the Central Zone shall include the Chicago, Cincinnati, Atlanta, St. Louis and Houston Clubs in the National League and the Chicago, Cleveland, Detroit and Minnesota Clubs in the American League; the Western Zone shall include the Los Angeles and San Francisco Clubs in the National League and the California and Oakland Clubs in the American League.

If, during the Major League playing season, a Player is required to report to a Major League Club from a National Association Club, or to a National Association Club from a Major League Club, such Major League Club shall pay the reasonable and actual moving expenses of the Player and other expenses resulting from such transfer and shall reimburse the Player for up to one month's rental payments for living quarters in the city from which the Player is transferred for which he is legally obligated after the date of the transfer and for which he is not otherwise reimbursed; except the foregoing shall not apply if the Player is required to report on or after September 1.

"Club"

(f) All references in other paragraphs of this contract to "the Club" shall be deemed to mean and include any assignee of this contract.

Termination

By Player

7. (a) The Player may terminate this contract, upon written notice to the Club, if the Club shall default in the payments to the Player provided for in paragraph 2 hereof or shall fail to perform any other obligation agreed to be performed by the Club hereunder and if the Club shall fail to remedy such default within ten (10) days after the receipt by the Club of written notice of such default. The Player may also terminate this contract as provided in sub-paragraph (f).(4) of this paragraph 7.

By Club

(b) The Club may terminate this contract upon written notice to the Player (but only after requesting and obtaining waivers of this contract from all other Major League Clubs) if the Player shall at any time:
   (1) fail, refuse or neglect to conform his personal conduct to the standards of good citizenship and good sportsmanship or to keep himself in first-class physical condition or to obey the Club's training rules; or
   (2) fail, in the opinion of the Club's management, to exhibit sufficient skill or competitive ability to qualify or continue as a member of the Club's team; or
   (3) fail, refuse or neglect to render his services hereunder or in any other manner materially breach this contract.
(c) If this contract is terminated by the Club by reason of the Player's failure to render his services hereunder due to disability resulting directly from injury sustained in the course and within the scope of his employment hereunder and written notice of such injury is given by the Player as provided in the Regulations on page 4 hereof, the Player shall be entitled to receive his full salary for the season in which the injury was sustained, less all workmen's compensation payment paid or payable by reason of said injury.
(d) If this contract is terminated by the Club during the training season, payment by the Club of the Player's board, lodging, and expense allowance during the training season to the date of termination and of the reasonable traveling expenses of the Player, including first-class jet air fare and meals en route to his home city, and the expert training and coaching provided by the Club to the Player during the training season shall be full payment to the Player.
(e) If this contract is terminated by the Club during the playing season, then, except in the case provided for in sub-paragraph (c) of this paragraph 7, the Player shall be entitled to receive as full payment hereunder such portion of the amount stipulated in paragraph 2 hereof as the number of days of his actual employment in the Club's playing season bears to the total number of days in said season, provided, however, that if this contract is terminated under sub-paragraph (b) (2) of this paragraph 7 for failure to exhibit sufficient skill or competitive ability, the Player shall be entitled to an additional amount equal to thirty (30) days payment at the rate stipulated in paragraph 2 hereof and the reasonable traveling expenses of the Player including first-class jet air fare and meals en route to his home city.

Procedure

(f) If the Club proposes to terminate this contract in accordance with sub-paragraph (b) of this paragraph 7, the procedure shall be as follows:
   (1) The Club shall request waivers from all other Major League Clubs. Such waiver request must state that it is for the purpose of terminating this contract and it may not be withdrawn.
   (2) Upon receipt of the waiver request, any other Major League Club may claim assignment of this contract at a waiver price of $1.00, the priority of claims to be determined in accordance with the Major League Rules.
   (3) If this contract is so claimed, the Club shall, promptly and before any assignment, notify the Player that it had requested waivers for the purpose of terminating this contract and that the contract had been claimed.
   (4) Within 5 days after receipt of notice of such claim, the Player shall be entitled, by written notice to the Club, to terminate this contract on the date of his notice of termination. If the Player fails so to notify the Club, this contract shall be assigned to the claiming Club.
   (5) If the contract is not claimed, the Club shall promptly deliver written notice of termination to the Player at the expiration of the waiver period.
(g) Upon any termination of this contract by the Player, all obligations of both parties hereunder shall cease on the date of termination, except the obligation of the Club to pay the Player's compensation to said date.

73

Baseball's Reserve System: The Case and Trial of Curt Flood v. Major League Baseball

Regulations 8. The Player accepts as part of this contract the Regulations printed on the fourth page hereof.

Rules 9. (a) The Club and the Player agree to accept, abide by and comply with all provisions of the Major League Agreement, the Major League Rules, the Rules or Regulations of the League of which the Club is a member, and the Professional Baseball Rules, in effect on the date of this Uniform Player's Contract, which are not inconsistent with the provisions of this contract or the provisions of any agreement between the Major League Clubs and the Major League Baseball Players Association, provided that the Club, together with the other Clubs of the American and National Leagues and the National Association, reserves the right to modify, supplement or repeal any provision of said Agreement, Rules and/or Regulations in a manner not inconsistent with this contract or the provisions of any then existing agreement between the Major League Clubs and the Major League Baseball Players Association. A copy of the Major League Agreement, the Major League Rules, the Rules or Regulations of the League of which the Club is a member, and the Professional Baseball Rules, as in effect on the date of this Contract has been delivered to the Player prior to execution of this Contract.

Disputes (b) All disputes between the Player and the Club which are covered by the Grievance Procedure as set forth in the Agreement between the twenty Clubs and the Major League baseball players, as represented by the Major League Baseball Players Association, dated February 19, 1968, shall be resolved in accordance with such Grievance Procedure, which is incorporated herein by reference.

Publication (c) The Club, the League President and the Commissioner, or any of them, may make public the findings, decision and record of any inquiry, investigation or hearing held or conducted, including in such record all evidence or information, given, received or obtained in connection therewith.

Renewal 10. (a) On or before January 15 (or if a Sunday, then the next preceding business day) of the year next following the last playing season covered by this contract, the Club may tender to the Player a contract for the term of that year by mailing the same to the Player at his address following his signature hereto, or if none be given, then at his last address of record with the Club. If prior to the March 1 next succeeding said January 15, the Player and the Club have not agreed upon the terms of such contract, then on or before 10 days after said March 1, the Club shall have the right by written notice to the Player at said address to renew this contract for the period of one year on the same terms, except that the amount payable to the Player shall be such as the Club shall fix in said notice; provided, however, that said amount, if fixed by a Major League Club, shall be an amount payable at a rate not less than 80% of the rate stipulated for the preceding year.
(b) The Club's right to renew this contract, as provided in sub-paragraph (a) of this paragraph 10, and the promise of the Player not to play otherwise than with the Club have been taken into consideration in determining the amount payable under paragraph 2 hereof.

11. This contract is subject to federal or state legislation, regulations, executive or other official orders or other governmental action, now or hereafter in effect respecting military, naval, air or other governmental service, which may directly or indirectly affect the Player, Club or the League and subject also to the right of the Commissioner to suspend the operation of this contract during any national emergency.

Commissioner 12. The term "Commissioner" wherever used in this contract shall be deemed to mean the Commissioner designated under the Major League Agreement, or in the case of a vacancy in the office of Commissioner, the Executive Council or such other body or person or persons as shall be designated in the Major League Agreement to exercise the powers and duties of the Commissioner during such vacancy.

Supplemental Agreements The Club and the Player covenant that this contract fully sets forth all understandings and agreements between them, and agree that no other understandings or agreements, whether heretofore or hereafter made, shall be valid, recognizable, or of any effect whatsoever, unless expressly set forth in a new or supplemental contract executed by the Player and the Club (acting by its president, or such other officer as shall have been thereunto duly authorized by the president or Board of Directors, as evidenced by a certificate filed of record with the League President and Commissioner) and complying with the Major League Rules and the Professional Baseball Rules.

Special Covenants

Approval This contract or any supplement hereto shall not be valid or effective unless and until approved by the League President.

Signed in duplicate this 3RD day of MARCH, A.D. 1969

Curtis C. Flood (Player)
4466 West Pine
St. Louis, Missouri
(Home address of Player)

ST. LOUIS NATIONAL BASEBALL CLUB, INC. (Club)
By _____ (Authorized Signature)
Gen. Mgr.

Social Security No. _____

Approved _____ 196__
President, National League of Professional Baseball Clubs

Chapter 8: The Trial—Day One—May 19, 1970

REGULATIONS

1. The Club's playing season for each year covered by this contract and all renewals hereof shall be as fixed by the National League of Professional Baseball Clubs, or if this contract shall be assigned to a Club in another League, then by the League of which such assignee is a member.

2. The Player, when requested by the Club, must submit to a complete physical examination at the expense of the Club, and if necessary to treatment by a regular physician or dentist in good standing. Upon refusal of the Player to submit to a complete medical or dental examination the Club may consider such refusal a violation of this regulation and may take such action as it deems advisable under Regulation 5 of this contract. Disability directly resulting from injury sustained in the course and within the scope of his employment under this contract shall not impair the right of the Player to receive his full salary for the period of such disability or for the season in which the injury was sustained (whichever period is shorter), together with the reasonable medical and hospital expenses incurred by reason of the injury and during the term of this contract, less all workmen's compensation payments paid or payable by reason of said injury; but only upon the express prerequisite conditions that (a) written notice of such injury, including the time, place, cause and nature of the injury, is served upon and received by the Club within twenty days of the sustaining of said injury and (b) the Club shall have the right to designate the doctors and hospitals furnishing such medical and hospital services. Any other disability may be ground for suspending or terminating this contract at the discretion of the Club.

3. The Club will furnish the Player with two complete uniforms, exclusive of shoes, which uniforms will be surrendered by the Player to the Club at the end of the season or upon termination of this contract.

4. The Club will pay all proper and necessary traveling expenses of the Player while "abroad", or traveling with the Club in other cities, including board, and first-class air and hotel accommodations, if practicable.
   During the championship season, the allowance for meals and tips shall be $15 per day for each date a Club is on the road and for each traveling day. No deductions will be made for meals served on an airplane. If, when a Club departs from the home city, departure is scheduled prior to 12:00 Noon, the Player will receive $15 for that date; if departure is after 12:00 Noon, the Player will receive $7.50 for that date. Returning to the home city, if arrival is later than 6:00 p.m. the Player will receive $15; if arrival is prior to 6:00 p.m., the Player will receive $7.50. The Club may require the Player to sign checks for meals at a hotel in lieu of the cash meal allowance.
   During the training season, the Player will receive an allowance of $40 per week, payable in advance, to cover training camp expenses. If the Player has his family in camp and is granted consent to live away from the Club's headquarters, he shall receive a meal money allowance of $12 per day, without deduction for lunch or sandwiches served at the ball park, and a room allowance equal to what the Club actually saves on hotel expenses by reason of the Player not staying at the Club hotel. Where the Club owns its own facilities (such as Los Angeles or Houston) where there is no saving, the Club will allow $2 per day per room, in addition to the $12 allowance for meals.
   The Club will also pay the first-class jet air fare of the Player to his home at the end of the season, provided, however, that if the Club finishes its season "abroad" and appropriate transportation is not provided back to the Club's home city, the Player shall be paid an amount equal to the first-class jet air fare back to the Club's home city plus the first-class jet air fare from the Club's home city to the Player's home, provided the Player elects to return home via the Club's home city.

5. For violation by the Player of any regulation or other provision of this contract, the Club may impose a reasonable fine and deduct the amount thereof from the Player's salary or may suspend the Player without salary for a period not exceeding thirty days, or both. Written notice of the fine or suspension or both and the reason therefore shall in every case be given to the Player.

6. In order to enable the Player to fit himself for his duties under this contract, the Club may require the Player to report for practice at such places as the Club may designate and to participate in such exhibition contests as may be arranged by the Club, for a period beginning not earlier than March 1, without any other compensation than that herein elsewhere provided. The Club will pay the necessary traveling expenses, including the first-class jet air fare and meals en route of the Player from his home city to the training place of the Club, whether he be ordered to go there directly or by way of the home city of the Club. In the event of the failure of the Player to report for practice or to participate in the exhibition games, as required and provided for, he shall be required to get into playing condition to the satisfaction of the Club's team manager, and at the Player's own expense, before his salary shall commence.

7. In case of assignment of this contract the Player shall report promptly to the assignee club within 72 hours from the date he receives written notice from the Club of such assignment, if the Player is then not more than 1600 miles by most direct available railroad route from the assignee Club, plus an additional 24 hours for each additional 800 miles.

   Post-Season Exhibition Games. Major League Rule 18(b) provides:

   Exhibition Games. (b) No player shall participate in any exhibition game played during the period between the close of the Major League championship season and the following training season; except that a Player, with the written consent of the Commissioner, may participate in exhibition games which are played within thirty days after the close of the Major League championship season and which are approved by the Commissioner. Player conduct, on and off the field, in connection with such post-season exhibition games shall be subject to the discipline of the Commissioner. The Commissioner shall not approve more than three Players of any one Club on the same team. No Player shall participate in any exhibition game with or against any team which, during the current season or within one year, has had any ineligible player for which is or has been during the current season or within one year, managed and controlled by an ineligible player under an assumed name or who otherwise has violated, or attempted to violate, any exhibition game contract; or with or against any team which, during said season or within one year, has played against teams containing such ineligible players, or so managed or controlled. Any player violating this rule shall be fined not less than fifty dollars ($50) nor more than five hundred dollars ($500), except that in no event shall such fine be less than the consideration received by such player for participating in such game.

Revised 10/1/68

Baseball's Reserve System: The Case and Trial of Curt Flood v. Major League Baseball

During the 1969 season, Flood testified that he was fined $250 for missing a team promotional banquet. The day before the banquet, while sliding into second base, Flood received a "5 inch spike" injury on his thigh from New York Met shortstop Bud Harrelson. Cardinal management's position was that Flood's injury was not serious enough to excuse his absence from the team banquet.

Flood reiterated that he first learned of his trade by telephone on October 8, 1969. Flood told the court that the call was from Jim Toomey, assistant to the Cardinals' General Manager, Vaughn (Bing) Devine; and Flood was informed that the trade was a seven player deal between the Phillies and the Cardinals. Flood, Tim McCarver, Joe Hoerner and Byron Browne had been traded to the Phillies for Richie Allen, Cookie Rojas and Jerry Johnson.

Flood testified that later that same day, he called General Manager Devine and told Devine "that I didn't think I was going to report to Philadelphia, mainly because I didn't want to pick up twelve years of my life and move to another city." Goldberg then offered as evidence Flood's Notice of Player Release or Transfer dated October 8, 1969, and a "best of luck" letter from Bing Devine to Flood dated October 8, 1969. Flood also noted that prior to receiving the written notice and telephone call from Cardinal management, Flood was never consulted by anyone regarding the trade to Philadelphia.

Goldberg then attempted to establish Flood's monetary "damages" as a result of the trade. Flood testified that he was a commercial artist; that he operated two photographic studios and one portrait studio in St. Louis. The business consisted of taking school "cap and gown" pictures and school photographs. Flood stated that these studios were being franchised—the first being located in Evanston, Illinois. Flood had started the portrait painting business in the early 1960s, and had started the photography studios in 1968.

CHAPTER 8: THE TRIAL—DAY ONE—MAY 19, 1970

At the time of the trade, Flood testified that he intended to play baseball in 1970 for the St. Louis Cardinals. In late October and November 1969, Flood met with Phillies General Manager John Quinn. Flood's testimony was that he told Quinn that he did not intend to play baseball with Philadelphia in the 1970 season. In an effort to change Flood's mind, Quinn offered Flood an annual salary of $90,000 plus $8,000 in spring training expenses—to no avail. Flood testified that it was Flood and not Marvin Miller or the Players' Association, who decided to file this suit because "I didn't think that after twelve years I should be traded and treated like a piece of property"; that he wanted to continue to play for the St. Louis Cardinals, but would play for another team "if I had the choice of playing for whom I chose or whoever offered me the best deal."

Flood told Judge Cooper that he was in excellent physical condition, that he was thirty-two years old, and that he could "easily" play another five years; that not being able to play the 1970 season was adversely affecting his skill as a ballplayer; and that he could command a salary of $90,000 during each of those years. Flood specifically mentioned Stan Musial, Hoyt Wilhelm, Ted Williams, Willie Mays, Hank Aaron and Mickey Mantle as examples of players who had productive years between the age of 32 and 40.

Toward the conclusion of Flood's direct testimony, Goldberg asked Flood if he had ever had discussions with the Cardinals about retiring from baseball. Flood recounted that in February 1968, while negotiating his 1968 contract, Flood told Cardinal General Manager Devine that he wanted a salary of $100,000 for the 1968 season, and that Flood would retire from baseball unless he was paid that salary. Apparently, Goldberg wanted to establish that Flood's threat of retirement in 1968 was merely a negotiating tactic (one of the few negotiating weapons available to a ballplayer), and that Flood had played the 1968 and 1969 seasons despite this retirement threat. After all, Flood was now telling the Court that he would incur irreparable injury and significant monetary damages unless he was allowed to continue to play baseball for the team of his choice.

Goldberg then directed his witness to the post-trade communications with Commissioner Bowie Kuhn. Plaintiff's counsel offered as evidence Flood's now famous Christmas Eve 1969 "I am not a piece of property letter" to Commissioner Kuhn; and then offered Commissioner Kuhn's letter in response dated December 30, 1969. The contrasts of these letters could not be more striking. Flood's letter formally asserted that he had the right to consider offers from teams other than the Phillies, and that the Commissioner's enforcement of baseball's "reserve system" violated "the laws of the United States and of the several states". Kuhn's letter acknowledged receipt of Flood's December 24th correspondence; included Kuhn's acknowledgment that Flood was "a human being" and "not a piece of property"; ignored Flood's specific requests; and audaciously stated that *if* Flood had "any specific objection to the propriety of the assignment, I (Kuhn) would appreciate your specifying the objection." In short, Kuhn *totally ignored* Flood's letter and the position therein asserted.

With no objection from the defense, Goldberg offered as exhibits and into evidence Flood's contract and a copy of Major League Rules and the Professional Baseball Rules. Flood then testified that under the contract and Major League Baseball rules, and despite the fact that Flood had not consented or agreed to his assignment or "trade" to Philadelphia, and despite the fact that he had no written contract then in effect with the Cardinals or the Phillies, Flood was prohibited from negotiating with any major league baseball team.

It must be emphasized that the essential facts in Flood's case were not in dispute. Offering sufficient evidence to

CHAPTER 8: THE TRIAL—DAY ONE—MAY 19, 1970

prove the existence of the reserve system and the practices of the owners was not a particularly difficult task. After all, baseball's reserve system had been in existence for over 80 years, and had actually been reduced to writing. Moreover, the defense was not only admitting that the reserve system was in existence, but was arguing that the continued existence and enforcement of the reserve system was absolutely essential for the integrity and betterment of baseball!

While Flood's testimony was not critical to proving many of the key facts, his testimony was crucial with respect to the players, the public and the media. The manner in which Flood delivered his testimony, his demeanor, his believability, and the conviction of his presentation would have been even more crucial had it been a jury trial. But it was not—Judge Cooper was the jury *and* the judge in this case.

The overwhelming majority of Flood's cross examination was handled by defense counsel Mark Hughes. First, Hughes questioned Flood about his familiarity with the Major League Baseball contract provisions—particularly the renewal option clause. Flood admitted that he had signed a total of 14 player contracts during the course of his career (two with Cincinnati and twelve with St. Louis) and that those contracts contained the same provisions which he was now challenging.

Second, the defense questioned Flood about his "happy years" in St. Louis, and tried to establish that Flood was "well paid" by the Cardinals for his services. Hughes pointed out that in addition to the annual salaries, Flood was paid for personal appearances and endorsements related to playing professional baseball; and that in 1964, 1967 and 1968, Flood received additional compensation for playing in the World Series.

Third, the defense impeached Flood's prior testimony that by late October 1969, Flood "decided" that he would not accept the trade to Philadelphia. The defense offered into evidence a letter from Flood to Phillies General Manager John Quinn dated December 4, 1969.[8] Confronted with the letter, Flood admitted that he had indeed met with John Quinn even *after* "deciding"not to accept the trade to Philadelphia.

The fourth area of cross examination turned out to be one of the defense's central arguments. The defense maintained that the "real plaintiff" was the Major League Baseball Players' Association, not Curt Flood. On this issue, the defense got Flood to admit i) that the Players' Association was "a very interested party" in this litigation; ii) that Flood had consulted with Marvin Miller and Richard Moss before meeting with his trial counsel Arthur Goldberg; and that Miller, Moss and Flood later met to discuss the possible suit with Arthur Goldberg; iii) that at the time the suit was filed, the Players' Association was in negotiations with the club owners; iv) that prior to filing this lawsuit, Flood met and consulted with the Players' Association in December 1969; and v) that the Players' Association was paying Flood's legal fees and expenses.

Next, the defense clearly established that Flood was seeking to abolish, not to modify, baseball's reserve system. Defense counsel Hughes questioned Flood as follows:

"Q. Do you want an injunction against the defendants from enforcing the reserve system against you?

A. Yes.

---

[8] December 4, 1969

"Dear Mr. Quinn:

Please accept my apologies for not returning your recent calls but the press of business made it difficult.

As you learned this morning, I am out of town at present and am dictating this letter by phone.

With regard to our conversations, I feel that I must resolve a number of personal problems *before I make a final decision*. Therefore, *I intend to give the entire matter serious consideration during the next two weeks* and will be in touch with you during the week of December 22nd."

Chapter 8: The Trial—Day One—May 19, 1970

Q. Do you want an injunction against the defendants from conspiring not to allow any club but Philadelphia to negotiate with you?
A. Yes.
Q. Is that what you want or do you only want some modification of the system?
A. I think some modification would do that for me.
Q. Well, which is it that you want? Do you want a modification or do you want the whole system to be struck down and declared illegal?
A. I would like the whole system to be struck down and declared illegal.
Q. So…you do want something more than a modification of the system, is that right?
A. Yes, I guess you are right.
Q. So you are correcting the answer you gave to me a little while ago in which you said you didn't want to have it declared illegal but merely to modify it?
A. Yes.
Q. You are correcting that?
A. I am correcting that.
Q. You want to be a free agent?
A. Yes."

Hughes then attempted to impeach Flood with an inconsistent statement made back in early January 1970 during a television interview with sportscaster and journalist Howard Cosell.

"Q. Mr. Flood, do you recall a television interview with Howard Cosell on January 3, 1969 (sic)? (The correct date was January 3, 1970.)
A. Yes, I do…
Q. And did you, in the course of that interview, have this colloquy with Mr. Cosell…
'If in the current negotiations Mr. Miller succeeds in inducing baseball to modify the reserve clause, would you

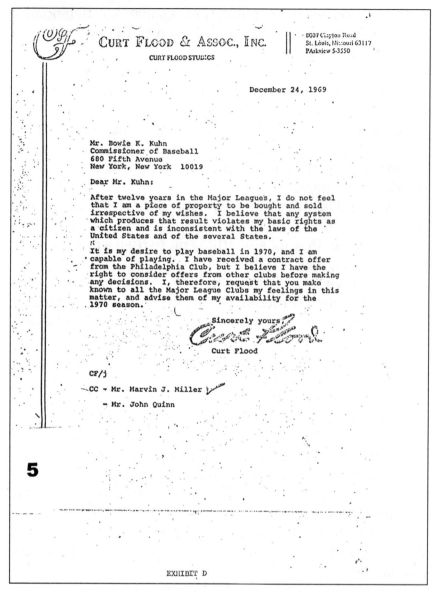

Flood's Christmas Eve 1969 letter to Commissioner Bowie Kuhn asserting Flood's right to negotiate and consider offers from other teams.

```
                    BASEBALL
              OFFICE OF THE COMMISSIONER
                   680 FIFTH AVENUE
                  NEW YORK, N.Y. 10019
BOWIE K. KUHN
 COMMISSIONER                                          TELEPHONE 212-265-8400
```

December 30, 1969.

Dear Curt:

This will acknowledge your letter of December 24, 1969, which I found on returning to my office yesterday.

I certainly agree with you that you, as a human being, are not a piece of property to be bought and sold. That is fundamental in our society and I think obvious. However, I cannot see its applicability to the situation at hand.

You have entered into a current playing contract with the St. Louis club which has the same assignment provision as those in your annual Major League contracts since 1956. Your present contract has been assigned in accordance with its provisions by the St. Louis club to the Philadelphia club. The provisions of the playing contract have been negotiated over the years between the clubs and the players, most recently when the present Basic Agreement was negotiated two years ago between the clubs and the Players Association.

If you have any specific objection to the propriety of the assignment, I would appreciate your specifying the objection. Under the circumstances, and pending any further information from you, I do not see what action I can take and cannot comply with the request contained in the second paragraph of your letter.

I am pleased to see your statement that you desire to play baseball in 1970. I take it this puts to rest any thought, as reported earlier in the press, that you were considering retirement.

                                          Sincerely yours,

                                          Bowie K. Kuhn

BKK/ms

Mr. Curt Flood
Curt Flood & Assoc., Inc.
8007 Clayton Road
St. Louis, Missouri 63117

cc: Mr. Marvin J. Miller
cc: Mr. Vaughan P. (Bing) Devine
cc: Mr. John J. Quinn

6

EXHIBIT E

Commissioner Kuhn's response—rejecting Flood's asserted right of free agency.

drop your suit?'

And then you are recorded as answering:

'Well, that is the basic reason for the suit, to get something short of what it is now. *Any revision of the reserve clause, something both parties can live with would be just fine with me.*'

Do you recall saying that?

A. Yes, I recall saying that.

Q. And is that the way you feel now?...

A. No, that's not the way I feel now...

Q. How do you feel now?

A. Well, I feel that we ought to start all over again and just wipe this thing out and do something different.

Q. You believe the whole reserve system should be scrapped?

A. Absolutely."

At the very end of this line of questioning, Flood reaffirmed that he was eager to play major league baseball in 1970, but that he was not prepared to sign a contract with the Philadelphia club for $90,000; that Flood wanted to play for the team "that makes me the best offer"; and that if no offers are received, Flood would not play at all. Many commentators opined that Flood simply would not play in Philadelphia under any circumstances, regardless of the offer because of Philadelphia's history and reputation for racial bias. This observation, however, is *not* supported by the trial record. It was Flood's testimony that he was prepared to play the 1970 season (and presumably thereafter) for the Phillies if the Philadelphia club made him the best offer.

Defense counsel then offered into evidence several documents, including a letter to Flood from Phillies General Manager John Quinn dated March 4, 1970, to establish that the Phillies had offered Flood a one year contract for $90,000. The letter also directed Flood to report to Clearwater, Florida for the Phillies' spring training practices.

Chapter 8: The Trial—Day One—May 19, 1970

Flood testified that he received these documents and acknowledged the contract offer, but noted that he did not sign the contract and did not report to the Phillies' training camp in Clearwater.

Defense counsel then questioned whether Flood had any communications with Commissioner Kuhn in response to the "I am not a piece of property letter" of December 24, 1969. Flood recalled that Commissioner Kuhn called Flood on or about December 30, 1969. During that conversation, Flood testified that Kuhn "merely read to me over the phone" the substance of his December 30, 1969 letter. Other than the December 30, 1969 letter and this telephone call, Flood received no communications from Commissioner Kuhn. Flood did, however, receive a call from Mr. Monte Irvin in Commissioner Kuhn's office. Mr. Irvin invited Flood to meet with Commissioner Kuhn in New York or Los Angeles at a time convenient for Flood. Flood testified that he declined Mr. Irvin's invitation and never again spoke or met with Commissioner Kuhn after that call.

Throughout Flood's testimony, Judge Cooper's treatment of the lawyers and the witness was nothing short of remarkable. Judge Cooper's comments to and treatment of the attorneys were nauseating, while at the same time, Judge Cooper's remarks and behavior toward Curt Flood were both rude and pompous. Judge Cooper's "ass kissing" of the lawyers started early in the trial:

"Now gentlemen, I would be remiss if we started trial without my having a word of comment on the record with respect to your splendid show of cooperation. Not only have you exemplified courtesy from one to the other and to the Court, but you have been extremely helpful in cutting through a lot of red tape and making this early trial possible. Without you, this could not have come to pass. You haven't given an inch on the merits; and that is understandable.

However, you have procedurally and wherever else you could accommodate one another, done so. We appreciate it [to] no end. We shall do our utmost to help you continue that show of excellent spirit throughout the trial.

I take it you are comfortable and that whatever you need you recognize we shall be glad to supply insofar as we possibly can...*We want you, you who have the burden, the tremendous burden of proof here and who labor under heavy responsibility, to feel as comfortable as you possibly can. And I would appreciate it if you call to my attention anything that we can do to help us sustain that notion.*"

In response to an early objection raised by Attorney Mark Hughes, Judge Cooper's sermon continued:

"You have a perfect right to have the record reflect whatever you think is in the best interests of your respective clients. Do not hesitate to interrupt because that is your duty."

Later, Judge Cooper continued his disrespectful treatment of Flood. The first instance occurred very early in Flood's direct examination. Immediately following one of Flood's answers, defense counsel Hughes rose to state his objection. After sustaining the objection, Judge Cooper turned to the witness and began to lecture Flood in a most condescending tone:

"Mr. Flood, you see, there are certain rules of evidence that govern us in a trial of a case, *and when you are asked a simple question* by counsel you must not give your thinking or the thinking that might have gone on in the mind of someone else...You are really arguing, you see...[A]ll you do then is respond according to your best recollection as to what you said, and what the other side said and tell us everything that took place on that occasion. *Do you think you can do that?*"

At another point, and even in the absence of any objection by defense counsel, Judge Cooper interrupted Gold-

Chapter 8: The Trial—Day One—May 19, 1970

berg's interrogation. The following exchange between Judge Cooper and defense counsel Hughes was quite bizarre:

Judge Cooper: "...I am sorry, Mr. Flood, but, you see, counsel doesn't want to interrupt and I see why *they are unhappy and they have a right to be unhappy.*"

Attorney Hughes: "Judge, I am not unhappy ..."

Judge Cooper: "Do you want me to strike what I said? *I thought you were trying to prevent getting up on your feet, and I wanted the record to show you were not particularly pleased with the testimony, but if you don't want it that way we will strike it.*"

Attorney Hughes: "Your Honor, I am not unhappy. I made certain objections which I thought were valid and I think your Honor indicated that you thought they were valid .... I am not unhappy, but I would like the witness to concentrate on what he said and what Mr. Devine [Cardinal General Manager] said."

Judge Cooper: "All right. You seem to object to the word "unhappy". We will strike "unhappy" and substitute the words "somewhat discomfited".

Then Judge Cooper appeared to openly taunt the witness:

Now, Mr. Flood, I presume you are not finding this as easy as getting up at bat, is that right?"

What is perhaps even more incredible is that Curt Flood then *apologized* to the Judge.

The trial transcript is also replete with other instances of Judge Cooper "speaking down" to Curt Flood. Instead of politely directing the witness to speak loudly and clearly when responding to counsel's questions, Judge Cooper took it upon himself in open court to lecture Flood like a school child:

"Mr. Flood, we are undoubtedly going to be with you for some time as a witness. The trial is a public trial. People have a right to come into this courtroom. That is the American way. I presume a good number of them have come here purposely to see you. They want to hear you. They have a right to know what is going on, and I am going to ask you, *and I hope it will be for the last time*, to really almost shout, if you have to, because we want to hear what you have to say."

Finally, and again in stark contrast to his treatment of Curt Flood, Judge Cooper continued to pamper trial counsel.

"If at any time the recesses *are too short*, you are to so indicate to the Clerk, *because I want you to be fully accommodated*. And also when there is extensive reading, *may I suggest that* it is alright with me if *you will have one of your* associates do the reading *and relieve you from the constancy of exercising your voice.*"

Curt Flood completed his testimony during the morning of May 19, 1970. He would not again testify in his trial.

Testimony of Marvin J. Miller

Next to the witness stand came Marvin J. Miller, Executive Director of the Major League Baseball Players' Association. Early on, Miller's testimony focused on his background and his role as Executive Director. Miller possessed a bachelor's degree in economics. Miller had previously been employed as an economist and worked as such for a couple of agencies of the federal government. From 1950-1966, Miller was employed by the U.S. Steelworkers of America. For the Steelworkers' union, Miller was the associate director of research, and in 1960 became the union's president.

On July 1, 1966, Miller became the Executive Director of the Players' Association. Despite the name, Miller explained that the Association was comprised of major league players, coaches, trainers and managers. As Executive Director, Miller testified that he directed the affairs of the Association; coordinated the needs and interests of players through collective bargaining; served as chief negotiator for the union; and represented the membership in grievance proceedings.

CHAPTER 8: THE TRIAL—DAY ONE—MAY 19, 1970

Goldberg then directed his witness to the heart of the case—baseball's reserve system. The first aspect of the reserve system discussed by Miller was the so-called "free agent draft". Held twice a year, the free agent draft affected players who had never before signed a major league or minor league contract. Once "drafted" by a team, that player was permitted to negotiate a contract or deal only with that team. Once drafted and offered a contract, the "drafted" player had only two choices: accept the team's offer or decline the offer. If the player declined the offer, that player was prohibited from contacting and attempting to negotiate with any other team, and likewise, no team was permitted to contact or attempt to negotiate with that "drafted" player. Prior to the free agent draft, a player who had never before signed a contract was free to negotiate with any and all teams. Miller also pointed out that once the "free agent draft" was instituted in 1965-66, signing bonuses, as expected, were reduced and paid less frequently.

Miller continued his attack on the reserve system, and then addressed the specific circumstances of the Cardinal center fielder. Miller pointed out that once a player, like Curt Flood, signed a major or minor league contract, that player became the property of the organization with whom the player signed the contract. The player's contract could be assigned, reassigned, optioned to play in other leagues, sold or traded. The player's options? Miller hit this one out of the park—"The player can accept the consequences or find another way to make a living."

Miller then cited Major League Rule 3(a). This rule required that *all* player contracts be identical in form. The Major League Rules were adopted by the club owners, not by the players, and existed long before the Players' Association was formed. Rule 3(a) provided that no club could use, negotiate or enter into a contract which contained a *non*-reserve clause *except with the written approval of the*

Commissioner. The unrefuted testimony of Marvin Miller was that never before in the history of baseball had a Commissioner approved a contract that did not include these uniform provisions.

The heart of the reserve system's stranglehold was paragraph 10(a) of the Uniform Player's Contract. This paragraph 10(a) was often referred to as the "reserve clause". It provided that the owner may tender a contract to a player on or before January 15th; if the player and owner did not enter into a signed agreement by March 1st, then the club could unilaterally renew the contract simply by so advising the player by way of a written notice on or before March 10th. Miller further emphasized that this Paragraph 10(a) permitted the team owner to insert any salary figure in that contract renewal, except that the owner could not cut the player's salary by more than 20% below the prior year's salary. In other words, this provision allowed the owner to unilaterally renew the contract and bind the player for another season, *and to cut the player's salary by up to 20%!* In addition, failure to sign a contract, among other things, banned the player from participating in any post regular season competition. Miller explained that by signing the contract, the agreement then gave the owner another option renewal right for the next playing season, and so on for each time the player signed. The player's choices were very simple: sign the contract or find another way to make a living.

Goldberg then questioned Miller about another contract provision -paragraph 5. This paragraph provided that while the player was under contract and prior to expiration of the club's right to renew the contract, the player was prohibited from playing baseball otherwise than for that club. Under paragraph 5, once a player had signed his first major league contract, and as long as the club never let its option renewal lapse, the player could never play for any other

Chapter 8: The Trial—Day One—May 19, 1970

club. Further, Miller cited a previous Commissioner's decision pursuant to which the player was not only restricted from playing *baseball* for any other club, the player was prohibited from playing *any sport* for any other club.

Major League Rule 3(g) prohibited "tampering". A player who talked or met with another team or a team that talked or met with another team's player was guilty of "tampering". A player who violated the "no tampering" rule was "blacklisted", and would not likely play major league baseball again. A team or owner that was guilty of "tampering" was subject to fines imposed by the Commissioner.

To illustrate, Miller's testimony referenced several players in the 1940s who went to play professional baseball in the Mexican League. Some of those players were "blacklisted". Miller explained that a player who failed to report to the team by whom the player was "reserved" was placed on a *restricted list*. A player who violated his "reservation" (for example, chose not to sign another contract with his team, and chose to play in the Mexican League) was placed on a *disqualified list*. A player, for whatever reason, who was placed on either list could not play for any other club in major league baseball.

Up to this point, Miller discussed seven of the most restrictive aspects of baseball's reserve system:
1) the "free agent" draft;
2) the required use of the uniform contract;
3) the requirement that the "reserve system" be included in all contracts;
4) the option renewal clause [Paragraph 10(a)];
5) binding a player to the team with whom he first signed a major league contract (Paragraph 5);
6) the "tampering rule" [Rule 3 (g)]; and
7) the Commissioner's authority and status as the sole and final arbiter of any disputes. (The Commissioner, of course, was appointed and paid by the club owners).

Despite the Association's past and ongoing attempts to negotiate modifications to the reserve system, the owners' response, according to Miller, had been "completely negative". He stated that the owners "had not put forth a single counter proposal for any modification whatsoever in any of the various ramifications and rules that make up the reserve system". The owners had advised the union that the owners "liked the system the way it is and that they do not feel that they want to change it". Miller also insisted that the pendency of Flood's suit did not prevent negotiations on or modifications to baseball's reserve system.

Corroborating Flood's testimony, Miller testified that his first conversation with Flood was in late November 1969 at the Summit Hotel in New York City. This meeting's attendees were Flood, Miller, Allan Zerman, Flood's business lawyer from St. Louis, and Richard Moss, legal counsel for the Players' Association. Miller recalled that Flood opened the conversation by stating that he had already made a decision to file a lawsuit alleging that the reserve system was illegal and that he would act on that decision soon. At this meeting, Miller was emphatic that Flood's decision was a most serious step, and that the risks were great. The case would take several years to litigate and would probably be decided by the U.S. Supreme Court—and there was no assurance of victory. At age thirty-two, Flood's career as a player would be over. Miller also warned Flood that win or lose in court, the owners would almost certainly "blacklist" Flood for any front office, coaching or management position in major league baseball. According to Miller, he "presented every negative reason he could think of" and advised Flood to reconsider his decision to file a lawsuit. Flood's response was that Miller had not pointed out anything that Flood had not already taken into consideration.

Approximately three weeks later, Miller consulted with the Players' Association at the Association's December

CHAPTER 8: THE TRIAL—DAY ONE—MAY 19, 1970

meeting in San Juan, Puerto Rico. Miller invited Flood to address the Executive Board. At the conclusion of the presentation, the Association voted to support Flood's lawsuit and to assist Flood with his legal expenses.

While Miller's earlier testimony regarding the all-encompassing aspects and intricacies of baseball's reserve system was both critical and compelling, it was Miller's "expert opinion" testimony that began to reveal an "Achilles heel" in Flood's case. At this point, Goldberg questioned Miller as to how the reserve system affected baseball players and their profession. Miller's response would come back to haunt Flood's case.

"Q. Now in your opinion, Mr. Miller, what is your own view, based upon your expertise in the area, of how the reserve system operates today to affect baseball players and their profession?

A. In my opinion, I think it is unnecessarily and unduly restrictive. I do not believe that you can operate without rules. It is quite clear that you need rules and need rules relating to the contracting of players with employer clubs, *but I do believe that the set of very tight restrictive provisions which currently exist are unnecessary and can be modified in a manner that would preserve the intent of the club owners, the players and the fans.*"

Next to Curt Flood, Miller was the single most important witness called to testify in the plaintiff's case. Yet, astonishingly, Miller's opinion was that baseball's reserve system did *not* need to be *abolished*—it only needed *modification*! Flood's position had just been severely undercut—by his *own* expert witness.

Having been qualified and having stated his expert opinion as to *baseball's* reserve system, Goldberg then attempted to qualify Miller as an expert on the reserve systems in *other professional sports*. Defense counsel objected arguing that Miller had no personal knowledge or personal involvement with the contractual provisions and reserve system in any sport *other than baseball*; and that his knowledge of the reserve systems in other professional sports was based solely upon what Miller had been told by others and based upon what he had read. Judge Cooper agreed with the defense and sustained the objection. Because the implementation of Flood's trial strategy included a comparison of baseball's reserve system to the reserve systems in other professional sports, it now became necessary for the plaintiff to present experts from other professional sports.

Miller's testimony produced two significant developments: 1) Flood's own expert witness concluded that baseball's reserve system need not and should not be abolished (directly contrary to Flood's written Complaint and Flood's direct testimony); and 2) Flood's lawyers would now need to call additional expert witnesses who could present details and the specifics of the "reserve systems" in other professional sports.

The defense would pounce on these developments and continually point out that this lawsuit was, in reality, initiated by the players' union in an effort to obtain modifications to the reserve system and other concessions from the club owners—and that Flood was merely a pawn in the union's strategy.

The first day was a rough one for Plaintiff Curt Flood.

Chapter 9
Day Two—Thursday, May 21, 1970

Testimony of Jack R. Robinson

Next to the stand came baseball icon and Curt Flood idol, Jack R. Robinson—better known as Jackie Robinson. Those present that day recalled that when Jackie Robinson entered the courtroom, "you could hear a pin drop". Flood's wife Judy later remarked that Curt was deeply moved and appreciative that his childhood hero came to testify on his behalf.

Goldberg's examination began with Robinson joining the Brooklyn Dodgers in 1947. Robinson played a variety of positions and played 10 seasons with the Brooklyn Dodgers; had a career average of .311; hit .342 and was voted Most Valuable Player in 1949; played in six World Series; retired from professional baseball after the 1956 season; and was inducted into Baseball's Hall of Fame in 1962.

Goldberg wasted little time before asking Robinson his views on baseball's reserve system. According to Robinson,

"…anything that is one-sided in this country is wrong, and I think the reserve clause is a one-sided thing in favor of the owners, and I think it certainly should at least be modified to give a player an opportunity to have some control over his destiny .... [U]nless there is a change in the reserve clause...it is going to lead to a serious strike.... [T]hey are pretty well fed up with the fact that they now no longer can ever elect the team that they want to play for to start...."

(Robinson's testimony regarding a strike was prophetic. There was a work stoppage in 1972; and there have been eight work stoppages since 1970.)

Interestingly, Robinson then described the impact of baseball's reserve system on "players who sit on the bench". In Robinson's words:

"...the reserve clause does not affect the $90,000 ballplayers as much as it affects that guy who sits upon the bench...he has to sit there to wait until a regular becomes injured or something before he gets a chance to display his abilities. Therefore, as long as he is sitting there on that bench, his salary has got to remain, in my opinion, basically what it is because he has no real value, or they can't express his value by the way that he performs, and when that player becomes injured and he replaces him, in my opinion, the strain affects his ability anyway because he now has to prove to his manager, prove to the public that he is a major league ballplayer and it sometimes adds stress to his playing ability, and therefore it hurts his opportunity of becoming more proficient and a better ballplayer, therefore commanding more money."

Robinson cited the specific examples of Don Zimmer, Eddie Miksis and Don Hoak. Because the Dodgers had a strong starting lineup, it was Robinson's view that these "substitutes" had very little chance of playing for the Dodgers at that time. Robinson testified that Zimmer, Hoak and Miksis could have started on other teams. Because of baseball's reserve system, these "substitutes" had no ability to offer their services to another team. They had to wait to be traded or sold by their club. (Incidentally, Hoak, Zimmer and Miksis did later become regulars with other major league teams.)

Robinson's remarks were anything but ambiguous. He testified that modifying the reserve system "would in no way be derogatory to the game"; and that he considered baseball a big business, and not a sport. During his cross examination, defense counsel Hughes asked Robinson a series of questions trying to establish that back in 1958, Robinson had testified before a U.S. Senate Committee that he was "highly in favor of the reserve clause". At first, Robinson stated that he did not remember so testifying. Defense counsel Hughes than produced a copy of Robinson's testimony before that 1958 U.S. Senate Committee.

What followed was a flurry of objections and arguments among counsel regarding Robinson's 1958 Congressional testimony. According to Marvin Miller, Robinson's retort was that if he did make such a statement before Congress in 1958, he was then much younger and not as smart, "but now I am a lot older and a hell of a lot smarter about the business of baseball and the reserve system". However, Robinson's statement apparently did not make it into the trial transcript. Judge Cooper ultimately ruled that all, not just a part, of Robinson's 1958 Congressional testimony would be marked as a trial exhibit and admitted into evidence. Later in the trial, Robinson's complete statement was submitted for the trial record. That 1958 statement to Congress was as follows:

"I think they [players] should in some way be able to express themselves as to whether or not they do want to play for a certain ball club. I am highly in favor of the reserve clause. I do not want this to get out that I don't believe that there should be some control, but on the other hand I don't think the owners should have all of the control. I think that there should be something that a ballplayer himself could say that would have some effect upon his particular position with a ball club. As it stands now, the players, in my opinion, don't really have the opportunity to express themselves in a way they should be able to." (P. 295, Hearings before the Subcommittee on Antitrust and Monopoly of the Committee on the Judiciary, U.S. Senate, 85th Congress, 2nd Session.)

At the very end of his testimony in the *Flood* trial, Robinson was asked what type of modifications to the reserve system would accommodate the needs of the players and the club owners. Robinson's response was that after a certain number of years, a player should have a chance to improve his situation. The owner ought to have a first option to retain that player, but arbitrarily selling or trading a player's contract without consultation or consent "is just plain wrong".

Finally, in open court, Jackie Robinson paid a personal tribute to Curt Flood:

"It takes a tremendous amount of courage for any individual—and that's why I admire Mr. Flood so much for what he is doing—to stand up against something that is appalling to him, and I think that they ought to give a player the chance to be able to be a man in situations like this, and I don't believe this is what has happened."

Testimony of Henry Greenberg

The plaintiff's next witness was first baseman and another Baseball Hall of Famer—Henry "Hank" Greenberg. Greenberg was signed in 1930 by the Detroit Tigers at age 18. After playing three years in the minors, Greenberg played from 1933-1946 (except for 4½ years in military service during World War II). Greenberg was the American League's Most Valuable Player in 1935 and 1940; hit 330 career home runs; on more than one occasion led the American League in runs batted in, home runs and doubles; and had a lifetime bat-

Chapter 9: Day Two—Thursday, May 21, 1970

ting average of .313. After the 1946 season, Greenberg was traded to and played his last major league season in 1947 with the Pittsburgh Pirates. In 1956, Greenberg was inducted into Baseball's Hall of Fame.

Immediately after he retired as a player, Greenberg joined the Cleveland Indians organization as a vice president in 1948; and in 1949, he became the director of Cleveland's farm system. In 1950, Greenberg became the club's General Manager; and by 1955, he became a part owner and a director of the Cleveland baseball club. He left the Cleveland club to become a part-owner and an officer with the Chicago White Sox organization. He served in the Chicago White Sox organization in a variety of management positions until 1963. As a witness, Greenberg could testify from the perspective of a club owner, general manager and a player—a great player.

Once Goldberg directed the reserve system questions to the witness, Greenberg did not hesitate and was not shy about his position. He testified that baseball's reserve system was "obsolete and antiquated", and that the game of baseball was in serious need of a change in the basic contract. Greenberg believed that a change in the contract would improve the player-owner relationship as well as the game. As an owner, Greenberg recalled a number of instances when certain players would grouse about the reserve clause. Greenberg also testified that the owners constantly tried to lobby Congress against the passage of federal legislation that would specifically make professional baseball subject to the Sherman Act and other federal antitrust statutes. Greenberg encouraged the players and owners to work together and to make, in his judgment, improvements like those being accomplished in professional football and basketball; and concluded that baseball would function better without the current "reserve clause".

At this point, Judge Cooper asked the witness why the "reserve clause" was not in the best interest of baseball. Greenberg responded that from the player's perspective, the "reserve clause" provision is unilateral. It may be invoked and enforced solely by the club owner, and the player has no choice other than to accept the contract because the player cannot play elsewhere. Greenberg emphasized that in the 1930s, the seasons were four months long and that since that time, the game and conditions had changed significantly. Greenberg pointed out that most players are young and inexperienced in business matters; noted the difficulty in discussing or negotiating a contract with management; and that a player really had no means to represent himself effectively with management.

On a personal note, Greenberg testified that after sixteen years with the Detroit Tiger organization, he, like Curt Flood, was notified by a telegram that he had been traded and that his contract had been assigned to the Pittsburgh club. Regarding Curt Flood, Greenberg stated that the baseball club owners must recognize that the player "has built up some equity in playing with the club over a period of years—they can't just arbitrarily say 'you play in Philadelphia next season'". In Greenberg's opinion, "the reserve clause in the present contract should be eliminated entirely", and that a replacement could be negotiated between the players and owners "very easily".

On cross examination, Greenberg testified that the existence of baseball's "reserve clause" is *not* a consideration taken into account by a prospective investor in a professional baseball club; and stated that he "would be perfectly willing to invest in baseball tomorrow if we had no reserve clause". However, because of the club's financial investment in a player, Greenberg agreed that the club owners ought to have the right to a player's services for a specified number of years. Finally, Greenberg testified that any substitute for the current reserve system ought to be *negotiated and agreed to* by the players and club owners.

Testimony of Marvin Miller (recalled)

Over the objection of defense counsel, Judge Cooper then allowed plaintiff's counsel to recall Marvin Miller as a witness. This time, Miller's direct examination was conducted by another one of Flood's counsel, Jay Topkis. (It is noteworthy that Goldberg would not conduct the examination of another witness in this case.)

Attorney Topkis questioned Miller about some of the "mechanics" of the "free agent draft"; and rehashed the point that a player drafted in this "free agent" draft is unable to talk to or negotiate with any other club. Topkis then questioned Miller about modifications to the reserve system that the players' union—through Marvin Miller—had proposed and presented to the owners. Miller's description of these proposed modifications included the following:

1) The renewal option would exist for an agreed upon number of years (instead of for life) after which the player could freely negotiate with any other club;

2) Same as #1 above, coupled with the original club's ability to maintain its exclusive rights to the player by matching the offer of any other club;

3) In order to prevent the "wealthiest" teams from "buying" all the free agents, the number of free agents that any one team could sign would be limited;

4) To address the "bench warmer being trapped issue", a player would be guaranteed a minimum salary increase for each year of service; and

5) Reduce and thereafter limit the number of players that each team could "reserve".

Miller continued on, citing examples of how the owners' exercise of "total control" impacted the players' personal lives. Miller gave examples of various "rules" concerning a player's hair length, facial hair, clothing styles, and even the content of a player's remarks to news reporters. Next, Miller spoke about the "hardships" that a player and his family would endure when the player is traded to another club—including the need to relocate his family, selecting new schools for school age children and the adverse impact on other business interests of a player.

What did this specific litany of horrors and hardships have to do with Curt Flood? What did the free agent draft, long hair and Miller's list of union proposed modifications to baseball's reserve system have to do with Flood's lawsuit challenging the existing reserve system as it applied to Curt Flood? They had absolutely nothing to do with Flood claims and his efforts to be immediately declared a free agent by the federal courts.

What may be considered fair, just and reasonable working conditions, and whether good faith negotiations were in fact being conducted by the union and the owners were not issues before Judge Cooper, nor were these issues relevant. Moreover, even if Judge Cooper would have issued an order directing the owners to conduct good faith negotiations with the union, how would such an order help Curt Flood? And how would such an order bolster Flood's contention that the reserve system violated his constitutional rights?

Further, on the issue of whether baseball's reserve system violated federal antitrust statutes or the Thirteenth Amendment, a willingness (or unwillingness) to negotiate modifications to that reserve system was likewise irrelevant. The more that Miller and the plaintiff's case focused on the negotiations between union (through Miller) and the club owners, the easier it became for the defense to argue and for the Court to conclude that it was the Players' Association, and not Curt Flood, that was the real party in interest.

CHAPTER 9: DAY TWO—THURSDAY, MAY 21, 1970

At this point, the plaintiff's case was a ship lost at sea, and in need of a captain who could read a compass.

Testimony of James P. Brosnan

For the final witness on Day Two, Attorney Jay Topkis called James P. ("Jimmy") Brosnan. In 1947, at the age of seventeen, Jimmy Brosnan was signed as a pitcher by the Chicago Cubs organization. Between 1947 and 1951, Brosnan bounced around in the minor leagues before being drafted into the Army in 1951. After his military service, Brosnan made it up to the Cubs in 1956. He pitched during the 1956 and 1957 seasons for the Cubs before being traded to St. Louis in 1958. After the 1958 season, Brosnan was traded to the Cincinnati Reds. Brosnan was the Reds' top relief pitcher during the 1961 and 1962 seasons. In 1961, the Reds won the National League pennant before losing the World Series to the New York Yankees in five games. In 1963, Brosnan was traded to and played his final major league season with the Chicago White Sox. In a total of 8½ major league seasons, Brosnan had a career record of 56 wins and 48 losses.

Brosnan was perhaps better known for his writing abilities and for two books he authored: *The Long Season*—published in 1960; and *Pennant Race*—published in 1962. According to Brosnan, it was the publication of these books that got Brosnan crosswise with the Cincinnati Reds organization and particularly with the Reds' General Manager, William Dewitt, in the early 1960s. Brosnan testified that in 1960, the Reds' organization confronted Brosnan and asserted the contract provision which prohibits a player from writing a column, article, book or other publication, or from appearing on a radio or television show without prior approval from the club. The Uniform Player's Contract contained the following provision:

"...The player further agrees that during the playing season, he will not make public appearances, participate in radio or television programs or permit his picture to be taken or write or sponsor newspaper or magazine articles or sponsor commercial products without the written consent of the club, which shall not be withheld except in the reasonable interest of the club or professional baseball".

Brosnan testified that he was traded and reassigned many times in his career, and noted the insensitive nature by which notices of those trades were delivered—phone messages, telegrams, etc. He also pointed out the difficulties experienced by players, and specifically, the amount of unreimbursed expenses frequently incurred by a player following a trade or relocation. Brosnan, like Jackie Robinson, testified that there were "bench warmers" that could have started on other clubs, specifically mentioning Bob Speake and Steve Bilko of the Cubs. When asked what would occur if the reserve system were modified so that a player could "play out his option", Brosnan disputed the idea that all of the better players would flock to one or more of the "wealthy" organizations because salary is just one of the factors a veteran player may take into account in deciding where he may want to play.

In 1962, the Reds informed Brosnan that he could not work or appear in a television documentary for NBC without prior approval from the Reds. Brosnan's testimony was that Reds' General Manager Bill DeWitt was concerned that Brosnan, in the television documentary, would say something critical of the Reds organization. Consequently, the club demanded that it be allowed to see the documentary before it was aired. NBC refused to agree to the Reds' demand and as a result, Brosnan testified that he lost a $4,000 opportunity. Brosnan testified that he wrote letters to both Ford Frick (then Commissioner of Baseball) and to Warren Giles (then National League President) seeking to

Chapter 9: Day Two—Thursday, May 21, 1970

have the contract clause waived, and that Brosnan never received a response of any kind from either Frick or Giles.

Prior to the 1964 season, the White Sox General Manager sent a letter to Brosnan informing him that he was not allowed to publish any article or book during the season. Brosnan testified that he had already sold several articles and works to various publishers for printing and circulation. Brosnan's testimony was that he formally requested that the White Sox waive the contract provision. The White Sox organization refused to waive the contractual language, and Brosnan then refused to sign his player contract for the 1964 season. A week later, Brosnan was unconditionally released from the White Sox. Following his release, Brosnan advertized his availability as a major league pitcher, but never pitched again in major league baseball.

During his testimony, Brosnan suggested that he was "blacklisted" by the owners at the beginning of the 1964 season because of his writings and publications. While there may indeed have been a causal relationship between Brosnan's writing and his unconditional release, all that was presented to establish this "blacklisting" charge was Brosnan's own admittedly biased testimony—and nothing else.

The purpose of calling Jimmy Brosnan as a witness for the Plaintiff Curt Flood is not completely clear. Presumably, Flood's lawyers decided to call Brosnan in order to show the owners' ability and willingness to enforce the Uniform Contract to the detriment of the players—and particularly to Jimmy Brosnan; and to show that the owners had a variety of weapons at their disposal to assert pressure on and control the players.

Brosnan was first contacted by Flood's lawyers just three weeks before the start of the trial. While sincere and well intended, Brosnan's testimony at times rambled aimlessly. Neither the witness nor his presentation was well prepared. Most importantly, however, it is unclear as to what, if any, part of Brosnan's testimony had to do with Curt Flood, or had to do with what Curt Flood needed to prove. Flood needed to prove that baseball's reserve system, *as applied to Curt Flood*, violated federal or state antitrust laws or the Thirteenth Amendment to the United States Constitution—not what the Cincinnati Reds or Chicago White Sox organizations may or may not have done to Jimmy Brosnan because of what Brosnan wrote or may have published. Overall, Brosnan's testimony was ineffective and mostly irrelevant.

Day Two was now concluded.

Chapter 10
Day Three—Friday, May 22, 1970

Testimony of Robert R. Nathan

On the morning of May 22, 1970, Jay Topkis called to the stand an economist and expert witness, Robert R. Nathan. Nathan graduated in 1931 from Wharton School of Finance and Commerce at the University of Pennsylvania; and in 1933, he received a Master of Science degree in economics from Georgetown University. Nathan had also worked as an economist for the U.S. Department of Commerce and was Chairman of the War Production Board during World War II. After World War II, Nathan organized his own consulting firm. Throughout his professional career, Nathan had performed extensive work, written books, and produced numerous studies for a variety of federal agencies, labor unions and industries in the fields of wage policy and wage rates.

Several years earlier, in 1966, Nathan had been retained by and testified at trial as an expert witness for the State of Wisconsin in the litigation over the relocation of the Milwaukee Braves franchise to Atlanta, Georgia. Nathan's credentials and background were impressive and the defense did not contest (in lawyer's lingo, the defense "stipulated" to) Nathan's qualifications as an expert witness.

Nathan testified as to the economics of baseball's reserve system, and Topkis's questions would get Nathan right to the point.

"From the economic point of view, the lack of an alternative set of opportunities for a ballplayer would tend to depress the wage level of the ballplayer in view of the fact that he has no opportunity to negotiate and bargain among alternative users of the talents and services....
To my knowledge—and I have worked in a great many industries, many service industries as well—I know first hand of no parallel in any other general field or any other sector of activity where the economic relationships between employers and employees have anything like...what this reserve system provides."

Nathan continued on the issue of employer-employee relations.

"To an economist, [baseball's reserve system] represents a degree of imbalance in the bargaining capability which is very substantially different from the bargaining relationships which generally prevail in a free society between buyers and sellers of goods and services, where there are obviously varying elements of strength, depending on how much administrative pricing there might be or how much exclusiveness there might be, but by and large in our society there is a tendency for substantial strength on both sides of the bargaining table. But from an economic point of view, [baseball's] reserve system is one which is totally and completely unbalanced in terms of strength of bargaining between the player and the employer....

As an economist,...I have grave doubts about the reserve system. I believe that we will find that even if we don't redistribute economic compatibility by size of city [and share television revenue and gate receipts], and if we

CHAPTER 10: DAY THREE—FRIDAY, MAY 22, 1970

will permit players to more freely reduce the rigidity of employer-employee relationships, we would find a considerable amount of competition and a considerable amount of varied strength and a considerable change over time in this win-lose relationship of individual teams."

Nathan's next opinion was that baseball's reserve system had a depressant effect on players' wages and that if players were free to negotiate freely among owners, not all players would gravitate toward the teams in a position to offer the highest wages. Nathan cited studies that indicate that population did not correlate precisely with attendance figures at major league baseball games, but that population was just one factor.

Regarding the minor league system and the attendant expense to the club owners, Nathan noted that it is common practice in almost all sectors of American industry to conduct training programs for employees. However, it was not common practice to bar employees from moving to another employer.

Toward the end of Nathan's direct examination, Topkis asked the following hypothetical question:

"Q. If the present reserve system were eliminated and it were replaced by a system in which the only restraint permitted on employees moving from one team to another was the right of the employer to sign employees to contracts for a term of years ranging up to perhaps five years, would you expect that the level of performance of the different clubs on the field in playing games would be significantly affected?"

Defense counsel Hughes's objection brought an outburst of laughter:

"I object to that question. I submit that Mr. Nathan, with all of his distinguished qualifications, is incapable of giving a meaningful answer to that question. It seems to me we are getting not into the area of an economist, but we are getting into the area of clairvoyance."

After Judge Cooper overruled defense counsel's objection, Nathan summed up his direct testimony. If the reserve system were eliminated (with the only restriction being the right of the club owners to sign players to contracts for up to five years in duration), Nathan testified that this system would increase players' salaries; would be advantageous in the distribution of player talent among teams; would cause other personal and economic factors to become part of the players' and owners' decision making; would enhance competition among the clubs; and would enhance competition "in the performance of this sport, in the assembly of players and assembly of talents and in their competition with each other."

The cross examination of Nathan was conducted by defense counsel Louis L. Hoynes. Hoynes got Nathan to admit that he had previously discussed his proposed testimony with Marvin Miller and with "Goldberg's lawyers", and that this discussion occurred about two weeks before the trial commenced. On cross examination, Nathan also acknowledged that he had never previously consulted or reviewed the rules of baseball or baseball contract provisions; that he had never previously been employed by a professional baseball club; and that he had no personal experience or knowledge of the process by which players and owners negotiated salaries.

The remainder of Nathan's cross examination was largely theoretical and philosophical in nature. While the defense succeeded in getting Nathan to acknowledge his lack of experience with and personal knowledge of major league baseball's negotiating process, the defense could do little to impeach Nathan's conclusions that the reserve system diminished salary levels, restricted competition, and restricted a player's opportunity to market his abilities

CHAPTER 10: DAY THREE—FRIDAY, MAY 22, 1970

among competing club owners. The defense would need to call its own expert witness later in the trial to counter Nathan's conclusions.

Nathan's testimony was impressive and gave the plaintiff some "science" and "economic theory" to support his argument that baseball's reserve system was a restraint of trade, and that baseball's reserve system violated Curt Flood's rights under federal and state law.

Day Three was now concluded. The trial would resume the following Monday.

Chapter 11
Day Four—Monday, May 25, 1970

Testimony of Alvin R. (Pete) Rozelle

When the trial resumed on Monday morning, Jay Topkis continued the presentation of the plaintiff's case by calling to the stand Mr. Alvin Ray Rozelle, better known by many as Pete Rozelle, then Commissioner of the National Football League (NFL). In the 1950s, Pete Rozelle worked in the Los Angeles Rams organization and ultimately became the Rams' General Manager. In 1960, at the ripe old age of thirty-three, Rozelle became the Commissioner of the NFL. In the first ten years under Commissioner Rozelle, the NFL and a rival league—the American Football League (AFL)—merged operations, and expanded from 12 teams in 1960 to 26 teams in 1970. Rozelle was also credited with the creation of the Super Bowl—the first of said games being played in January 1967.

In the 1960s, the business of professional football was undergoing great change. Rozelle testified that the initial phase of the NFL-AFL merger took place on June 8, 1966, and that the final phase was completed on February 1, 1970. The upcoming 1970 season would be the first time in which teams from the "old AFL" and NFL would com-

Chapter 11: Day Four—Monday, May 25, 1970

pete during the regular season. Since the merger in 1966, the winner of the AFL played the winner of the NFL in the Super Bowl. In those Super Bowl games from 1967-1970, the AFL won 2 and the NFL won 2. (Trivia: Can you name the teams that competed in each of the first four Super Bowl games? Hint: Two teams appeared twice in these first four games.)

Jay Topkis called Rozelle to testify about professional football's reserve system, the standard NFL player contract, and the Commissioner's powers and duties under the NFL Constitution and Bylaws. Before Rozelle took the witness stand, the defense stated its objection to Rozelle's testimony on the grounds that it was irrelevant to any issue in dispute. For the record, Judge Cooper noted the defense's continuing objection on the basis of relevancy, and overruled the objection. Rozelle testified that the NFL Commissioner, like the Commissioner of Major League Baseball, was charged with the duty and responsibility of interpreting and enforcing the standard player contract. Unlike baseball, however, the standard NFL player contract allowed a player to play out his option. Paragraph 10(a) of the standard NFL contract provided that at the end of the contract's term, the club may renew the contract *or* exercise an option for *one* additional year. During that final year, the player was entitled to a salary of 90% or more of the player's salary for the previous year. At the end of the option year, the player was a free agent and free to negotiate, sign a contract and play for another club.

Rozelle noted that the one year option provision (which ultimately allowed a player to play out his option and become a free agent) had been a part of the standard contract "for many, many years". Rozelle went on to explain the role and obligation of the Commissioner to award "compensation" to a club who had "lost" a player to "free agency". Prior to 1961, there existed no "compensation provision". In 1961, however, the NFL Bylaws/Constitution was amended by adding the following provision: "Any player whose contract with a club has expired shall thereupon become a free agent and shall no longer be considered a member of the team of that club following the expiration date of such contract. Whenever a player becoming a free agent in such manner thereafter signs a contract with a different club in either the NFL or the AFL, then, unless mutually satisfactory arrangements have been concluded between the two clubs, the Commissioner may name and then award to the former club one or more players from the active reserve or selection list, including future selection choices of the acquiring club as the Commissioner in his sole discretion deems fair and equitable. Any such decision by the Commissioner shall be final and conclusive." (NFL Constitution—Article XII.1H)

Rozelle further testified that since becoming Commissioner in 1960, he was required to determine and award compensation on three or four instances; that there were instances, both before and after the merger, that players had played out their options; that in 1969 alone, ten players had played out their options. More specifically, Rozelle opined that "the existence of the option clause and the right of a player to play out his option have not injured or in any way impaired the integrity of professional football". Of particular importance to Curt Flood, Rozelle testified that he, as Commissioner, had approved contracts which contained "no trade" or "no assignment" clauses.

On the issue of competition for players, Rozelle's testimony was also of particular interest. Rozelle stated that from 1960-65, there were two separate leagues (NFL and AFL) and two separate player drafts. Consequently, the AFL and NFL competed for players in the draft (and also competed with the Canadian Football League). Since the merger, however, the NFL and AFL conducted a common draft

CHAPTER 11: DAY FOUR—MONDAY, MAY 25, 1970

among the league's 26 teams in which the teams drafted based upon the inverse order of their standings at the end of the previous season. The first such joint NFL-AFL draft occurred after the 1966 playing season. Finally, he stated that since 1960, professional football game attendance had increased; that television and radio revenues had increased; and that gate receipts had increased.

Rozelle's testimony allowed Flood's lawyers to make the following points and arguments:

In professional football's reserve system (unlike baseball's), a player was *not* the property of or owned by the club with whom the player originally signed a player contract.

Again, in professional football's reserve system (unlike baseball's), a player could play out his option and ultimately become a free agent, negotiate a contract with and play for another club. Moreover, there were previous instances in which players did indeed play out their options and became free agents.

A professional football player's right to play out his option had existed for many years before the AFL-NFL merger in 1966.

There was competition for the services of players between the NFL teams and the Canadian Football League (CFL) teams.

The business of professional football was flourishing—attendance, receipts and revenues had all increased since 1960.

Despite the competition for players among the NFL and CFL teams, and despite the player's right to play out his option and become a free agent, the business of professional football was profitable.

The cross examination of Rozelle was conducted by defense counsel Hoynes. The questions put to Rozelle on cross were excellent and established three key points. While Flood's lawyers wanted to show that football's reserve system and standard player contract were less restrictive, Rozelle admitted that one of the intended purposes and specific outcomes of the AFL-NFL merger in 1966 was the creation of a common draft and *the elimination of competition* between the NFL and AFL in the draft of college players.

Second, Rozelle testified that if the merger between the NFL and AFL had not occurred, several clubs would have failed financially. (Rozelle was able to sidestep the question of which teams would have folded.) Rozelle stated that reducing the competition among the teams and between the leagues was necessary to avoid the financial collapse of several franchises.

Third, Rozelle conceded that he, as the NFL Commissioner, had to go to Congress on two different occasions (1962 and 1966) to lobby for specific legislation authorizing the implementation of certain arrangements and agreements among the teams, leagues, and television stations, etc. which, in the absence of federal legislation, would have constituted unlawful restraints of trade in violation of federal antitrust laws.

When Rozelle testified that in the absence of the NFL-AFL merger, certain teams would have failed financially, Flood's lawyers were immediately off their chairs (and perhaps almost through the ceiling) raising numerous objections and pleading with Judge Cooper to allow them to recall and to question Rozelle on this conclusion. Topkis was not merely seeking to question Rozelle again, he wanted the judge to order Rozelle to produce the pertinent financial records of each of the NFL teams and return to court for this additional testimony on another day after producing those documents.

In response to Topkis's requests, the defense argued that 1) Topkis, on behalf of the plaintiff, had already completed his direct examination of Rozelle, and that plaintiff

CHAPTER 11: DAY FOUR—MONDAY, MAY 25, 1970

was not entitled to again question the witness about issues Topkis could have covered during Rozelle's direct examination; 2) it is completely improper to call a witness to testify on behalf of the plaintiff and then to cross examine or impeach your "own witness"; and 3) if Judge Cooper allowed the additional testimony and evidence of each team's financial condition, this would result in significant and needless delay in the trial, and would require the production and consideration of an enormous amount of information completely irrelevant to any trial issue in dispute. Defense counsel Hughes elaborated:

"Your Honor, first, may I address myself to plaintiff's Counsel's indication that in some way or other he is taken by surprise that we should interpose any objections. Certain things ought to be made transparently clear. The plaintiff wanted an early trial. The plaintiff deliberately chose an early trial. [Plaintiff's] Counsel did say that they expected to take a day and no more. To say that on the fifth day of the trial, our interposing objections…somehow or other has impeded the efficacy and acceleration and speed of their case seems to me to be very specious indeed. They knew that if all of this had appeared to be relevant to them when they were preparing for trial, they could have taken the very liberal pretrial procedures that the Federal Rules provide. They could have taken the Commissioner's deposition. They could have done all kinds of things to get the kind of testimony that they now are seeking to elicit at the tail end of this trial.…As far as cooperation is concerned, we have furnished them with an enormous amount of data at their request and at some difficulty and at some interfering with our own preparation. Now when it comes immediately to the problem at hand, what are they really doing? They are really trying to impeach their own witness, the Commissioner. They were the ones that got into this.…The

Commissioner testified that in his opinion certain of these clubs would have gone under in both leagues had they not had the merger. That was the subject that they went into. Now what do they want to do? They want to go into the amount of television receipts for the purpose of showing that with those receipts somehow or other they could have...bailed these club out. ...In the first place, you can't impeach your own witness that way, and in the second place, if they try to do that and create that impression, we have got to [analyze] the operating statements of all these clubs...and that is where we are...headed if this...is allowed to continue."

After a long argument among the lawyers and a short recess which followed, Judge Cooper agreed with the defense and denied the plaintiff's request to recall Rozelle.

It is amusing to note that just moments *before* this tumultuous outburst among the lawyers, Judge Cooper was again heaping praise upon the combatants for their cooperation and fair play. Judge Cooper expressed his compliment for the record:

"...[I]n light of the splendid cooperation between counsel and with a sense of fair play *that has never been exceeded*...I don't care what enterprise, football, baseball, we have our fine standards and the lawyers have exemplified it at its best...."

At the risk of sounding overly critical, Day Four clearly revealed that Flood's legal team was woefully unprepared in its presentation of Commissioner Rozelle. Under the federal "discovery" rules for trials, the parties customarily take depositions (sworn statements) from opposing parties and witnesses, and request the production of documents, records and other relevant data in the possession of other parties and witnesses. Furthermore, the procedural rules require the disclosure of all witnesses which a party intends to call at trial. The discovery process affords an

CHAPTER 11: DAY FOUR—MONDAY, MAY 25, 1970

opportunity for the parties to be thoroughly conversant with the evidence *before* the trial commences.

In the Curt Flood case, and for reasons not completely clear, the trial record shows that there were no depositions of any witnesses taken before trial. With regard to Rozelle, he was subpoenaed to appear (and to bring with him certain documents) just a few days before he appeared in court. Incredibly, the transcript of the trial also reveals that Flood's lawyers were reviewing the Rozelle documents and actually developing their questions for the witness *as Rozelle was giving testimony on the witness stand.*

Day Four was now concluded. When the trial resumed the next day, Flood's lawyers would continue to call witnesses and present evidence regarding the reserve systems in other professional sports—this time, however, it would be ice hockey and basketball.

Chapter 12
Day Five—Tuesday, May 26, 1970

Testimony of Walter J. Kennedy

Next to the witness stand came Walter J. Kennedy—then Commissioner of the National Basketball Association (NBA). Kennedy was a 1934 graduate of Notre Dame University. In the early 1940s, Kennedy worked as the sports information director at his alma mater. In 1946, he became the public relations director of the Basketball Association of America (which eventually merged with the NBA), and in the 1950s, for the Harlem Globetrotters. After a world tour with the Globetrotters, Kennedy returned home to Stamford, Connecticut where he was elected and served as that city's mayor from 1959-1963. Kennedy became the NBA Commissioner in 1963 and served in that capacity continuously until 1975.

To put Walter Kennedy's testimony in some perspective, by the spring of 1970, the NBA was engaged in negotiations and litigation with the rival American Basketball Association (ABA) regarding a possible merger of the two leagues. The ABA was created in 1967 and played nine full seasons, through 1976. Many forget (or did not know) that players such as Julius Ervin ("Dr. J"), George McGinnes, Artis

CHAPTER 12: DAY FIVE—TUESDAY, MAY 26, 1970

Gilmore, Moses Malone, Marvin "Bad News" Barnes, David "Skywalker" Thompson, and George Gervin were among the ABA's marquee players. Ultimately in June 1976, the two leagues "made peace" and merged. As a result, teams like the New York Nets, Denver Nuggets, Indiana Pacers and San Antonio Spurs survived the merger, while franchises such as the Kentucky Colonels, Virginia Squires, Dallas Chaparrals and the Spirits of St. Louis dissolved.

Also by the spring of 1970, a number of professional basketball players had "jumped" their contracts and began playing with another team in the rival league. Not surprisingly, litigation and business disputes resulted and relations between the rival leagues were anything but smooth. On April 21, 1970, just weeks before the start of the Flood trial, Cincinnati Royals' star player, Oscar Robertson, was traded from the Cincinnati Royals to the Milwaukee Bucks. When that deal had been completed, Robertson negotiated a contract with the Milwaukee Bucks that included a "no trade without consent" clause.

Topkis immediately directed the witness to the NBA standard player contract and the duties of the Commissioner. The defense stated its continuing objection for the record on the grounds of relevancy. Kennedy stated that all player contracts had to be executed on the standard NBA form and had to be approved by the Commissioner; that the standard NBA player contract (Paragraph 10) authorized the assignment, sale or transfer to another club; that the contract included a one-year renewal option provision; and that there were instances in which a NBA player, upon the expiration of the one year renewal option, had signed a contract with another club. Finally, Kennedy acknowledged that he had approved the Oscar Robertson—Milwaukee Bucks contract—including the "no trade" clause.

During the remainder of Kennedy's direct examination, he confirmed that beginning in 1967, there were instances of NBA players "jumping contracts"—both before and after the expiration of their terms—to sign and play in the ABA; that the NBA and ABA conducted separate drafts and directly competed for players; noted that there were other amateur and "lesser" basketball leagues from which players were sometimes recruited and signed; acknowledged that, unlike Curt Flood, a professional basketball player was not the property for life of the team with whom the player originally signed a professional contract; and that a professional basketball player (like a professional football player) could serve out his contract and, upon expiration, sign a contract with another club.

Amazingly, as was the case during the testimony of Commissioner Rozelle, Flood's lawyers were again developing questions for the witness while Commissioner Kennedy was on the witness stand. Jay Topkis sought the Court's indulgence on more than one occasion:

"I trust your Honor will forgive me if I go slowly. This is the first time I have ever seen these [NBA Player Contract form and NBA Constitution/Bylaws] documents....

Your Honor, the (NBA) constitution and bylaws are a rather lengthy document, and I haven't had a chance, as I said to peruse it....Might I now recess the witness's examination for a few minutes to give me an opportunity to study this document...?"

The cross examination of Walter Kennedy was conducted by defense counsel Hoynes. On cross, Commissioner Kennedy testified that the approval of the Oscar Robertson "no trade" clause was the first and only instance in which he approved such a contract provision. Distinguishing the NBA from major league baseball, Kennedy testified that neither the NBA nor the individual NBA teams provided financial support for the amateur or lesser leagues, and that professional basketball had no "farm system". Also, unlike professional baseball, Kennedy stated that college

CHAPTER 12: DAY FIVE—TUESDAY, MAY 26, 1970

players were the primary, if not exclusive, source of NBA players.

Defense counsel then questioned the Commissioner regarding the proposed merger of the NBA and the ABA.

"Q. Do not the club owners of the two major basketball leagues, the American Basketball Association and...the NBA, propose, subject to Congressional approval, to merge their operations?...

A. There have been and are still discussions taking place between representatives of both the NBA and the ABA with the ultimate thought of going to Congress for Congressional approval of a possible merger."

By May 1970, litigation in relation to the merger was pending. This litigation included lawsuits filed by individual players against the two leagues. With the consent of the parties, however, the courts had entered injunctions prohibiting the NBA-ABA merger, but preserving the right of the leagues to jointly appeal to Congress for legislative approval of the merger. Attorney Hoynes' cross examination continued.

"Q. Yesterday, the plaintiff in this case subpoenaed and called to the stand the Commissioner of the National Football League, Pete Rozelle. Mr. Rozelle testified about the merger in 1966, I believe, of the two rival football leagues, the NFL and the AFL, and at that time he testified in substance that the merger of those two leagues was an economic necessity. In your opinion, as the Commissioner of the National Basketball Association, is the proposed merger of the NBA and the ABA likewise an economic necessity to some of the member clubs of one or both leagues?"

This question drew an objection from Attorney Topkis, and further argument from Hoynes:

"...Your Honor, it seems plain to me that these witnesses from other sports have been called, particularly basketball, to demonstrate that two rival leagues can get along in fact. That [the co-existence of rival leagues] is one of the proposals that has been propounded to your Honor. I think we are entitled to show that the whole history of professional sports is that rival leagues in one sport in fact do not work out and that ultimately one of those leagues either disappears by dropping by the wayside or by merger, and that in the present instance, the only present instance in professional sports where there are two rival leagues, history is indeed repeating itself...I think [the defense is] entitled to elicit not only the fact that the two leagues propose to merge, but that it is necessary for them to merge."

In most respects, Walter Kennedy's testimony paralleled the points and issues covered by NFL Commissioner Rozelle. Now Flood's legal team wanted to compare the reserve system of baseball to professional ice hockey.

Testimony of Robert Alan Eagleson

Plaintiff's Counsel William Iverson then called Robert Alan Eagleson as Flood's next witness. Eagleson was the Executive Director of the National Hockey League Players' Association (NHLPA) which was created in 1967. (While Eagleson testified that he was a lawyer and that he was "reasonably familiar" with the NHL Standard Player Contract, Constitution and Bylaws, Eagleson's presentation would suggest otherwise. Even more stunning was the fact that plaintiff's counsel apparently had no idea what Eagleson would say on the stand. Again, the record reveals the lack of preparation in that Iverson was reviewing the NHL standard contract and other documents for the first time as he was directing questions to Eagleson.

The purpose of presenting evidence pertaining to the reserve systems of other professional sports was to show that baseball's reserve system was unnecessarily (and illegally) restrictive when compared to those reserve systems

CHAPTER 12: DAY FIVE—TUESDAY, MAY 26, 1970

in other professional sports. What is absolutely amazing was that Alan Eagleson, a witness called by Flood's lawyers, and presumably called to testify *for* the plaintiff's position—would actually provide testimony in support of the position asserted by the defense.

During his brief but damaging direct examination, Eagleson testified that Paragraph 17 of the NHL standard player contract was "a life time option clause and that a player, once he signs the contract, since that is the standard contract for the league, signs with a team *for life*." How on earth was this standard NHL contract clause any less restrictive than the very baseball contract provision that Curt Flood was challenging? Why did Flood's lawyers insist on presenting this evidence?

Eagleson also testified that the NHL standard player contract allowed "greater privileges" for certain "superstars" to depart from the standard contract by demanding "no trade clauses", and the right to renegotiate a contract if traded to a new club. The remainder of Eagleson's testimony included a confusing and worthless description of the NHL's disciplinary hearing process, and meandering gibberish about each team's "reserve list". Eagleson's testimony was so damaging to Flood's position, and so helpful to the position asserted by the defense that the defense declined its opportunity to cross exam Eagleson.

Testimony of Clarence Sutherland Campbell

For the final witness on Day Five, Flood's lawyers called the President of the National Hockey League (NHL), Clarence Campbell.

The sixty-five year-old, Canadian born Campbell was a Rhodes scholar, lawyer, former NHL referee and a former Canadian military officer. After World War II, Campbell was appointed and served as a prosecution lawyer for the

Canadian War Crimes Commission at the Nuremburg trial of Nazi Kurt Meyer. When Campbell returned to North America in 1946, he was offered the job and became President of the NHL.

During his tenure, Campbell increased the number of NHL regular season games; created the NHL All-Star Game; initiated the development of the players' pension plan; and oversaw the first major expansion of the NHL in 1967 which doubled the number of teams from six to twelve. (Trivia: Can you name the first six NHL expansion teams which began play in the 1967-68 season?) Campbell was elected into the Hockey Hall of Fame in 1966 and served as NHL President until 1977.

Almost immediately, Campbell made it known that he took serious issue with the testimony given just moments earlier by Eagleson. Jay Topkis would be on the receiving end of Campbell's answers:

"Q. Now, you were in court when Mr. Eagleson testified?
A. Yes, I was.
Q. You heard the questions that were put to him and the answers which he gave?
A. Yes.
Q. Were you asked the same questions would you give the same answers?
A. I am afraid not...there were a number of errors...."

Campbell then described the provisions of the NHL standard player contract and bylaws. He testified that the standard player contract contained a renewal option clause, and a provision allowing any salary dispute to be decided by the NHL President or by binding arbitration; that the bylaws and contract contained "no tampering" provisions; that the bylaws allowed each club to maintain a player "reserve list"; that the contract and bylaws provided that a player's contract may be traded, sold, or assigned; and that the bylaws required all player contracts to be in standard form, and

CHAPTER 12: DAY FIVE—TUESDAY, MAY 26, 1970

that no modifications to the standard form were authorized except by resolution of the NHL's Board of Governors.

Campbell testified that during his term as NHL President (since 1946), the Board of Governors had never approved a variation of the standard player contract for any individual player. Although Campbell acknowledged that certain teams had on occasion made "collateral agreements" with individual players which purported to change the terms of the standard player agreement, Campbell testified that he, as Commissioner, had never given approval to, and that he would not give effect to any such collateral agreement.

Campbell confirmed that the reserve list of a NHL club consisted of 37 players; and that the effect of the reserve system, combined with the renewal option clause, was "a contract with a team for life". (This conclusion was unrefuted by Plaintiff Flood.) Like professional baseball, the NHL had a draft system for amateur players ready to enter the professional ranks. Campbell testified that the NHL draft occurred annually where each member team would draft amateur players in reverse order of the finish of the team in the preceding season. Once selected, a player was registered on the reserve list of the selecting team, and thereafter, the selecting team had the exclusive right to negotiate a contract with the "draftee".

Finally, Campbell emphasized the importance of the financial support and subsidies paid by the NHL and individual NHL teams to the Canadian Amateur Hockey Association and other minor professional hockey leagues. Like professional baseball (but unlike professional basketball and football), Campbell testified that the costs of player development, scouting, and minor league operations were significant, costing each NHL team in excess of $200,000 per year.

"One of the really serious problems of professional hockey is that we do have to develop our own talent. There's no sources...of playing material available to us any place else except from institutions and organizations which we support, none whatever."

It was because of these costs and because of the necessary and substantial player development efforts that Campbell supported the continuation of hockey's reserve system.

"Q. Mr. Campbell, considering the extensive and expensive player development cost and arrangements which hockey has, and referring only to your sport and to none other for the moment, what is your opinion about the reasonableness and necessity of player contract arrangements which the NHL clubs enjoy through their contract and bylaw provisions?

A. Well, let me say this: if it were not for the security which the league affords to its members, in other words, that all members afford to one another as to the proprietary interest which they can maintain in the talent which they develop, it just couldn't be done. Nobody would run that hazard. It would be quite impossible, and the cost is tremendous....

Q. So, that in your sport, with its particular needs and requirements, including specifically the player development costs, player contract arrangements are a necessary and vital part of your existence?

A. If it were not for that assurance, no one would spend that kind of money. They just couldn't."

Through the testimony of Pete Rozelle and Walter Kennedy, Flood's lawyers were attempting to establish that professional football and basketball players, unlike professional baseball players, were not the property of the club owner for life; and that upon expiration of any existing contract, professional basketball and football players could negotiate and play for another club. In so doing, this gave Flood a basis to argue that baseball's reserve system was far more draconian and was an "unreasonable" restraint of trade.

The problem, however, was that Curt Flood's core claim

CHAPTER 12: DAY FIVE—TUESDAY, MAY 26, 1970

was that baseball's reserve system was *illegal*. Flood was asking the Court to *abolish* baseball's reserve system in its entirety, and to declare Flood a free agent. Consequently, what difference did it make to Curt Flood if professional basketball or football had a common draft, or had two different leagues, or whether or under what circumstances a professional basketball or football player could play out his option or "veto" a trade? *None* of these or any other proposed *modifications* to baseball's reserve system would help Curt Flood in his immediate effort to be declared a free agent and play professional baseball in 1970; and *none* of these *proposed changes* went to the heart of his claim that baseball's reserve system was illegal in its entirety.

Through the testimony of Alan Eagleson and Clarence Campbell, Flood's lawyers had also hoped to establish that hockey's reserve system was less restrictive than baseball's reserve system. As it turned out, Flood's lawyers presented two "hockey witnesses" who contradicted each other regarding the standard player contract. More importantly, however, and aside from the contradictions, the testimony elicited from *both* Eagleson and Campbell firmly established that hockey's reserve system, as a whole, differed very little from that of professional baseball, and was actually no less restrictive than baseball's reserve system.

At the conclusion of Clarence Campbell's testimony, Plaintiff Curtis Charles Flood rested his case. It was not a strong note on which to rest—and Day Five of the trial had not yet concluded.

At this stage of a trial (after the plaintiff concludes the presentation of his case) and in order to preserve all procedural options, the defense customarily makes a motion (requests the court) to dismiss the plaintiff's claims on the grounds that the plaintiff failed to present sufficient evidence (or failed to meet his burden of proof) in support of his case. This motion is frequently presented in a routine manner, with the defense expecting the court to summarily deny the motion and direct the defense to then begin presenting its case.

As expected, in the Flood trial, the defense made its motion to dismiss the plaintiff's claims. What was different, however, was that the defense went into painstaking detail in its argument in support of its motion. The most notable aspect and strongest point made by the defense focused on Flood's claim relating to involuntary servitude and peonage. Defense counsel Hughes pointed out that Flood's complaint (Count IV) alleged that baseball's reserve system "is a practice constituting and resulting in peonage and involuntary servitude" in violation of federal statutes and the Thirteenth Amendment of the United States Constitution.

Attorney Hughes addressed Judge Cooper:

"It seems plain to me that the plaintiff has failed to adduce any proof or facts beyond the bare allegations of [the complaint] itself…. There really is no proof at all. The only testimony on this subject was given by the plaintiff himself…."

Hughes then referred to the following portion of Flood's testimony given on Day One of the trial:

"Q. …Mr. Flood, you say, in substance, that the requirements of playing for one club to the exclusion of others is peonage and involuntary servitude…is that right?

A. Yes.

Q. Is that your sole basis, those allegations of the complaint, your sole basis for claiming peonage and involuntary servitude?

A. No.

Q. What other factors and circumstances do you claim as constituting a basis for your allegation that you are subjected to peonage and involuntary servitude?

A. Because I have no choice of where I can work.

Q. Isn't that what Paragraph 39 and Paragraph 40 [of the

CHAPTER 12: DAY FIVE—TUESDAY, MAY 26, 1970

Complaint] say?

A. Well, I imagine it to be. I thought you wanted something further.

Q. No, I am saying is it anything more than what is alleged in Paragraphs 39 and 40? Doesn't 39 and 40 cover the totality of your claim in that respect?

A. In this respect, yes."

The defense continued its argument as follows:

"And then he [Flood] was asked whether he was ever indebted to the St. Louis Club, and he answered that he was not and never had been. There is no evidence, of course, in the record produced by [Flood] or by anyone that he is indebted to the Philadelphia Club.... I submit to your Honor that the plaintiff is obviously not a slave. He is free to play or not to play baseball as he sees fit, and he has deliberately chosen not to play baseball. No law makes him play and no law restrains him in any way. He is free to pursue any other calling and, according to his testimony, he is now pursuing another calling, his photography business and his portrait businesses. So it is just palpably plain that he doesn't meet the definition of involuntary servitude either under the Constitution or any other definition....Moreover, he is not a peon because a peon is a person who is compelled to work for an employer, to work off a debt.... [I]n that connection, your Honor, I would like to call attention to one decision which so clearly points that out. It is the decision of *Clyatt v. United States*, where the [United States Supreme] Court held that "peonage is defined as a status or condition of *compulsory service based upon the indebtedness* of the peon to the master.

...I submit that on the record that has been adduced before your Honor that he [Flood] simply is not a peon....To the extent that he [Flood] claims that he was deprived of his opportunity of freedom of labor, he is relying on the Norris-LaGuardia Act [which]...provides...that workers shall enjoy freedom to organize, to bargain collectively and to engage in concerted activity without interference, restraint or coercion...[H]e has adduced no proof that he has been so restrained in any way, and to the contrary, there is abundant proof in this record of the extent to which there is collective bargaining now between the Players' Association on the one hand, of which the plaintiff is a member, and the defendant clubs...."

The defense continued to attack the legal sufficiency of each of the counts of Flood's Complaint. At the conclusion of the defense's motion, Flood's attorney, Jay Topkis, rebutted the defense's characterization of the plaintiff's evidence, insisted that Flood had presented a compelling case, and noted that it was now time for major league baseball to "step up to the plate" and present its defense of baseball's reserve system.

On the legal issue of peonage and slavery (Count IV), Flood's case was indeed weak and certainly could have been dismissed at this point of the trial by Judge Cooper. Judge Cooper, however, had already embarked upon a course that would permit the parties to make as complete an evidentiary record as possible at trial. In denying the defense's motion to dismiss Flood's complaint, Judge Cooper explained his ruling:

"At the close of plaintiff's case and pursuant to Rule 41(b) of the Federal Rules of Civil Procedure, defendants move to dismiss plaintiff's remaining four causes of action for failure upon the facts and the law to show a right to relief....[This Court] has concluded that in the interests of obtaining a full and complete picture for both the trial and Appellate Court, it is advisable to deny defendants' motions, put defendants to their proof and decide this case only after all the evidence has been adduced."

It was now time for the professional baseball establishment to present the defense of its reserve system.

CHAPTER 13
DAY SIX—WEDNESDAY, MAY 27, 1970

Testimony of Bowie K. Kuhn

At approximately 10:15 a.m., major league baseball began the defense of its reserve system. The defense called its first witness—Commissioner Bowie K. Kuhn. At the time of the trial, Kuhn was 44 years old. Born and raised in Tacoma Park, Maryland, a suburb of Washington D. C., Kuhn was a graduate of Princeton University (1947) and of the University of Virginia Law School (1950). After being admitted to the New York Bar in 1951, Kuhn practiced law in the D.C. firm of Willkie, Owen, Farr, Gallagher and Walton (by 1970, the firm's name was Willkie, Farr & Gallagher). Kuhn became a partner in the firm in 1961. During his time with the firm, Kuhn worked extensively with one of the firm's senior partners, Louis Carroll. (Not surprisingly, in the Flood case, Carroll and the firm of Willkie, Farr and Gallagher were counsel of record for Defendant Bowie K. Kuhn.) For many years, Carroll and the firm served as counsel for the National Baseball League. Following the firing of Commissioner Eckert in 1968, Bowie Kuhn was elected by the owners and, on February 4, 1969, Kuhn became Commissioner of Baseball.

The direct examination of Commissioner Kuhn was presented by attorney Victor Kramer. Kuhn's direct testimony was well organized, scripted and would take in excess of a day to complete. Early in his testimony, Kuhn was asked to summarize the duties of the office of Commissioner of Baseball. Kuhn stated that the most important duty of the Commissioner "now and as it has always been", is to protect the integrity, the honesty and the public acceptability of the game of baseball; that the Commissioner is charged with enforcing the rules and agreements of organized baseball; that the Commissioner is an arbitrator of disputes arising within the game of baseball; and that the Commissioner has certain ceremonial and public relations functions and duties.

Kramer then turned the witness to the subject of baseball's reserve system:

"The reserve system in baseball, your Honor, is a complex set of agreements and rules affecting clubs. The system I think is most commonly associated with Paragraph 10(a) of the Uniform Player's Contract...which provides an option to the club to renew the contract. But in fact, the system goes considerably beyond that provision. It includes the provision...that a major league club may have forty (40) players under contract and twenty-five (25) active players during the season...; it would include [the provision] that each... club...must...by November 15...file its reserve list of forty players...; and it includes the assignment provisions...of the Uniform Player's Contract...and Major League Rules...; and [it includes]...the tampering rule...which...provides in effect that one club cannot try to negotiate or deal with an employee of another club, including a player, while he is under contract...or reservation to the club."

Kuhn's next statement crystalized the stark contrast between the position of Plaintiff Flood and that of the owners and the Commissioner.

Chapter 13: Day Six—Wednesday, May 27, 1970

"...These are the basic provisions of the reserve system taken together with the *safeguards which are built into the system for the protection of the players.*"

Flood's basic premise was that baseball's reserve system was a set of agreements and procedures among the club owners which were designed to make a player the life long property of the club with whom the player signed his first contract to play baseball. On the other hand, Commissioner Kuhn characterized baseball's reserve system as a system of "safeguards for the protection of the players". During Kuhn's direct examination, the Commissioner continually referred to various reserve system provisions as "player safeguards"—a characterization which would later provide some fertile ground for cross examination by Flood's lawyers.

Kuhn then identified and elaborated upon each of the "player safeguards and protections", including the limitation of 40 players on the reserve list and 25 players on the active list. He even described the minor league draft as "designed to *guarantee* that a minor league baseball player be given a chance for advancement in his profession if he has the qualifications to advance."

Kuhn characterized Paragraph 10(a) of the Uniform Player's Contract as yet another "safeguard". Under this provision, a club exercising its option to renew could not do so at a salary less than 80% of the player's salary under the prior year's contract. In other words, a club intending to exercise its option to renew a player's contract may unilaterally "cut" the player's annual salary by up to 20%. Kuhn completed his litany of "safeguards" by identifying the minimum salary provision and the player's right to receive a maximum of 30 days of termination pay in the event a player was released by a club during the playing season.

Counsel Kramer then directed witness Kuhn to the various modifications to baseball's reserve system suggested by several of Flood's witnesses. In his well rehearsed but articulate response, Kuhn cited four standards or criteria against which the Commissioner, throughout his testimony, would evaluate any proposed modifications to baseball's reserve system: 1) integrity; 2) economic effect; 3) mechanical workability; and 4) effect on equalization of team strength.

Next, Commissioner Kuhn addressed Flood's current status under the Major League Rules. In particular, Kuhn cited Major League Rule 15. That Rule provided that if, without permission from his club, a player failed within 10 days of the opening of his club's season to report or to contract with his club for that season, the player may be placed on the restricted list by the Commissioner. A request to so place a player on the restricted list required the Commissioner's concurrence. Kuhn testified that this

"...is one of the reasons that I contacted Mr. Flood at the time I did, by sending him the telegram and trying to get him to sit down and talk with me because I was anxious that he should play. I remain anxious that he should play. And I was endeavoring to avoid having Mr. Flood placed on the restricted list. Under the circumstances, I was left with no alternative but to approve the placement of his name on the restricted list".

Kuhn testified that he was familiar with the history of organized baseball, and in particular, with the history of baseball's reserve system. In addition to being an avid reader on the subject of baseball, Kuhn specifically relied upon and referenced the *MacMillan Encyclopedia* (1969); the Third Edition of Turkin & Thompson's *Baseball Encyclopedia*; Seymour's *History of the Early Years of Baseball* (1960); "*An Informal History*", by Doug Wallop (1969); and the *Celler Report* (1952).

Kuhn testified as to the early days of baseball beginning with the National Association of Professional Ballplayers in

CHAPTER 13: DAY SIX—WEDNESDAY, MAY 27, 1970

1871, as well as to the origins of the reserve system in the 1870s. He testified that the reserve system was adopted in 1879 in an effort to avoid some of the evils of "revolving"—a term used to describe when some players leave one team and all end up playing on another team; and noted that the assignment clause first appeared in the uniform contract of the National League in the 1880s.

Attorney Kramer then directed his witness to a specific passage from the *Celler Report* which stated as follows: "Baseball's history shows that chaotic conditions prevailed when there was no reserve clause." Kuhn then offered a well prepared and windy opinion:

"Q. In your study of the early history of baseball, did you come across evidence in support of the conclusion that chaotic conditions prevailed when there was no reserve clause?

A. Yes…Taking the history of the game from the earliest organization…in 1857,…up to the organization of the present major leagues in 1903,…the history shows…quite conclusively that in the absence of a reserve system…that permits more than a minimal number of players to be reserved, that a number of problems crept into the game which threatened its very existence. Among these…was the problem of revolving, both during a playing season and after a playing season was over, where players would go from club to club.…[T]he effect of this was quite clearly to shake public confidence in the game, because the player playing for one team one year would be playing for another team the next, with the attendant suspicion that, particularly with the heavy amount of betting that went on, that he may have done something to benefit his second team while he was playing for his first team in the course of the race. This has a great effect on public confidence. Attendance was obviously affected. The ability of clubs to survive under these circumstances was very limited. I think during the history of the National Association of 1871, which lasted only five years, there were 25 teams in that league during that time, the great majority of which failed, went out of business. Only three started and were able to finish the five-year period. Profitability was very low, and in this climate of scrambling, not just ballplayers but clubs scrambling to see who could beat out the other guy ignoring the rules, there was created a most unhealthy climate for a professional game. The rules became secondary. The clubs violated their own rules. The leagues violated their rules in competition with one another. The players had little respect for the system of which they were a part, and as a result, dishonesty became rampant in the game. Indeed, it got so bad during a certain stage of this history that they said that the only people that bothered going to the ball games any more were the gamblers. The ballplayers were fixing games. The clubs were fixing games. When the clubs did it, it was known as "hippodroming", a term that has continued today, happily not in baseball...*The entire climate was an extremely evil one for a professional sport, and it was cured, in my judgment ultimately by an effective reserve system, plus a strong central government organization in baseball along with the safeguards that have built into the system both with the reserve system and with the strong central government."*

In 1883, Kuhn continued, the reserve system was extended to eleven players—at that time, nearly the entire team roster. According to Kuhn, this extension, taken together with the National Agreement which ended the "war" between the National League and the American Association, "permitted an era in the last part of the 1880s of relative profitability of club operations and relative stability of players on teams, with attendant rises in attendance and public acceptance of the game". As to the effect on the players, Kuhn quoted the following portion of the Celler Committee Report:

CHAPTER 13: DAY SIX—WEDNESDAY, MAY 27, 1970

"The ballplayers, too, benefitted from this new stability and prosperity. *While the reserve rule had been directed against them to reduce salaries*, in the long run they realized a greater income, partly due to the owners' desire to keep them satisfied, partly due to competition by rival leagues and partly due to the competition resulting whenever a weaker club forfeited its franchise and players. The average player salary doubled from 1880 to 1889...."

Kramer continued his artful examination of Kuhn and the defense's attempt to establish not only the reasonableness, but the *necessity* of baseball's reserve system.

"Q. The House Judiciary Committee [1952 Celler Report]...expressed the opinion [that] experience points to no feasible substitute to protect the integrity of the game or to guarantee a comparatively even struggle. Now that report and that opinion was given in 1952. My question to you is, in your experience do you know of anything since 1952 that has arisen that would point to any feasible substitute for the reserve system viewed as a system to protect the integrity of the game or to guarantee a comparatively equal competitive struggle?

A. No, I do not."

To bolster that view, Kramer then asked Kuhn to identify the changes in organized baseball since 1952 that have benefitted the players. Kuhn stated that the single most significant change was expansion. Up until and through 1952, professional baseball clubs were largely confined to what Kuhn referred to as "the northeast quadrant" of the United States—St. Louis to Chicago to Boston to Washington, D.C. But beginning in 1953, baseball began to move into new geographic areas. In 1953, the Boston Braves relocated to Milwaukee; and in 1958, the New York Giants became the San Francisco Giants while the Brooklyn Dodgers became the Los Angeles Dodgers. After the 1953 season, the St. Louis Browns moved and became the Baltimore Orioles. After the

1954 season, the Philadelphia Athletics moved and became the Kansas City Athletics.

Kuhn's summary of major league baseball's changing landscape also referenced the addition of four new franchises in 1962: the New York Mets and the Houston Colt 45s (later the Astros) in the National League; and the Los Angeles Angels and Minnesota Twins in the American League. After the 1965 season, major league baseball would now be played in the southeastern U.S. following the relocation of the Milwaukee Braves franchise to Atlanta, Georgia. Just one year before the trial (and Flood's last year with the Cardinals), major league baseball again expanded by another four teams. 1969 marked the first time that a major league baseball franchise would be located outside the continental United States. In 1969, the Montreal Expos and the San Diego Padres joined the National League; and the Seattle Pilots and Kansas City Royals began play in the American League. At the same time, the Kansas City Athletics relocated and became the Oakland Athletics. (The Seattle Pilots played only one season, had a record of 64 wins and 98 losses, and after bankruptcy, relocated and became the Milwaukee Brewers.)

According to the Commissioner,

"...the effect of all of this [expansion] has been to increase not only the geographic areas in which the game is played...but it has expanded the number of major league teams from sixteen to twenty-four, which means that vast new opportunities for players in the major leagues have been created and at least a long term potential for a more profitable operation of the clubs has been created by reason of expansion into new territories. I think this has been beneficial to everyone in baseball."

Kuhn next described other player benefits which relate to "equalization" of club talent. Kuhn testified that the adoption of the free agent draft in 1965 (Major League Rule

4) and the adoption of the unrestricted minor league draft in 1958 (Major League Rule 5) "benefit the upward movement of players and benefit clubs...by permitting them to equalize playing strength...." Kuhn then cited the existence and effectiveness of the Major League Baseball Players' Association and its Executive Director.

"...In 1966, Mr. Miller came into the picture and in my judgement has done a strikingly effective job in representing the ballplayers and in obtaining significant economic gains for them, quite dramatically, I think, Your Honor. In 1966, he negotiated a new benefit plan which increased the annual club contribution from $2.6 million to $4.1 million. That was a two-year arrangement and when that expired, he negotiated a three-year arrangement which increased the annual contribution from $4.1 million to $5.5 million. He negotiated a new basic agreement...in 1968...which contains very significant benefits for the players, and he has negotiated a tentative agreement on a new basic agreement.... So the presence of this Association has been an effective force, and Mr. Miller has, in my judgment, improved it in player representation and rights...."

The subject matter of Kuhn's direct testimony again turned to the crux of the case—baseball's reserve system. From the witness stand, professional baseball's "czar" would now arrogantly pontificate that baseball's existing reserve system in its entirety was not only designed to benefit the players, but was an absolute necessity for the operation of professional baseball.

"Q. Mr. Kuhn,...you have had approximately 19½ years of experience in one capacity or another in organized baseball, is that right?

A. Yes.

Q. My question to you is...whether or not in your opinion organized baseball *could continue and function satisfactorily without the reserve system* ?

A. *In my opinion, it could not.*

Q. What are the reasons for your opinion?

A. The reasons, Mr. Kramer, *are measured by the standards by which the necessity of the reserve clause must be measured. There are four of these, as I see it.* One is to provide an equalization of team strength; another is to assure the growth of player and team strength and development; thirdly, the protection of the integrity and public acceptance of the game; and fourthly, attraction of capital to the game so that it might operate."

Kramer then asked his witness to address the relationship between the integrity of the game of baseball and the reserve system.

"Q. Please explain how the integrity of the game has anything to do with the reserve system.

A. I think I can short circuit that to some extent, Mr. Kramer, by referring to history. The history...of baseball without a reserve system...has demonstrated that *it is impossible to maintain integrity of operations...it is impossible to maintain honesty among the clubs or players....* The whole process of revolving and shifting and what has accompanied it leaves, in my judgment, *no hope of the maintenance of integrity as is necessary for a professional sport to operate.*"

Kuhn then read a statement (contained in the 1952 Celler Report) by A.G. Mills. Kuhn described Mills as "the man who originated the reserve rule."

"...As now, each summer's campaign was planned during the preceding winter and the habit was general on the part of the clubs to take on obligations in the way of players' salaries that were not justified, as the spring games would inevitably demonstrate that the majority of such clubs could have no hope of winning even a respectable number of games. Moreover, this condition was greatly aggravated by the general practice on the part of the richer clubs, of strip-

Chapter 13: Day Six—Wednesday, May 27, 1970

ping the weaker ones of their best playing talent. Then would follow the collapse of a number of these clubs in midseason, leaving their players unpaid, while the winning clubs, owing to the disbandment of the weaker ones, would also frequently fail from inability to arrange a paying number of games. In such a condition of things, it was manifestly impossible to establish and maintain that discipline which is indispensable to success in every form of team contest, and the laxity of discipline was largely responsible for the grosser evils which were then rife, such as dissipation, gambling, and even in some cases selling of games."

Kuhn addressed yet another desired and intended effect of the reserve system—equalizing competition among the clubs. The Commissioner took the position that unrestrained competition among the clubs, as opposed to standardized cooperation, would destroy professional baseball.

"...Again, I think that history, your Honor, provides a clear answer. Unrestrained competition as we have in the marketplace applied to baseball would produce the evils which I believe I have described in the game where at the time we had unrestrained competition. It is inevitable in a league, in a professional team sport, that you must compete within the league. The clubs must compete with one another. This is critical. They must compete in trying to acquire the best players and in various other ways, but if they compete too vigorously against the other partners in the league and put them out of business, *as history shows that men's instincts will lead them to do,* then you have destroyed the league. But the leagues must likewise have cooperation among its members in order to exist and be effective with the public. So you have the need both for keen if not fierce competition but also cooperation, which has the effect of limiting that competition in order to permit the various entities within the league to compete as successfully with one another as possible, in other words, to *standardize the conditions of competition so that you can have equal competition* and hopefully have good races, exciting to the public, and therefore *carry out your trust to the public.*"

It is critically important to understand this portion of Kuhn's testimony. The Commissioner's testimony was that major league baseball was not just some multi-million dollar, international, business conglomerate. To Kuhn, professional baseball was a unique American enterprise which, as an institution, had a *duty* to "maintain the public trust" and, which as a result, was entitled to some special status under the law.

Kuhn also steadfastly maintained that "unrestrained competition" and "men's instincts" would lead to the destruction of major league baseball. Ironically, and according to Kuhn, the reserve system was essential to protect the club owners from their *own destructive instincts* and to maintain the "public trust." While Kuhn believed that "unrestrained competition" would destroy baseball, it is important to note that in one sense, *there were no "restraints"* on baseball and there had never been any legal "restraints" on the club owners—a fact that was buttressed by the U. S. Supreme Court's holding in 1922 and reinforced in 1953 in the *Toolson* case. Under these decisions, professional baseball was *exempt* from the Sherman Act and was not subject to antitrust regulation or enforcement.

The kind of "restraints" that Kuhn believed were necessary, and which were necessary to keep baseball from being destroyed were embodied in baseball's reserve system—a set of "restraints" not imposed by governmental regulation or enforcement, but rather a set of "restraints", practices and agreements entered into among and enforced *by the owners* "for the good of the game" and to "maintain the integrity of the game." In fact and in reality, the club owners were free to organize, collude and jointly impose their own set of agreements and restraints upon the players—unre-

CHAPTER 13: DAY SIX—WEDNESDAY, MAY 27, 1970

stricted by any threat of antitrust enforcement or violation. The indisputable fact was that by 1970, professional baseball was indeed a major business and industry—and, just one year prior, it had completed the largest expansion (from 16 to 24 teams) in the history of professional baseball. Why the unprecedented expansion? Because sophisticated business interests realized that a professional baseball franchise could be operated profitably—not because the individual owners decided to fulfill some nostalgic notion of "public trust" or to maintain "the integrity of the game".

Kuhn's position was troubling. On the one hand, Kuhn believed that the owners could not be trusted to conduct themselves rationally. After all, according to Kuhn, their "instincts" would destroy baseball. Therefore, a reserve system—devised and enforced by the owners—was essential to protect the owners from themselves. On the other hand, Kuhn's view was that the club owners were like stewards or fiduciaries who would, collectively and through the office of the Commissioner, fulfill some public trust or obligation to act in the best interest of the *game of baseball*. Certainly, no law or federal antitrust scrutiny was required—particularly in light of all of the "player safeguards" built into baseball's reserve system. In Kuhn's view, to think otherwise was an insult to the "game", unthinkable and downright blasphemy!

Kuhn next described the wide divergence of financial resources among the clubs and the potential impact of the various modifications to the reserve system suggested by Marvin Miller and other Flood witnesses. Kuhn was then asked about the operation of professional baseball in the absence of a reserve system.

"...Q. Now I turn to the question of financial resources as distinguished from profitability, and I ask you whether or not there is a wide divergence of financial resources ...among the major league clubs?

A. Yes.

Q. What accounts for this wide divergence in financial resources?

A. Several things.... These variations occur because from club to club there is a great variation in the amount of gate receipts.... The broadcast market, including radio and television, varies from city to city according to its size, and therefore the source of revenue here varies greatly.... In addition, the principal operator of a club frequently has been responsible for loaning money to the club and permitting it to operate...so...the assets of the various operators play a significant part....

Q. What significance, if any, Mr. Kuhn does this divergence in financial resources have in considering the workability of alternatives to the reserve system, concerning which there has been testimony by plaintiff, and by Mr. Miller and Mr. Greenberg and Mr. Nathan?

A. Well, the workability of any particular proposal can in my judgment...be affected by the lack of evenness of financial strength among the clubs....

Q. Well, let us take a proposal that I believe was advanced by the plaintiff himself, *that we simply do away with the reserve rule*. What would the effect of that be in your opinion, in light of the widely varying financial resources of the...clubs?

A. I don't think there is the slightest question that the more well-to-do clubs would attract the star players and *the less well-to-do clubs would simply go out of business*. You certainly couldn't operate a league in my judgement.... *Baseball as we know it simply could not survive....*"

The Commissioner's testimony continued with a "check list" of advantages and successes which Kuhn attributed to baseball's reserve system. Drawing upon his interpretation of certain baseball history, Kuhn concluded that major league baseball was able to attract investment and capital

CHAPTER 13: DAY SIX—WEDNESDAY, MAY 27, 1970

because of the stability which resulted from a strong reserve system. The Commissioner's testimony continually revealed a distinction which somewhat defied logic and which Flood's lawyers would attempt to exploit later on during the Commissioner's cross examination. Succinctly, this distinction was between the "game" of baseball as our national pastime, and the "business" of baseball as part of the entertainment industry. It was Kuhn's view that professional baseball was subject to fierce competition.

"Q. ...With what other activities or types of business enterprises, if any, does organized baseball compete today?

A. Baseball competes with a host of activities *in the entertainment field.* To enumerate some of these, it competes to a degree with other professional sports, notably professional hockey, professional basketball, professional football and to some extent professional soccer. It competes, however, outside of the sports field with a great many other types of activity, such as horse racing...the movie industry, all forms of outdoor recreation, which of course are at their peak during the warm months when baseball is played. This would be golf and tennis and camping and fishing and the use of automobiles. The vast expansion of our highway systems and our automobile supply has put America on the roads and not necessarily to ballparks.... These examples could be multiplied by all the things that go on during the warm weather that attract people to other forms of entertainment.... [T]he medium of television...may be the most important form of entertainment with which baseball competes.... In my judgment, if I may, your Honor, I believe this competition has never been so intense for baseball as it is today and as it has been in recent years, and the intensity, the degree of competition is heightening at all times...."

It is interesting to note that *none of the professional sports nor any of the fields of entertainment* which Kuhn acknowledged as fierce competition to professional baseball were *exempt* from the Sherman Act and federal antitrust regulation. Moreover, and by way of example, how could professional basketball or professional football *survive* in the absence of a reserve system pursuant to which a player remained, for the rest of his life, the property of the team with whom he signed his first professional contract?

At the very end of Kuhn's direct testimony, defense attorney Kramer highlighted each of the various reserve system proposals and modifications suggested by each of the witnesses presented in Flood's case in chief. Kramer asked Kuhn about the modification that would allow a club to have an option on a player's services only for an agreed upon number of years (suggested by Miller); the proposal that established an exclusive option for a maximum of five years (suggested by Nathan); the proposal that would prohibit a club from signing more than a specific number of free agents during a specified period (suggested by Miller); minimum salary progressions for all players; reducing a club's reserve list from 40 to a lower number of players; the establishment of separate and competitive leagues; and informal arbitration of salary disputes. Kramer asked Kuhn to state his opinion as to the effect of each of those proposals on professional baseball.

Not surprisingly, Kuhn's testimony was that each of the proposals presented "serious" problems, and that some of the proposals would "destroy baseball as we know it." Kuhn's concluding opinions and views on the proposed modifications to baseball's reserve system are contained in the following and rather lengthy narration:

"...[I]t has been my conviction and continuous practice...that the problems of the type presented on the reserve system as they arise between the players and clubs should be solved by the players and clubs *in the formal course of collective bargaining* and that the Commissioner of Baseball, carrying out the functions of his office, should not

CHAPTER 13: DAY SIX—WEDNESDAY, MAY 27, 1970

involve himself in the merits of those considerations and in the strategy of the parties relating to this type of problem.

Since October [1969], when the present bargaining began, I have studiously adhered to that principle.... I have not expressed my views on these subjects...to anyone except to my attorneys during the course of preparing for this testimony. However, it seems to me that there comes a time in the course of litigation...where I am bound to express my views on these things, because the questions have been presented to this Court in part for decision.

As to Mr. Miller's proposal,...it is a difficult proposal for me to address myself to because of the vagueness of the detail.... Addressing myself as best I can to the general idea and taking those standards...by which I would try to test a modification in the reserve system, I would say that in terms of...the effect on [the] integrity of the game, this has perils because inevitably it opens the door to a player dealing with another club while he is with a first club.... The mechanics [of this proposed modification] do not make it clear to me how this could be prevented, and it is an invitation to the avoidance of the tampering rule.

Any time a player comes to the end of a period of service and looks for another employer, the danger of impairing the integrity of the game immediately emerges.... [The] opportunities are very widespread...for that to happen, because our teams travel around the country, spend a number of days playing a stand in different cities as they travel on the road, which presents a considerable opportunity for tampering and for discussions, which could affect the integrity of the game or affect the appearance of the integrity of the game, which is just as important.

On workability, I have indicated that the mechanics are simply not stated in Mr. Miller's proposal.... He doesn't suggest how many years.... *I think this is the kind of thing that can be worked out in bargaining, if it can be worked out at all.*

In terms of equality of competition, I am afraid that this would have an adverse effect because the richer teams would tend to sign up the players who became available under such a free agency arrangement.

In terms of the economic effect, *I think the economic effect could be serious* if, as a result of this, the stronger teams financially attracted the players, your Honor, leaving the weaker teams to flounder and possibly perish financially, *but basically this is the kind of question that in my judgement can be resolved, if it can be resolved at all, in bargaining."*

Even from the witness stand, the Commissioner could neither resist the temptation nor pass up the opportunity to express his irritation with his nemesis, Marvin Miller, with the Players' Association, and to comment upon the litigation and the collective bargaining process.

"Q. In your opinion, if changes are to be made in the reserve system, how should those changes be made?

A. They should be made...by...bargaining between the players and the clubs. I do not believe they should be made or that they can be made unilaterally by the clubs. We are dealing here with terms and conditions of the players' employment. So the change should be made in bargaining.

I feel that the reference to court litigation points up a misfortune in the present bargaining context. It has been my stated opinion repeatedly that *the decision of the Players' Association to back Mr. Flood's litigation here was a serious mistake on their part.* This decision was made as long ago as their San Juan meeting in the first half of December 1969, and *to think that they were seriously embarking on realistic negotiations to find a solution when they had committed themselves to litigation is nonsense in my judgement.* And, indeed, when they effectuated *their determination* at San Juan *by bringing this litigation* in the middle of January, it quickly resulted in the Players' Association and the clubs bargaining team working out an arrangement whereby they

CHAPTER 13: DAY SIX—WEDNESDAY, MAY 27, 1970

simply put the reserve system question up on the shelf and thereafter ceased, so far as I can determine, to bargain on the subject. *Therefore, I think the Players' Association made a serious mistake in its position.*"

Kuhn had just articulated a critically important argument. Through the Commissioner, the defense had just pronounced its position (and its legal argument) that this litigation was not brought by Curt Flood, but that this litigation was the Players' Association's suit against major league baseball. Kuhn would now attempt to distinguish the union's interests from the plaintiff's interests.

"...Mr. Flood is something else again. *He is perfectly free to sue anybody he wants. I don't criticize him for doing it or not as he sees fit. I criticize the Players' Association.* I criticize them further for the kind of proposal which is presented here in Mr. Miller's testimony. The proposals are all around, undefined and interrelated by Mr. Miller's testimony as I heard it. He didn't say any one of these generalized proposals was the thing he was presenting. He said it is some combination of these. So it has a double fault. You don't know what he is presenting because it is a combination of several things, and in its individual elements it is imprecise."

In Kuhn's continuing criticism, the club owners would not be spared.

"...Now, *I further criticize the clubs* in the bargaining here because I don't think they should have permitted Mr. Miller to make this kind of a proposal. I *think they should have insisted on a precise proposal which could have been discussed in joint meetings of the clubs to see if it had any possible merit.* Instead, this kind of proposal was permitted, it came to a point with this litigation commencing where both of them in essence took it off the table and we have had no bargaining since. The important thing to recognize there is that *since this litigation was commenced there have been very important concessions made in other areas.*"

(As will be discussed later, to say that there had been "very important concessions" made in other areas since the commencement of the Flood suit was an understatement of magnanimous proportion.)

Because Flood's lawyers chose to present evidence of numerous and purportedly "corrective" modifications to baseball's reserve system, the defense was forced to respond. Kuhn's direct examination was organized and presented in a manner to refute each of these proposed modifications. Consequently, Kuhn's direct examination, while well organized and thorough, was lengthy and replete with Kuhn's wordy opinions and commentary.

Commissioner Kuhn's testimony on direct examination was the embodiment of the baseball establishment's rationale and justification for baseball's reserve system. The Commissioner's defense of baseball's reserve system was based upon the historical "need" for the system to combat evils like "revolving", "hippodroming," and player tampering; to maintain the integrity of the game and the financial stability of baseball in the late 1800s and the early 1900s; and finally, to "safeguard" and benefit the players. Moreover, the Commissioner predictably and conveniently asserted that "chaos" would result in the absence of the reserve system and that there existed no feasible alternative to the reserve system.

The Commissioner's testimony, however, did not (and could not) address how the reserve system "justified" a player being the club's "property for life"; nor how the reserve system, a series of agreements and practices among club owners, could lawfully be enforced by those same owners; nor could the Commissioner address the legal or policy basis for why baseball, unlike any other professional sport, was "exempt" from the Sherman Act and thereby "exempt" from federal antitrust regulation and enforcement.

CHAPTER 13: DAY SIX—WEDNESDAY, MAY 27, 1970

Perhaps the most irreconcilable and contradictory positions asserted by the Commissioner pertained to his paramount duty as Commissioner and the negotiations between the club owners and the players regarding modifications to baseball's reserve system. First, Kuhn stated that allowing a player to play out his option and become a free agent would permit tampering and thereby threaten the integrity of the game. Kuhn also stated that if players were free to play out their options and become free agents, this would abolish the reserve system and "destroy the game of baseball as we know it". Second, Kuhn testified that the duty of the Commissioner that was paramount to all others was to act in the best interests of baseball, and to maintain the public trust and the integrity of the game. Third, the Commissioner testified that any modifications to the reserve system ought to be negotiated and bargained between the club owners and the players—and should not involve the Commissioner nor be the subject of litigation.

On these key points, Kuhn's testimony was blatantly inconsistent. Assume, for example, that the players and the owners *negotiated* a modification to baseball's reserve system pursuant to which a player could play out his option and become a free agent. In that scenario, how could the Commissioner allow the players and owners to effectively negotiate the "destruction" of baseball's reserve system, and at the same time, fulfill his duties as Commissioner and act in the best interests of baseball to maintain the integrity of the game?

It was now time for Flood's team to question the Commissioner.

Cross Examination of Commissioner Kuhn

Early in his cross examination, Topkis questioned the Commissioner about professional football's reserve system which permitted a player to "play out his option" and become a free agent. Kuhn had previously testified that allowing a player to play out his option would result in "tampering", would call into question the public's confidence in and destroy the integrity of the game of baseball. Topkis was inquiring as to how such a procedure could be viable in professional football, and at the same time, destroy the integrity of the game of baseball. Topkis specifically asked whether Kuhn believed that baseball players and owners were more corrupt than football players and owners. After a lengthy set of questions and answers, the Commissioner replied "No".

The subject then shifted to the independence and the impartiality of the position of Commissioner. Topkis confronted Kuhn with the testimony of then Commissioner Ford Fricke in 1952 before the Celler Committee. During those 1952 Congressional hearings, Commissioner Fricke stated that "the [Office of] Commissioner is a law unto himself". Topkis asked Kuhn whether he agreed with the 1952 statement of then Commissioner Fricke. In response, Kuhn said…"I don't see how I could agree with it". Moreover, and at the probing of Topkis, the Commissioner admitted that the Commissioner's salary was "paid from a bank account maintained by the Commissioner's Office, for which the funds are drawn from World Series receipts and from a central bank account of the twenty-four clubs." On the issue of impartiality, Kuhn acknowledged that the players were not consulted when the club owners hired Kuhn as Commissioner in February 1969.

Topkis then questioned the Commissioner on one particular provision of baseball's reserve system that Kuhn previously referred to in his testimony as a "player safeguard".

"Q. Commissioner, you testified this morning that one of the safeguards, I think you called it, for players or protec-

CHAPTER 13: DAY SIX—WEDNESDAY, MAY 27, 1970

tions for players that has come along in recent years has been the adoption in the standard contract of a provision that a player's salary can't be cut more than 20 percent in any year; do you remember that testimony?

A. Yes.

Q. Have you ever calculated, Commissioner, what the impact on a player's salary would be if he started out with an annual salary of $50,000 and had it cut the maximum 20 percent each year for eight years?

A. I have not calculated that, no....

Q. ...So...we could agree that if a player were paid $50,000 in the first year, in the eighth year he would be paid $10,688 ?...

A. It adds up to eight years and that would bring it down to the figure you used, yes.

Q. $10,688?

A. Yes.

Q. And, Commissioner, that could happen to a ballplayer under the rules of organized baseball today, could it not, unless he chose to quit the sport?

A. Yes.

Q. Do you wish to withdraw the term "safeguard"?...

A. *Of course not.*"

Kuhn's insolence continued during Topkis's next line of questioning—the Commissioner's authority as an arbitrator. Major League Rule 22 read in pertinent part:

"All disputes between players and clubs shall be referred to the Commissioner and his decisions shall be accepted by all parties as final. Negotiations between player and club regarding *the player's compensation under his contract shall not be referable to the Commissioner.*"

Despite the clear wording of Rule 22, Kuhn maintained that he would and could intervene as an arbitrator involving salary disputes. Kuhn adamantly proclaimed that each player had an "absolute right" to *ask* the Commissioner to "use his good offices". Kuhn also humbly noted for the record that since becoming Commissioner, Kuhn, on his own initiative, intervened in several trade disputes (involving Ken Harrelson and Camillo Pasquel) and resolved the disputes. Separate and distinct from the Commissioner's Rule 22 powers, it must be noted that the Commissioner always had the power to "act in the best interest of baseball", and the Commissioner and only the Commissioner determined *when* to invoke this authority and what constituted the "best interest of baseball."

As the end of Day Six approached, Topkis asked the Commissioner his views on the adoption of a provision that would allow a player to "veto" a trade to another club. While Kuhn reluctantly conceded that such a provision, in and of itself, would not affect the integrity of the game, Kuhn testified that he opposed such a "veto" provision because it would "negatively impact team morale." By any standard, the Commissioner's rationale was pathetically lame.

When Topkis informed Judge Cooper that he would not finish his cross examination of the Commissioner before the end of the day, the Judge adjourned Day Six of the trial and directed the Commissioner to return the next day to resume his testimony.

Chapter 14
Day Seven—Thursday, May 28, 1970

Cross Examination of Bowie Kuhn (Continued)

It was approximately 10:00 a.m. when Commissioner Kuhn returned to the witness stand. Topkis wasted no time pressing the witness on his repeated pronouncements that the reserve system was inviolate.

"Q. ...What changes could be made to the reserve system without destroying the fabric of baseball?

A. The changes that the parties can agree to...The players are well represented and I am sure Mr. Miller and the Players' Association are capable of bargaining changes in the reserve system."

The Commissioner knew full well where this line of questioning would take him. Kuhn quickly began to "back peddle", and his answers became increasingly vague and evasive.

"Q. Mr. Kuhn, were the players and the owners to agree that at the end of five years a player would become a free agent and be able to bargain with any other team that he wished and that were arrived at as the result of collective bargaining, you would regard that as perfectly reasonable and proper, is that right?

A. You would have to give me the full details of the workings of that and I really can't answer the question.... I simply don't understand what you mean by reasonable and proper arrangement. I don't know what you are getting at in terms of my position.

Q. Would it operate to destroy baseball?

A. I would have to refer back to my answers of yesterday where I dealt with that particular subject and gave my views on that.... I would have to say that I do not anticipate any such result in bargaining. It is a hypothetical question and I will give you that answer."

After some substantial effort to recover, Kuhn testified that allowing a player to play out his option "would be very damaging to the operation of professional baseball." Kuhn noted three reasons: the potential for player tampering; the resulting loss of public confidence in the integrity of the game; and Kuhn's desire to keep baseball "free from any taint". What Topkis never asked was whether Kuhn, as Commissioner, in carrying out his duty to act in the best interest of baseball, would take action to void any collective bargaining agreement provision which allowed a player to play out his option and become a free agent.

Topkis then directed the witness to the reserve system's impact on players' wages.

"Q. ...I believe [Mr. Nathan] testified that the operation of the reserve system had as one of its consequences a depressant effect upon the wage level of the players. Would you agree with that statement?

A. No.

Q. Would you believe that the operation of the reserve system *tends to raise the wage level of the players?*

A. Yes.

Q. And would you believe that a seller normally does better in selling his services when he has one buyer or when he has more than one potential buyer?

CHAPTER 14: DAY SEVEN—THURSDAY, MAY 28, 1970

A. In the normal market situation, when he has more; but not in baseball."

The discussion between Topkis and Kuhn again referenced the 1952 Celler Report. Topkis directed the witness to a passage from the Report stating that since the inception of the reserve system in 1879, the share of major league clubs expenses going for *team salaries* has exhibited a continual *decline*. The Report listed the following percentages:

1879—68%	1939—32.4%	1946—24.8%
1929—35.3%	1943—28.9%	1950—22.1%

Kuhn did not quarrel with these figures from the Celler Report, and estimated that the figure for the 1970 season was approximately 25%.

Topkis then began a line of questioning regarding the business acumen of the club owners and the so called "sports league theory". For illustration purposes, Topkis inquired about player salaries.

"Q. Commissioner,...if a ball club pays too much for the player talent, it will go broke. Would that be a fair summary of part of your testimony?

A. That could happen, yes.

Q. Well, that is true of any businessman, isn't it, that if he pays too much for something that he uses he will go broke?

A. Yes. I believe so.

Q. Why, then, Commissioner, would you believe that these businessmen who today own major league baseball [clubs], would pay too much?...

A. The difficulty is that you are talking about *a sports league, and that differentiates baseball from other business operations.* If the New York Yankees, let us say, attract all the best talent, so that the other clubs in the American League cannot compete effectively with them, the Yankees are hurt, the other clubs are hurt, and the sport will ultimately fail.

Q. Wouldn't it be stupid for the Yankees to do that because nobody would come to watch the Yankees play, would they?

A. No, it wouldn't be. Perhaps it would be unwise, but...in the past it has happened where the opportunity presented itself."

Again, the Commissioner was articulating his view that baseball's reserve system was, at least in part, necessary to protect baseball club owners from making bad business decisions to the detriment of themselves—the owners, as well as to professional baseball.

Topkis took this discussion with the Commissioner one important step further. Topkis posed a series of questions as to why professional baseball club owners, as distinguished from other business owners, should be free of such business risks. Kuhn's responses were astonishing.

"Q. Well, one business or another in the course of American history has encountered adversity. I suppose we could agree on that.

A. Yes.

Q. Is there any particular reason *why baseball should be free of that risk?*

A. *Within a sports league, you have a different problem....* If you are talking about the application of the antitrust laws....

Q. I am just asking you about the laws of economics. *What is there about baseball that entitles it to immunity from the ordinary laws of economics?*

A. The ordinary laws of economics, and as applied by the antitrust laws, *would plainly impair if not destroy the operations of sports leagues.* That was the conclusion...of the Celler Report. *That is why baseball is exempt from the antitrust laws, in my judgment."*

Topkis was clearly stunned by the Commissioner's last response. In fact, the transcript reveals that Topkis's

CHAPTER 14: DAY SEVEN—THURSDAY, MAY 28, 1970

remark in response to Kuhn's answer was stricken from the trial record. Nevertheless, Topkis persisted in questioning Kuhn regarding the Commissioner's interpretation of baseball's antitrust exemption.

"Q. Who exempted baseball from the operation of the federal antitrust laws, Commissioner, *for the reason that but for such exemption, the game would die?*

A. *I believe the ruling of the Supreme Court in the Toolson case was grounded on such consideration. That's my judgment.*"

Kuhn's "sports league theory" as well as his description of the findings and conclusions of the Celler Committee were seriously flawed. If, as Kuhn concluded, the laws of economics and federal antitrust laws would "destroy" sports leagues, why didn't the Celler Report recommend that *all* professional sports be exempt from the Sherman Act? Why didn't Congress take action to "reverse" the federal court decisions which specifically held that these same professional sports leagues were subject to and not exempt from federal antitrust laws? Kuhn's apparent understanding of the Court's holding in *Toolson* was also without merit. Nowhere in *Toolson* does the Supreme Court even hint that subjecting professional baseball to the Sherman Act would destroy the game. Nor did the Court's decision suggest that the purported "destruction" of baseball was even a consideration in (much less the basis for) the Court's decision.

Topkis then interrogated the Commissioner about a proposed modification whereby a salary dispute could be the subject of impartial arbitration. Kuhn responded that "it would be particularly harmful in the area of player-club relations", and that "it would create a gulf between the players and clubs." In Kuhn's words, "it would be a bad thing." Kuhn expanded on his answers to further note that there was no need for arbitration because there existed meaningful negotiations between players and club owners. The Commissioner refuted Topkis's assertion that the player in effect is forced to take the club's final offer or retire from baseball.

"Well, that simply isn't the situation. The player does have an alternative to taking the final offer. The players are in a perfectly respectable individual bargaining position with the clubs. They are normally able to bargain from the clubs a higher salary than the club offers. The bargaining is certainly two-sided. The player is every bit as important to that club as that club is to that player in almost every case."

When questioned about the club owners' recoupment of development costs, Kuhn continued to be vague and evasive. Topkis asked whether the players and owners could negotiate a set period of time in which a club could have exclusive rights to a player in order to recoup the club's expenses and investment in that player's minor league training.

"I don't know what the precise period is in terms of simple recoupment. I don't know how to answer that question."

Topkis then confronted the Commissioner with a provision of the 1968 Basic Agreement. In late 1967, before Kuhn was Commissioner, the players and the club owners completed their negotiations on the 1968 Basic Agreement. In this negotiation, Kuhn participated as a representative of the National League. In that Agreement, the players and owners agreed to review and study *alternatives to the reserve clause*. Article 8 stated that "the parties shall review jointly the matters of...possible alternatives to the reserve clause as now constituted.... The joint review of the reserve clause shall be completed prior to the termination date of this agreement". Kuhn acknowledged that the "termination date" of the agreement was December 31, 1969, almost one year after Kuhn became Commissioner. Yet, when Topkis inquired as to the outcome of that joint study and review of baseball's reserve system, Kuhn replied that *he did not participate in those reserve clause discussions and had no knowledge of who participated or what was discussed.* (How could

CHAPTER 14: DAY SEVEN—THURSDAY, MAY 28, 1970

the Commissioner be that uninformed?)

Kuhn also seemed to develop a bad case of memory lapse. Topkis referred back to the Commissioner's prior testimony that the financial resources of the club owners varied widely, and that the reserve system was necessary as an equalizing factor. Topkis asked the Commissioner to name the clubs which had the greatest and the least amount of resources.

" A. ...I couldn't give you any precise answer to that...

Q. What, [then] Commissioner, is the source of your information on which you ground your belief that the resources of the clubs vary widely?

A. My experience in baseball, my general knowledge—as Commissioner and as counsel; my observation of the operations of the clubs.

Q. Are you given financial statements of the clubs, either operating or balance sheets?

A. Oh, I'm sure I have at some time in the past...but not on a regular basis...I would assume that in the past I have seen some audited information here or there. I would assume that must exist. I certainly don't know. I have no recollection..."

Next, Topkis directed the witness to the early stages of the reserve system. Topkis confronted Kuhn with the fact that the original reserve system, adopted in 1879-80, allowed for a club to "reserve" a maximum of 5 (out of 11) rostered players. In 1970, baseball's reserve system allowed a club to reserve all 40 of its players. Topkis also pointed out that the original reserve system was not part of any contract between the players and owners, but rather, the original reserve system was adopted in secret and made a league rule by the owners. The Commissioner did not refute the historical accuracy of Topkis's representations.

Topkis again went on to address Kuhn's assertion that due to the varying resources of the club owners, the reserve system was necessary to maintain equalization of team strength. Under the system in place in 1970, Topkis accurately noted that teams playing away games received only a small percentage of the gate receipts. As noted in the following series of questions and answers, Kuhn would concede nothing.

"Q. There is no reason, is there, Commissioner, why the teams in baseball couldn't split gate receipts...on a 50-50 basis?

A. ...I don't know that there is any legal reason. Practical reasons would present themselves...

Q. Can you think of any way in which the game would be adversely affected by the clubs splitting gate receipts 50-50?

A. Yes I can...."

Kuhn's response was pathetically contrived.

"A. The investments that have been made on the basis of the present system, so you have a problem there. You have contract problems. You would have to do it by a vote of the league. You would have to see what the league provisions are, whether it could be accomplished under the league constitution. I just don't have those in mind, but you certainly could have problems for the game presented by the process of trying to do this....There are no major league regulations on this....

Q. Right. But I am talking about the level of play on the field, the level of competition. Would the interests of the game as a game be adversely affected by such an agreement among the owners to split gate receipts?...

A. ...Mr. Topkis, the answer is really three-fold. In the first place, I find it difficult to form a very definitive opinion on this question; secondly, you have got the problem of how you would achieve it, and the difficulties you might have in trying to achieve it could adversely affect the game on the field by creating eruptions of some kind within the structure..."

CHAPTER 14: DAY SEVEN—THURSDAY, MAY 28, 1970

What nonsense.

Toward the very end of Kuhn's cross examination, the Commissioner again insisted that the reserve system was essential to "maintaining" the equality of team strength. Topkis was ready and confronted the Commissioner with some statistical data which suggested otherwise. With the assistance of *Baseball's Encyclopedia*, Topkis pointed out that in the past fifty years (1920-1969), sixty-three (63) percent of the league pennants were won by four clubs. (Can you guess these four clubs?)

"Q. According to my calculations, Commissioner, of the one hundred major league pennants during the fifty year period beginning in 1920 and ending in 1969, four teams have won on a total of sixty-three occasions. Do you regard that as compatible with your belief that the reserve system has equalized competition on the playing field?

A. I did not say that it has equalized competition, Mr. Topkis,...[I]t tends to equalize competition. Yes. It is compatible, and you will also find that in the last...decade that this concentration of winners has diminished, and that this has been a result of further modifications in the reserve system, such as the free agent draft..."

It is noteworthy that the free agent draft to which Kuhn referred did not come into existence until 1965. Despite Kuhn's belief that the concentration of winners had diminished in the last decade, it must also be noted that in the decade from 1960-69, the *same four franchises won 60% of the league championships!*

The completion of Kuhn's cross examination brought Day Seven to its conclusion. The overwhelming majority of Kuhn's testimony on cross involved historical circumstances and justifications for baseball's reserve system; "global considerations" which affected the players and owners as a whole; and all of the "changes" in the "game of baseball" that, according to Kuhn, required the continuation of baseball's reserve system to maintain the well being and integrity of the "game".

At times, Topkis's cross examination of Commissioner Kuhn was brilliant. On occasion, Topkis elicited responses from Kuhn which could only be described—even by Kuhn's defenders—as incomprehensible, contradictory and pathetic. Again, what was conspicuously missing were the details specific to Plaintiff Curt Flood—*his* trade, *his* contract, and how baseball's reserve system impacted *his* claim for free agency.

Prior to adjourning Day Seven of the trial for the Memorial Day holiday, Judge Cooper addressed counsel and those in attendance in open court. May of 1970 was a time of great civil unrest. On May 1, 1970, U.S. troops invaded Cambodia in pursuit of the Viet Cong—the Vietnam War continued to rage in Southeast Asia. Three days later, on May 4, 1970, the nation was shocked by the death of four Ohio students during an anti-war protest at Kent State University.

"Gentlemen, I don't want to release you without thanking you again and expressing to each and every one of you the wish that you take full advantage of the holiday. There is so much that upsets us these days that is going on in the streets, everywhere. People are angry. There is a lot of intemperateness that is distressing. Let us seize this occasion to contemplate the significance of this holiday and to some extent, with some of us more, with others less, concentrate on the holiday itself and its meaningfulness to all of us as American citizens regardless of our views."

CHAPTER 15
DAY EIGHT—MONDAY, JUNE 1, 1970

Testimony of Charles S. ("Chub") Feeney

The defense continued with its second witness, Charles S. ("Chub") Feeney, President of the National League. Feeney had served as President of the National League since January 1, 1970. Feeney was born in 1921 in Orange, New Jersey, a place that Feeney refereed to as "a suburb of New York City". After graduating from Dartmouth College in 1942, Feeney served in the U.S. Navy during World War II. In 1949, Feeney graduated from Fordham Law School and passed the New York Bar. While in law school, Feeney worked in a variety of capacities for the New York Giants organization, and later on became General Manager of the Giants in 1952. Feeney worked continuously for the Giants organization—which Feeney referred to as "a family business"—until being elected and beginning his term as President of the National League on January 1, 1970. At the time of the Flood trial, Feeney was 49 years old.

Feeney's testimony would in large part mirror the views of Commissioner Kuhn. Attorney Mark Hughes inquired about the San Francisco farm system and the costs of that system. Feeney noted that the Giants minor league system—including subsidies, salaries, and scouting expenses—totaled approximately $1 million per year. President Feeney also emphasized the need for the minor league system, and distinguished baseball from professional basketball and football where the college players literally "step directly onto the field of professional play".

Feeney offered his views on the free agent draft and signing players to their initial major league contract. The defense was attempting to downplay the arguments that the free agent draft (which began in 1965) had diminished the player's negotiating posture and reduced the amount of signing bonuses. (Interestingly, in the course of one of his responses, President Feeney cited as an example the circumstances of a young pitcher named Andy Messersmith). Feeney testified that the *total amount* spent on signing bonuses remained the same. While the average signing bonus after 1965 was generally lower, more players were receiving bonuses. (Feeney never indicated whether this particular conclusion was based solely upon his personal knowledge and experience with the Giants organization, or whether this conclusion was based upon information he had garnered from all National League teams in his new role as National League President—a job he had only held for five months).

Next, Hughes directed the witness to the assignment and renewal provisions of the Uniform Player's Contract. In response to a series of carefully worded questions, Feeney testified that as general manager, he had never traded or optioned a player because the player and the club could not come to agreement on salary; that to his knowledge, no player ever "objected" to signing the Uniform Player's Contract; and that no one ever objected to the assignment provision or the renewal provision of the Uniform Player's Contract.

Feeney cited a couple of examples of players who had asked him (as Giants GM) to assign their contracts to other clubs. First, he testified that in 1965, a young catcher named

CHAPTER 15: DAY EIGHT—MONDAY, JUNE 1, 1970

Randy Hundley was anxious to play regularly and asked to be traded. At that time, Hundley was playing behind the Giants regular catcher, Tom Haller, and was one of three young Giant catchers. Hundley got his wish and was playing for the Chicago Cubs in 1966. Feeney also cited Giants catcher Bob Barton who, in the spring of 1969, was one of three catchers on the Giants roster. Feeney testified that Barton did not feel that he would be given an opportunity to play regularly for the Giants. By the 1970 season, Barton was playing for the expansion San Diego Padres.

According to Feeney, the Giants acceded to the wishes of Barton and Hundley because "they were obviously unhappy with the ball club" and "there was merit to their request[s] that they be given an opportunity to catch regularly". The defense offered this evidence to counter the suggestion that baseball's reserve system in every instance operated to the detriment of the players commonly referred to as "benchwarmers".

As expected, Hughes then directed President Feeney to the subject of baseball's reserve system. Feeney described the objectives of baseball's reserve system before announcing his belief in the necessity of that system.

"...One of the objectives is to preserve the integrity of the game. [I]f...a player was going to be a free agent of his own volition at the end of the season, and in the heat of the pennant race made a costly error which cost his team a game and the pennant, and then the next spring appeared on that other team, even though the error was made inadvertently, I think public confidence would be shattered.... [A]nother reason is to even competition. If a player of his own volition could become a free agent at the end of a season, the more wealthy teams...would obviously have an advantage in signing him, which would eventually break down the competition in baseball. If the competition broke down far enough, it would probably mean that the weaker teams would no longer be able to compete financially and probably might go bankrupt. It is also an inducement for people to invest large sums of money both in baseball and in the farm system. If these investments were not made,...we would lose the talent that is coming in,...the minor leagues...would probably cease to exist...."

Feeney then critiqued the views and suggestions of Marvin Miller. When questioned about the player's right to play out his option after an agreed upon number of years, Feeney was lockstep with the baseball establishment.

"...Well, this is actually just what amounts to a watered down version of everybody being a free agent...."

Feeney was also quick and decisive in his rejection of the concept of two competing leagues, as well as the suggestion regarding impartial arbitration of salary disputes.

At this point, Feeney's testimony seemed to drone on aimlessly about the player safeguards and benefits of the reserve system. Like Kuhn, Feeney testified that modifications to baseball's reserve system should be accomplished by collective bargaining. Interestingly, Feeney acknowledged that in 1965, he was asked to become a candidate for the office of Executive Director of the Players' Association (Miller became the Executive Director in 1966). Feeney referenced a 1965 meeting with Harvey Keune (then Giants player representative), Jim Bunning (then American League Player representative) and Robin Roberts (then National League Player representative). Feeney testified that he was flattered but declined the offer.

At the very end of Feeney's direct testimony, Hughes asked his witness to compare the talents of Plaintiff Curt Flood with other major league baseball stars. Hughes refreshed the witness's recollection of Flood's testimony, and specifically, Flood's testimony that he had at least five more years of baseball playing skill and could command a salary of $90,000 for each of those five seasons.

CHAPTER 15: DAY EIGHT—MONDAY, JUNE 1, 1970

"Q. In your opinion, is this a realistic forecast?

A. I would say it's speculative.

Q. Do you consider him to be in the same class as a player and as a fan attraction as Willie Mays?

A. I think Curt's a very fine baseball player, but I think he would even admit that he is not quite the fan attraction as Willie Mays is.

Q. Would you say he is in the same class as a player or fan attraction as Stan Musial?

A. My answer would be the same.

Q. Or as Ted Williams was?

A. My answer would be the same.

Q. Or as Henry Aaron is?

A. My answer would be the same.

Q. Or as Mickey Mantle was?

A. My answer would be the same...."

On one level, this line of questioning was spiteful. Flood never testified that he was as big a star or fan attraction as any of the players named by Attorney Hughes. Flood's testimony was that he could play competitively and productively for at least another five years, and could command the same salary during those years that he was paid for the just completed 1969 season—$90,000. The defense never offered into evidence the salaries of any of these stars nor of any other active or retired major league player. On this note, Feeney completed his direct testimony.

Cross Examination of Charles S. ("Chub") Feeney

Jay Topkis immediately picked up on the longevity of Flood's baseball career. (On January 18, 1970, two days after Flood's suit was filed, he turned thirty-two years of age).

"Q. You say, Mr. Feeney, that Mr. Flood is not as remarkable a player and fan attraction as Willie Mays. How old is Willie Mays today?

A. Thirty-nine.

Q. Do you know of any reason in Mr. Mays' and Mr. Flood's physical condition which would bar Mr. Flood from playing as long as Mr. Mays?

A. I do not.

Q. Tell me, has the trend of Mr. Mays' salary in the last seven years been down or up?

A. In the last seven years, it has been up, and then maintained a level.

Q. And when did it hit the level that it has since stayed at, at what age?

A. I think three years ago.

Q. When Mr. Mays was thirty-six?

A. Correct.

Q. The Giants have never thought it appropriate to cut Mr. Mays' salary by so much as a dime, is that right?

A. That's correct."

Topkis then wanted the witness to acknowledge similarities between baseball's reserve system and the institution of slavery. Topkis began with a poorly worded question to Feeney essentially asking the witnesses to describe the differences, other than compensation, between being a professional baseball player and being a slave. Topkis stumbled through an awkward and unproductive exchange with Feeney before getting his bearings.

"Q. ...[W]hen we were discussing slavery a few minutes ago, you said that a ballplayer is free to pursue any other trade.

A. Yes, that's true.

Q. But, presumably baseball is the trade in which he is most skilled and in which he can command the highest income, isn't that right?

A. Yes, that's true, and then he is generally performing that trade if he is that skilled.

Q. And you said also that a player by contrast with a

CHAPTER 15: DAY EIGHT—MONDAY, JUNE 1, 1970

slave is free to negotiate.

A. Yes.

Q. But with only one owner, we could agree, couldn't we?

A. Yes, that's true...

Q. ...You testified,...in the course of your direct examination that no player ever objected to signing the Uniform Player's Contract, was that right?

A. That is correct.

Q. Did any player have any *choice* as to whether he would sign the Uniform Player's Contract?

A. Except for special covenants such as an agreement that a player would get paid more if he pitched so many innings or played in so many games, or so on, that's right, the Uniform Contract was to be signed.

Q. It was either that or quit organized baseball, is that right?

A. Voluntarily retire or not play, yes."

Finally, Feeney admitted that under the Uniform Player's Contract, the club could *unilaterally terminate the contract* after giving sixty days notice to the player.

Topkis then returned to the subject of the free agent draft which began in 1965. On this subject, Topkis was able to quickly extract a number of admissions from the witness. Feeney acknowledged that the 1965 free agent draft was adopted by a vote of the owners without consultation with or approval from the players; and that the free agent draft was tantamount to an agreement among the owners "to not compete" for the services of *new* players. Feeney further admitted that he knew of no other business or industry (other than professional basketball and football) in which this agreement "not to compete" existed.

Topkis cross examined Feeney regarding the amounts of signing bonuses paid by the Giants to specific players—both before and after the imposition of the 1965 free agent draft. The defense vehemently objected and a long "side bar" argument among counsel ensued. The defense insisted that the issue of privacy was paramount and argued that this line of questioning, if allowed at all, must take place in the judge's chambers and to the exclusion of the press and public. While the trial record reveals that the lawyers heatedly argued over this point, the trial record is somewhat unclear as to its resolution.

Topkis then directed Feeney to the subject of the Giants pitching staff during the 1963 season. In doing so, Topkis was attempting to "connect up" the prior testimony of Jimmy Brosnan and to confront Feeney with some compelling evidence as to the owners' "blacklisting" of Brosnan. Topkis got Feeney to assess the caliber of the Giants relief pitching staff in the 1963 and 1964 seasons. Feeney's testimony was that in 1963, the Giants relief pitching "was not outstanding but adequate"; and that in 1964, it was "good".

Topkis confronted the witness with specifics. In 1963, while Feeney was General Manager of the Giants, the top three Giants relief pitchers were Billy Pierce (8 saves), Bobby Bolin (7 saves), and Don Larsen (3 saves). Topkis noted that in this same 1963 season, Jimmy Brosnan had 14 saves and an earned run average of 2.84—better than any of the Giants pitchers in 1963. Nevertheless, after the 1963 season, Brosnan was unconditionally released by the Chicago White Sox. Despite Brosnan's 1963 statistics and placing an article in the *Sporting News* in the spring of 1964 advertising his availability, not a single club owner contacted Brosnan to acquire his services for the 1964 season. Feeney merely stated that he did not recall the specifics of Brosnan's "retirement".

On the subject of player-club negotiations, Feeney emphasized that as the Giants GM, he would negotiate with the player and no one else; that he had never negotiated a contract with a player's agent or attorney; and that no player had ever requested that the team negotiate with the player's attorney or agent. Immediately following this testimony,

CHAPTER 15: DAY EIGHT—MONDAY, JUNE 1, 1970

Topkis produced a copy of an article which appeared in the May 15, 1967 edition of *Sports Illustrated* entitled "The Dodger Story", by Buzzy Bavasi.

Topkis offered the *Sports Illustrated* article into evidence to establish that Dodger General Manager Buzzy Bavasi, like all other baseball general managers of the day, strictly and deliberately adhered to a practice of refusing to negotiate with anyone other than the player—especially with a player's agent or attorney. Topkis read a quote from the article which was attributed to the Dodger GM specifically referencing the "holdout" of Dodger star pitchers Don Drysdale and Sandy Koufax after the 1965 season, and a book which included a discussion of this episode. The article quoted Bavasi as follows:

"According to Sandy...they (Koufax and Drysdale) scored all kinds of other points...and established several precedents. The book tells how I refused to negotiate through their agent, *which is 100 percent true.*"

Bavasi continued by saying that if he had commenced negotiations with Bill Hays, the agent for Drysdale and Koufax,

"...I opened the door to more trouble than baseball ever dreamed in its worst nightmare. If I gave in and began negotiating baseball contracts through an agent, then I set a precedent that is going to bring awful pain to general managers for years to come because every salary negotiation with every Humpty Dumpty fourth string catcher is going to run into months of dickering. Sandy knows that I have better sense than that, and *Sandy knows that I have never in my life called his agent.*"

After another lengthy legal argument among trial counsel over the admissibility of this *Sports Illustrated* article into evidence—including objections as to hearsay, reliability, authenticity of the quote and failure to produce Bavasi as a live witness—Day Eight of the Curt Flood trial concluded.

CHAPTER 16
DAY NINE—TUESDAY, JUNE 2, 1970

**Cross Examination of
Charles S. ("Chub") Feeney (Continued)**

On the morning of June 2, 1970, Topkis resumed his cross examination of Chub Feeney. The first subject of the day was the tampering rule. Like Commissioner Kuhn, Feeney testified that public confidence in the game's integrity would suffer greatly if a player could become a free agent and play for another club the following season.

Topkis confronted Feeney with the issue of whether "tampering" with a club's field manager was any less serious than tampering with a player. Topkis walked Feeney through the circumstances surrounding the 1964 World Series between the Yankees and the Cardinals. Immediately after the Series, Cardinal manager Johnny Keane was signed by and became the manager of the New York Yankees for the 1965 season. Topkis asked Feeney to explain the distinction between manger tampering and player tampering, and to elaborate on why public confidence would be less shaken in the instance in which a manager had been the subject of the tampering. Unable to articulate a rational distinction, Feeney cited the fact that the Cardinals won the 1964 World

CHAPTER 16: DAY NINE—TUESDAY, JUNE 2, 1970

Series, and incredulously surmised that had the Cardinals lost that Series, the Yankees signing of Keane as manager for the 1965 season would have shattered the public's confidence in baseball.

Before concluding, Feeney was asked whether there were any "arbitration mechanisms" in professional baseball. In response, Feeney referenced the recent change to the Basic Agreement negotiated between the clubs and the Players' Association during the spring of 1970.

"A. Yes. There is an arbitration mechanism which goes through several stages and at the present time ends in all cases with the Commissioner. However, under the new agreement which has just been reached between the players and the clubs, the arbitration would go eventually through the steps to an impartial arbitrator as the final arbitrator in all cases except those involving the game's integrity.

Q. This doesn't involve arbitration of salary disputes?

A. No it does not."

At the time of the Flood trial, this 1970 change to the Basic Agreement may have appeared to most casual observers to be of marginal importance and certainly irrelevant to the core issues being litigated in the Flood suit. (Marvin Miller was not among those who may have believed that this change was insignificant). Without question, this 1970 change to the Basic Agreement was negotiated and materialized because of the filing of Flood's lawsuit. Perhaps the cruelest irony of all was that Curt Flood could not avail himself of that impartial arbitration provision. Moreover, it was the same arbitration provision which, for the first time in major league baseball history, permitted certain issues and disputes to be decided by an impartial arbitrator (and not solely and exclusively by the Commissioner) and would be at the heart of abolishing baseball's reserve system some five years later, thereby ushering in the age of free agency.

Feeney's testimony was in many respects a regurgitation of Commissioner Kuhn's justifications for baseball's reserve system. While Topkis was more successful in obtaining various concessions and admissions during his cross examination of Feeney than he was with Kuhn, the presentation of testimony and other evidence specific to Curt Flood and *his* challenge was conspicuously nonexistent.

Testimony of Vaughn P. ("Bing") Devine

Next to the stand, the defendant clubs called St. Louis Cardinals Vice President and General Manager, Vaughn P.("Bing") Devine. Mr. Devine attended high school and college in St. Louis, and after graduating from Washington University in 1938, he began working in the publicity department in the St. Louis Cardinals organization. Except during his service in the Navy from 1943-45, Devine had held a variety of jobs in the Cardinals organization including business manager in the minor leagues, scout and in player development. In 1958, Devine became the Cardinals General Manager and served as such until August of 1964 (fired just two months before the Cardinals beat the Yankees in the 1964 World Series). For the next three years, Devine served in the organization of the New York Mets, and became president of the Mets organization in 1967 before returning as Cardinal General Manager in 1968. Other than the three year stint with the Mets, the 52 year-old Devine had spent his entire baseball career with the Cardinals.

Defense counsel Hughes directed Devine to the date of October 8, 1969 and the circumstances of the Flood trade. For the first time in two weeks, the witness would actually be addressing the facts relating to Curt Flood as opposed to

CHAPTER 16: DAY NINE—TUESDAY, JUNE 2, 1970

the hypothetical affects of the various proposed modifications to baseball's reserve system.

"Q. Did you act on behalf of the Cardinals in the exchange of contracts which assigned Curt Flood's contract to the Philadelphia Phillies?

A. Yes I did.... The transaction actually occurred, I believe the date was October 8 of the past year, 1969....The player contracts involved in the deal were from the Cardinals to the Phillies—Curt Flood, Tim McCarver, Joe Hoerner and Byron Browne. Coming to the Cardinals from the Phillies, Richie Allen, Cookie Rojas and Jerry Johnson....

Q. Would you describe...the details of the transaction...going back to the time of the first discussions between you and the Philadelphia club...?"

Devine testified that in late September 1969, Devine contacted Phillies General Manager John Quinn to verify the rumors circulating around the league that Richie Allen "was available". Devine stated that Quinn confirmed that Allen could be acquired and that he and Quinn agreed to discuss a possible deal.

"Q. From your standpoint, was the primary consideration in the deal the acquisition of Richie Allen's contract?

A. Very much so. As I said, that was our first inquiry as to whether or not Allen could be had in the deal and that was the main basis on which we predicated our interest.

Q. Was there any motivation on your part for getting rid of the player contract of Curt Flood?

A. ...The Phillies indicated at all times the two most important names as far as they were concerned were the catcher Tim McCarver, and the center fielder, Curt Flood.

Q. Did they indicate to you, in word or substance, that unless those two players were included there could be no deal?

A. I think they not only indicated that, but stated that....We felt we had a firm agreement on a deal at about 1 o'clock in the morning...of October the 8th...and we also agreed to...talk first thing in the morning...to conclude the deal...."

Devine then testified about management's efforts to contact the players to inform them of the trade to the Phillies. Devine recalled that he asked his assistant Jim Toomey to contact Flood, Hoerner and Brown, and that Devine would contact McCarver. He noted that the Cardinal organization had always attempted to contact a player to inform him of the trade prior to making a public announcement or conducting a press conference.

It was not until after the call from Jim Toomey and after the conclusion of the press conference on the morning of October 8th that Devine talked with Flood by telephone. Devine recalled that conversation as follows:

"...As he told me the year before, he [Flood] had thought about quitting at that time, that baseball had become physically a problem to him, that he was tired mentally and physically, and as he often had thought...that there was something better in this world than playing centerfield. He thought that this was now the time for him to effect his retirement and quit and as a result he was going to quit and not report to the Phillies.

Q. What did you say to him?

A. I told Curt that I thought that this was an emotional reaction, that he really didn't feel this way...and that he had several more good years of baseball left in him...I also told him that Mr. [John] Quinn would be in touch with him...about the Philadelphia end of the deal and interest in him, and he said 'Well, there's not much use'. In fact, I said he [Quinn] would call him immediately, that he [Quinn] had gotten his number and wanted to talk to [Flood] quickly...and Curt said 'Well, I really have nothing to talk to Mr. Quinn about because I am going to quit and I am not going to report to the Phillies, so there's no need to talk to him,

CHAPTER 16: DAY NINE—TUESDAY, JUNE 2, 1970

and he had better reach me quickly anyhow, because I'm going to leave the country and be out for quite a while.

Q. Did he say where he was going?

A. I believe he said he was going to Copenhagen, and I was familiar with that because I knew he had some sort of a business over there.

Q. Now, have you exhausted your recollection of that conversation?

A. No.... There is one other thing I do recall. I recall Curt telling me, in this somewhat lengthy conversation now, that he wished I had shot him down the previous spring, and this was in terms of his quitting, and I asked him specifically because I thought—I thought I knew, but it was a little unusual expression—I said, 'When you say shoot me down' what do you mean? And he [Flood] said 'Well, you know, when we were having our contract discussion of a year ago and I wanted more money than you were prepared to give me and we couldn't get together, I wish then that you hadn't reached a figure that I could agree with and probably we would never have reached this point and I would have quit a year ago."

To say the least, it must have been very strange for Curt Flood to have been listening to Devine's version of their "trade day" conversation now eight months after it occurred and in open court for the world to hear. Flood was never called to the stand to refute Devine's testimony or any other evidence presented at trial.

Devine recalled that Flood's contract salary for the 1967 season was $50,000, and that after the Cardinals won the 1967 World Series, Flood and the Cardinals agreed on a salary for the 1968 season in the amount of $72,500. Following the 1968 season in which the Cardinals won the pennant (but lost to Detroit in the World Series), Devine testified that Flood wanted to become a "$100,000 ballplayer", but that the Cardinals and Flood finally agreed upon a salary of $90,000 for 1969 and for what would turn out to be Flood's final season in a Cardinal uniform.

Ironically, Devine recalled that he was the Cardinals General Manager in 1957 when Devine engineered the deal to acquire then nineteen year-old Curt Flood from the Cincinnati Reds. (For all of the trivia fans, in that 1957 deal, the Cardinals traded three pitchers—Willard Schmidt, Marty Kutyna and Ted Wieand for Curt Flood and Joe Taylor.) After describing Flood's early development and his accomplishments during his career with the Cardinals, Devine testified that he regarded Flood "then and now" as a player of exceptional ability. While its relevance was unclear, the remainder of Devine's direct testimony centered around other Cardinal players that were acquired by way of trade and played for the 1964 Cardinals, including Bill White, Lou Brock, pitcher Curt Simmons and Julian Javier.

Topkis's cross examination of Devine was puzzling and rambled frequently. In one instance, Topkis felt compelled to establish that it was a common negotiating ploy for a player to indicate that in the absence of a reasonable and acceptable offer, the player would "retire".

"Q. Isn't that a standard gambit for players in their early thirties who are out to obtain salary increases in negotiations to suggest that they are seriously thinking about retiring?

A. Not from my experience…No."

Topkis continued to inquire about this negotiating ploy, but then, for some reason, asked about Devine's experience and contract negotiations with former Cardinal great Stan Musial.

"Q. Did you ever negotiate a contract with Stan Musial, that is to say, while he was a player?

A. Yes.

Q. Did he ever threaten to retire in the course of those negotiations?

CHAPTER 16: DAY NINE—TUESDAY, JUNE 2, 1970

A. No.
Q. Never?
A. No."

As the following will verify, Topkis would not take "no" for an answer.

"Q. In the course of your negotiations with Mr. Musial, did he ever say to you that he planned to retire?
A. Some day.
Q. Did he ever say to you as you were commencing negotiations for a particular season that he had decided to retire and was not going to play that season?
A. Never.
Q. Did he ever say to you as you commenced negotiations...that he was thinking seriously of retiring?
A. No.
Q. Did the word 'retiring' as it applied to a present belief about an immediately proposed course of conduct ever come to Mr. Musial's lips while you were negotiating a contract with him?
A. No."

In his memoirs published in 2004, Bing Devine recalled his very first deal as a major league general manager in the winter meetings of 1957. Devine wrote that he met with Gabe Paul, then General Manager of the Cincinnati Reds. Fred Hutchinson was the Cardinals field manager at the time. Hutchinson had heard of the abilities of the nineteen year-old Curt Flood, and was supportive of Devine pursuing a possible deal.

When asked on the witness stand during the *Flood v. Kuhn* trial in 1970, and again 34 years later in his memoirs, Bing Devine did not mince words and did not equivocate: "I traded Flood to get Richie Allen". In his memoirs, Devine recalled Flood as being a "strong thinking personality", and noted that because Flood refused to report to the Phillies, it took the Cardinals six months to complete the trade.

Baseball's Reserve System: The Case and Trial of Curt Flood v. Major League Baseball

When it finally became apparent that Flood was not going to change his mind, the Cardinals, in April of 1970, sent first baseman Willie Montanez and pitcher Bob Browning to the Phillies as "compensation" for Flood.

Devine's final reflections on Curt Flood, the trade and baseball's reserve system are nothing short of amazing:

"Even though Flood lost, as time went on and the whole thing unfolded, I felt rather guilty. Especially, with what it led to...free agency for major league players. Flood's suit was an important part of that process. I don't think I ever had any negative intent toward Flood's suit. I also justified it by saying it probably would have happened anyway. *And the truth of the matter is it should have happened.* When you think about it, the players had no control over their careers...It's opposed to what the Constitution stands for—freedom. And I recognized that it was wrong.... Even though I traded him, Flood and I stayed in touch after that. I remember calling him and talking to him when he was ill not long before he died. Curt Flood was always special to me. He was my first big league trade and he was a great player for the Cardinals. Most of all, he was a good person with strong beliefs and the character to act on them."

Testimony of Joseph Henry Garagiola

Next to the stand, defense counsel called former major league baseball catcher and then co-host of NBC's *Today Show* and several other television and radio shows, Joe Garagiola. Garagiola played nine professional seasons from 1946-1954. Except for one of those seasons, Garagiola was primarily a backup catcher for the Cardinals, Cubs, Pirates and the Giants, and was a career .257 hitter.

Immediately after being sworn in as a witness, Garagiola and Judge Cooper carried on a strange conversation. It was as if Garagiola thought he was about to do an interview or

CHAPTER 16: DAY NINE—TUESDAY, JUNE 2, 1970

do some comedic routine as host of the *Today Show*, and Judge Cooper was a willing guest.

"Judge: Do you always have a smile like that?
Witness: Yes, always.
Judge: That is a blessing.
Witness: You have to do it because when you have those bad years, you have to laugh your way through them.
Judge: That is what I do with bad cases.
Witness: I know. I can tell. You are sitting here and you are really grinding it out, but you look happy. A lot of guys walk around and they are happy in here (pointing to his heart), but they don't tell on their face.
Judge: What did you decide with regard to me?
Witness: I liked you...I wish you were on a bubble gum card, Judge, I'd save you...."

Curt Flood had to have been shaking his head in bewilderment as to what he was watching and hearing. As his short testimony would reveal, Garagiola gave no outward sign or appearance that he had been called to give substantive testimony in a major federal antitrust suit against major league baseball.

After a few short introductory questions, defense counsel inquired as to baseball's reserve system.

"Q. And would you tell his Honor just briefly, and in a general way, your understanding of what the reserve system is.

A. You sign a contract and the club owns you till they get rid of you. That's about it. And they got rid of me a few times.

Q. Now, Mr. Garagiola, in your opinion, is the reserve system reasonable and necessary for the effective operation of organized baseball?...(After a lengthy objection and discussion among the lawyers and the court)...

A. For me, yes.

Q. Now have you ever given any thought to possible modifications or changes in the reserve system as you know it and understand it to be?...

A. I thought about it, yes, but I don't have anything, and when people ask me and use the words I have been hearing about modifications and we should have some changes and we should do this, to me this is the best system so far. Nobody's come up with anything. I think if they might change the name but have the same thing, everybody would be happy."

Perhaps Garagiola was called to testify in order to refute the testimony given by Jackie Robinson regarding players who were primarily substitutes or "bench warmers", and the negative impact which baseball's reserve system had on those players.

"Q. Mr Garagiola, during the course of this trial there have been references from time to time to "bench warmers", and in one instance Mr. Robinson described it as "the guys who sit on the bench,"...who are not regulars, who, if they had the free opportunity to move from place to place, could move to another team and become a regular on that other team....In your experience what have you got to say about such a suggestion?"

Garagiola responded by mocking the concept of a "bench warmer" being somehow deprived of an opportunity to play full time and be a starting player for another team. Perhaps the witness was drawing too much from his own experience as a professional player.

"A. I have to laugh because I have heard that all the time I have been playing. I was a bench warmer. I played regularly, in my opinion, one year, and the guys that tell you that they can play regularly with other ball clubs, sometimes the worst break they get is to get traded. We used to get these great Dodger phenoms who used to sit on the bench, and sit on the bench when they came to us, and that was it...."

Garagiola then summed up his point with great "eloquence".

CHAPTER 16: DAY NINE—TUESDAY, JUNE 2, 1970

"...If you can play, you can play, and if you can't play, baby, you ain't gonna play. It's that simple....[A] bench warmer is a blow out patch, that's all, by any other name...162 games you have to have someone fill in.... Somebody gets hurt, you're right there. I'd rather be on a big league bench sitting down and being there ready to play than in some minor league where I can't....

Q. Are they used for other purposes except filling in, in case of injury?

A. Yes. You make the speech when a star can't show up, you do that. You get to play second games at doubleheaders...."

Garagiola's attempt at humor continued with what the witness referred to as his "best story" to illustrate the worth and role of a "bench warmer".

"When I joined the Giants, [Manager Leo] Durocher clinched the pennant, and Durocher said to me 'You catch. I don't want to get (Wes) Westrum hurt.' Now that's a tipoff. Westrum was the regular catcher, so what was I? I mean, I wasn't going to the Hall of Fame. End of story."

By his own admission, Garagiola was a bench warmer, and obviously one without much ambition or desire to become a starter on another team. His testimony was both pointless and pathetic—a conclusion which must have been shared by other defense counsel as well as Jay Topkis. Flood's lawyers did not even bother to ask Garagiola a single question on cross examination. According to the transcript, Garagiola's testimony was completed in a total of 13 minutes. Garagiola's brief, but ridiculous, performance continued even as he left the witness stand when he uttered "Do I get paid?"

In the final analysis, Garagiola's testimony was embarrassing and a joke. Not unlike prior witnesses in this trial, the substance of Garagiola's testimony had nothing to do with Curt Flood's circumstances, and was not even remotely related to any relevant issue.

Testimony of Joseph E. Cronin

Next to the witness stand came Defendant and American League President, Joe Cronin. At the time of the trial, Cronin was not quite 64 years old. Cronin's Hall of Fame playing career began in 1925 when he signed with the Pittsburgh Pirates. After several seasons in the minors, Cronin was traded to and played shortstop for the Washington Senators from 1929-32. In 1933, at the ripe old age of twenty-six, Cronin became the team's player-manager. In his first season as manager, the Senators won the American League pennant, but lost to the New York Giants in the 1933 World Series, 4 games to 1. In 1946, Cronin became the Red Sox field manager until his transition to General Manager in 1947, a position Cronin held until February 1959 when he was elected American League President. Cronin had a .301 lifetime batting average and was inducted into the Baseball Hall of Fame in 1956.

One of the first areas of inquiry was the adoption of the free agent draft in 1965. It was Cronin's view that the free agent draft "helped equalize the competitive playing strengths of major league clubs." Specifically, Cronin cited the "success" of the 1970 California Angels which, according to Cronin, was in large part the direct result of the Angels' drafting a young pitcher named Andy Messersmith. Cronin cited yet another example—the free agent drafting of three young players by the Oakland A's—Sal Bando, Rick Monday and Reggie Jackson.

For reasons which are not entirely clear, defense counsel directed the witness to the pending transfer of the Seattle Pilots franchise to Milwaukee. Cronin told Judge Cooper that the Seattle Pilots played only one season (1969) in the American League; that the Seattle franchise was purchased for $5.4 million; that the Seattle franchise filed for bankruptcy and that the bankruptcy court had approved an assignment

CHAPTER 16: DAY NINE—TUESDAY, JUNE 2, 1970

to a group of Milwaukee investors; that the field where the Pilots played their home games, known as Sick Stadium, was only intended to be an "interim" facility; that the Seattle owners had committed to a bond issue to finance a new domed stadium by 1973; that Sick Stadium had serious drainage problems; that due to the poor condition of the stadium, players were fearful of getting hurt; and that Sick Stadium was a "subpar" facility with lighting problems, poor seating and seating capacity of only 18,000-20,000.

Although the circumstances surrounding the transfer of the Seattle franchise to Milwaukee had little, if any, relevance to Curt Flood's claims, Cronin's testimony did include some interesting history and discussion of the Pilots team and its only season. With a field named Sick Stadium, perhaps the Seattle franchise was doomed from the start.

Regarding the suggested modification to baseball's reserve system, Cronin testified that he agreed in total with the previous testimony, opinions and conclusions of National League President Chub Feeney and Commissioner Kuhn. Not unexpectedly, Cronin concluded that there was no need to modify the reserve system, that the reserve system benefitted the players and that the reserve system was indispensable to the operation of major league baseball. In summary, Cronin's testimony was at times interesting, but broke no new ground with respect to the issues of the case. Following the testimony of President Cronin, Judge Cooper adjourned Day Nine of the trial.

CHAPTER 17
DAY TEN—WEDNESDAY, JUNE 3, 1970

On Wednesday, June 3rd, the defense presented three witnesses. Each of these witnesses was a major league baseball club owner: Francis Dale (Cincinnati), John McHale (Montreal) and Robert Reynolds (Anaheim). For the first time in the trial, the court heard the defense of baseball's reserve system from the perspective of the club owners—at least these club owners.

Testimony of Francis L. Dale

Francis Dale was the President and majority owner of the Cincinnati Reds. Dale's background was impressive. After graduating from Duke University in 1943, and after serving in the military during World War II, Dale graduated from Virginia Law School in 1948. Dale was an antitrust lawyer and was the head of his own law firm; served as president of the Ohio State Bar Association in 1965; and was a member of the Antitrust Section of the American Bar Association. In 1965, Dale became both the president and publisher of the city's newspaper, *The Cincinnati Inquirer*, and served as part owner and director of the Cincinnati Bengals NFL franchise. (The inaugural season for the Bengals was 1968).

CHAPTER 17: DAY TEN—WEDNESDAY, JUNE 3, 1970

On the stand, Dale described his early involvement and eventual ownership of the Reds. In 1965, the City of Cincinnati undertook the task of building a new stadium. According to Dale, the new stadium was deemed necessary to compete with the other major cities. As president and publisher of the newspaper, Dale became directly involved in developing public support. Eventually, Dale put together a group of local residents and businesses to buy the franchise on the condition that the new ownership would sign a 40-year lease to finance the stadium. In January 1967, Dale's group bought the Cincinnati Reds, and shortly thereafter, the same group acquired the new NFL franchise—the Bengals. Both teams signed 40-year leases to play in the new stadium which opened in June of 1970.

During his direct examination, Francis Dale explained his understanding of and opined as to the necessity of baseball's reserve system; stated that the Cincinnati investor-owners had obtained prior legal advice as to baseball's exemption from federal antitrust regulation; testified that the investor-owners relied upon baseball's exemption from federal antitrust regulation and that those investor-owners would not have made their investments but for that antitrust exemption. Dale also cited the "uniqueness" of baseball as the specific justification for baseball's exemption from federal antitrust regulation.

"Q. Mr. Dale...in your opinion, is the reserve system as you understand it to be reasonably necessary for the effective operation of organized baseball?

A. ...My experience...has led me to the conclusion that baseball is a unique business, unique even from other professional sports.... [I]n other major professional sports, the players come to the major leagues with a certain amount of not only skill, but also great notoriety. In basketball, you take All American basketball players. They are known to the public. In football, it is the same case. In hockey, they are known. In baseball, *it requires a considerably longer time to bring a player to the point of skill as well as to the point of public acceptance, and those two factors are almost equally important in my view.* So if there is to be a large investment, as we were about to make, we must be assured that there is enough time to get that kind of return from the investment. Therefore, I think it is necessary that there be certain rules, restraints, if you will, both on the players and the owners that produce a balance where this system can work to the benefit of both the owners and the players. And my experience leads me to believe and to know that there are restraints on both sides and that it is a rather delicate balance and...that the balance is good and is working. It has within it the makings for the flexibility that is necessary to keep it moving with the times."

Dale went on to identify the "prime reason" for an owner's investment in a major league baseball franchise.

"...In the first place, the business investment, the return on investment, is not the prime reason for the investment. There are many more investments that are much better than getting into baseball...so...the incentive of the money is not the prime incentive. The prime incentive of the owners of baseball, whether they are in it as business or as a community service, which is closer to our situation, is to try to win for the city and for themselves the prestige that it brings, the upsurge of the economy that it brings to the city, and there is the pride that is there. That is the prime motivating factor in ownership...."

It was Dale's direct testimony that because it took time to develop a player's skill in a team's minor league system, and because it to took time for a player to acquire public acceptance, baseball was unique from other professional sports. For the first time, however, Dale suggested that the prime incentive for an owner included "community ser-

CHAPTER 17: DAY TEN—WEDNESDAY, JUNE 3, 1970

vice", the desire to win games for the host city, and the prestige that accompanied a winning team. These views and conclusions would be challenged throughout Dale's cross examination.

On cross examination, Topkis immediately addressed the issue of the club owner's motivation to invest in a professional baseball franchise.

"Q. Mr. Dale, do I understand it to be your testimony that baseball club owners are motivated primarily, predominantly by local pride and similar considerations rather than by the desire to make money?

A. My testimony was that some are. All are motivated primarily by the desire to win.

Q. And I suppose then that it would be your testimony that the Brooklyn Dodgers moved to Los Angeles for sentimental reasons.

A. I don't know all of the reasons...but I am certain that the move included that motivation, yes, sir...

Q. So it is your notion that when Walter O'Malley ...decided to move the Brooklyn Dodgers to Los Angeles, he did that in order to win and he thought he would do better economically in Los Angeles and then would win more, is that right?

A. I have no idea...what Mr. O'Malley had in his mind, but I would suspect that that is the case...."

Topkis then got Dale to admit that prior to the move to Los Angeles in 1958, the Brooklyn Dodgers had indeed been one of the most successful franchises in professional baseball. Topkis got the witness to acknowledge that in the ten years before the move to Los Angeles, the Dodgers had been in the World Series six times and won the World Series in 1955. Topkis continued on this point, noting that the move from New York by the Giants in 1958 may also have been for reasons other than a desire to *continue* to be a successful franchise. Topkis asked Dale for his view as to why

193

the Braves organization had moved from Boston to Milwaukee to Atlanta, all in a span of 17 years; and likewise, why the Athletics organization moved from Philadelphia to Kansas City to Oakland in that same 17 year period. In concluding this line of questioning, Topkis asked Dale whether in these instances, the club owners "were chasing dollars or victories"? Topkis had successfully made Dale all but concede this point.

Topkis then addressed a hypothetical modification of the reserve system to allow for impartial arbitration of salary disputes. Dale had just stated his opinion that the reserve system, as it existed, was "indispensable to the economic success of baseball and to the acceptance by the public of baseball." What immediately followed was a sharp exchange between Topkis and Dale.

"Q. Let me ask you what your opinion would be as to some possible modifications to that system. Let us suppose that the system were modified in this respect and in this respect only, namely, that when a player and a club got into a dispute as to what the player's salary should be for a given year, then…in advance of the season, either the player or the club would have the right to submit that dispute to impartial arbitration. In your opinion, would that one modification of the reserve system be fatal to baseball?…

A. Because baseball is run by people who have ingenuity and skill…I am certain that they could handle it. *My opinion would be, however, that such a plan as you propose would be perhaps the most unfair thing that you could do to the ballplayers as well as to the owners, and in that regard would weaken baseball considerably.*

Q. *You come here as a friend of the players* and tell us that, is that right…in their interest?

A. I come here as a witness.…*I am not here as a friend of anybody.*

Q. *You are here to protect your investment, aren't you?*

CHAPTER 17: DAY TEN—WEDNESDAY, JUNE 3, 1970

A. I am here to testify in this case. I am very much interested in baseball; I am very much interested in the ballplayers and their success; *and I...resent any implication that I am not here in the interest of our ballplayers...*

Q. *And you are here to protect that $7 million investment, aren't you?*

A. That is part of the reason. I have an investment, obviously, yes, *but I am not here primarily to follow some dollars, if that is what you are trying to infer,* because I am very much interested in the ballplayers.

Q. It is your testimony, then, again that people in baseball on the management side are not predominantly interested in dollars?

A. I am not predominantly interested in dollars. I am not interested in losing any, but I am interested in winning the pennant for Cincinnati."

Topkis again posed a hypothetical modification to baseball's reserve system, namely, allowing a player to play out his option and become a free agent after five years of service in the major leagues. Dale did not waffle in his response. Dale stated that *allowing* a player to become a free agent after five years of service would be "fatal" to the game and, if implemented, "...*baseball is going to die in the way we know it now and the way I think it should be presented to the fans, yes.*"

Dale went on to state that an owner would lose his investment and not be adequately compensated for a player that left to play with another club. In such a system, owners would no longer be willing to make the requisite investment in the minor league system and player development if the player, after five years, "could just walk away". Using statistical data prepared by the defense, Topkis called Dale's attention to the fact that the *average* length of a player's major league baseball career was less that five years (i.e., 4¾ years).

Dale then elaborated on the "fatal" nature of allowing a player to play out his option.

"It would expose the club, not protect it....[I]f I had an established ballplayer that had been with me for five years, and here I have invested some place between $350,000, $400,000 to even bring him to the major leagues, and then we work with him for five years and he becomes an established ballplayer and I have promoted him and we have done all of these kinds of things, and then he walks away, and then someone who wants to pick the right cherry off the tree, so to speak, comes in and offers some fantastic price, and then I am forced to match him and we get into a wild jungle which, in my judgment, in the long run, would be very detrimental to the ballplayers as well as to baseball as a whole."

Dale characterized professional baseball *not* as twenty-four competing businesses, but rather as an organization or system that operated for the benefit of all the franchises and players as a whole.

"...[I]n such a system (free agency), the poorer or weaker franchises would not be able to compete for the better players and therefore baseball would be destroyed.... [B]aseball is a league. Baseball is a unique business. It is not 24 businesses competing with each other. It is a league set-up and you are not going to have a league if the bottom three franchises fall out.... [Y]ou see when a ballplayer enters into baseball, he just doesn't become a Cincinnati Red. He becomes a member of organized baseball, and he works into that system, and he is entitled to what that system can produce, but if you destroy the system, the ballplayer is going to be deprived of that great opportunity to perform and to participate in this tremendously valuable opportunity for him."

Throughout the course of Dale's direct examination, he frequently reminded the court that a player's longevity with

CHAPTER 17: DAY TEN—WEDNESDAY, JUNE 3, 1970

a particular club was critically necessary in order to allow a club to recoup its investment and player development costs; and that "fan devotion" to "players held in high regard" would be destroyed if players could move around and change teams under a system where a player could become a free agent.

In addition to its "indispensability" to the *game* of baseball, Dale's view was that the reserve system promoted and maintained a player's longevity with a single club; and that fan devotion to those players "held in high regard" was critical to a club's popularity and economic success. Having so testified, Topkis confronted Dale with a number of facts which Dale had great difficulty trying to reconcile. First, since acquiring the Reds after the 1966 season (in June 1967), the Reds had traded away all but three starters on the 1966 roster (including Deron Johnson, catcher Johnny Edwards, outfielders Vada Pinson and Tommy Harper, shortstop Leo Cardenas). Second, of the 25 players on the Reds' 1966 roster, only four remained—Jim Maloney, Tommy Helms, Tony Perez and Pete Rose. (Of the remaining 21 players, only two were "lost" to retirement). Third, despite having only played nine weeks into their rookie seasons in 1970, Dale acknowledged that two young Cincinnati Reds—Bernie Carbo and Dave Concepcion—were "already held in high regard" and had already acquired "tremendous fan devotion".

Finally, Dale insisted that the club owners must be able to recoup their investment, a result that the reserve system guaranteed. If club owners were not able to recoup their investment, Dale concluded that the owners would stop investing—all to the detriment of major league baseball. What was strange, however, was Dale's *own* motives and reasons for investing in the Reds (and the Bengals).

"The primary reason for investment in the Bengals was the same as our investment in the Reds, that is, *community service*, trying to find a second tenant for the stadium so that we could finance a new stadium for the city..."

Dale's rationale for and defense of baseball's reserve system would be the foundation for the testimony to be presented by the other club owners.

Testimony of John J. McHale

It was shortly before the noon recess on June 3rd when the defense called its next witness—John J. McHale—President and chief executive office of the Montreal Expos club. McHale was a native of Detroit; played football and baseball at and graduated from the University of Notre Dame. McHale played in the Detroit Tiger organization from 1943-48. Following his playing career, McHale worked as director of the Tiger farm system, as director of player personnel and, in 1957, at the age of thirty-six, became the General Manager of the Tigers. In 1959, McHale became president and general manager of the Milwaukee Braves, and served in that capacity through 1966. In 1967, McHale became an assistant to then Major League Baseball Commissioner William Eckert. During that tenure, McHale became intricately involved in Major League Baseball's efforts to add an expansion team in Montreal. Shortly after the City of Montreal was awarded a franchise in 1969, McHale left his position with Major League Baseball and became a partner, president and chief executive officer of the new franchise—the Montreal Expos.

In the first playing season for the National League Expos in 1969, the Montreal club struggled to a 52-110 record. At the time of McHale's testimony, Montreal had just begun its second major league season. The beginning part of McHale's testimony centered on the positive spirit and enthusiasm of the Canadian people, the problem of having no permanent stadium, and the need for the Expos to establish and maintain a farm system to develop young players.

CHAPTER 17: DAY TEN—WEDNESDAY, JUNE 3, 1970

McHale then succinctly stated his understanding of baseball's reserve system.

" I understand the reserve system to be the provision in the Uniform Player's Contract, the professional baseball rules, the major league rules that give a club the exclusive right of the player's services while he is under reservation by a club."

Consistent with the prior testimony of Francis Dale, McHale told Judge Cooper that before making his decision to invest in the Montreal Expos, McHale had been advised as to the current status of baseball's exemption from antitrust regulation; that he had specifically relied upon that legal advice and baseball's exemption; and that he would not have made his personal investment in the Expos in the absence of the reserve system. Based upon his experiences as a player, general manager and part owner, McHale testified that baseball's reserve system was necessary, reasonable and fair.

"Your Honor, I think the reserve system as it has been working has been reasonable and fair. I haven't found it creating unfairness or a great hardship on players I have dealt with. I think that for three reasons; first of all, I think of the fan. I think the fan has got to be considered in this, that a player builds up a great affection and following, and for that player to move freely on his own volition I think would be very difficult and hard on franchises. I think the player would suffer. I think he would not really make as good a deal as he thinks he would. I think the game would suffer and therefore the general welfare and the general health of the game would suffer and therefore I think eventually the players' salaries would not be as high. And thirdly, I think the clubs would lose the financial stability that they have now. You would no longer attract the strength of ownership, the financial backing that is required today to take this highly speculative game and stand behind it. Those are my reasons."

During his cross examination, Topkis delved into further detail regarding McHale's personal investment in the Expos, as well as the importance of the reserve system in McHale's decision to invest.

"Q. Do I understand, then, just to sum it up, if I may, Mr. McHale, that for personal investment of $100,000 and an additional contingent liability of $25,000 you got 10 per cent of a business with an operating net worth of ten million?
A. Yes.
Q. And do you testify to this Court that were it not for the reserve system in precisely its current form and no other, you would not have made this investment?
A. I would not."

Topkis continued to question McHale on what some would conclude was a relatively small, if not paltry, investment in return for a 10% ownership of a business having a net worth of $10 million. The animosity between McHale and Topkis finally erupted during cross examination with McHale sarcastically referring to Topkis as "Mr. Attorney", and Topkis addressing his questions to "Mr. Witness."

Under questioning by Topkis, McHale repeatedly asserted that *any* change in baseball's reserve system would *seriously increase the risk* of his investment. Topkis then confirmed that McHale was General Manager of the Milwaukee Braves in 1963 when the Milwaukee Braves issued a prospectus and offered common stock for sale to the public. Despite McHale's insistence that any change in baseball's reserve system would constitute a serious risk to his investment, McHale admitted that the Milwaukee Braves' prospectus which accompanied the public stock offering in 1963 *contained no reference whatsoever* as to the possibility of a change in or the elimination of baseball's exemption from federal antitrust regulation.

Distinguished from Dale, McHale's testimony consistently emphasized that the reserve system was necessary to preserve an owner's financial investment in the business of baseball. Dale, on the other hand, cited the concept of "community service" as a primary motivation for an owner to invest in baseball. The afternoon of Day Ten would continue with the testimony of yet another owner—Robert Reynolds.

Testimony of Robert A. Reynolds

In 1970, Robert A. Reynolds was the President and single largest corporate stockholder of the California Angels club. Reynolds played collegiate football and graduated from Stanford in 1936. As a member of the Stanford football team, Reynolds played in three straight Rose Bowl games (1934-36). Having played the tackle position, Reynolds was selected as a member of the Pacific All-Time, All-Coast Football Team, and a member of the College Football Hall of Fame. Upon graduation from Stanford, Reynolds signed a professional contract and played two years in the National Football League with the Detroit Lions. Following his football playing days, Reynolds befriended and became involved in the broadcasting business with western-movie star and baseball fan, Gene Autry. In late 1960, Reynolds and a group of investors were awarded the new California Angels baseball franchise for the total amount of $3.5 million. The new franchise began play in 1961 in Anaheim. In addition to his ownership of the Angels, Reynolds, in 1965, became a part owner, officer and director of the Los Angeles Rams NFL franchise.

The initial portion of Reynolds' direct examination was a virtual "carbon copy" of the presentations of the Reds owner, Francis Dale and Expos owner, John McHale. At times, his responses almost seemed rehearsed. Exactly like McHale and Dale, Reynolds recalled that he was aware of baseball's reserve system prior to his investment in the Angels; that he was advised by legal counsel that baseball was exempt from federal antitrust regulation; that he personally relied up that legal advice; and that he would not have made any investment in the Angels franchise without baseball's exemption. Reynolds articulated his understanding of baseball's reserve system as follows:

"...[M]y understanding then, as it is now, that under the provisions of the Uniform Player's Contract and the rules of ...organized baseball, that the clubs having players or drafting them had the rights under this reserve system.... It is my understanding that the Supreme Court of the United States had exempted baseball under the antitrust laws and that unless Congress should enact legislation to the contrary, that the exemption would remain."

Defense counsel then asked Reynolds a hypothetical question regarding professional baseball without the reserve system:

"Q. If it were to be held by this Court that baseball was no longer exempt from the antitrust laws and that the reserve system was illegal, what in your opinion would be the effect upon organized baseball?"

Although his answer failed to provide specific examples, analysis or rationale, Reynolds concluded the worst.

"A. It would be, in my judgment, extremely detrimental to baseball. It could well be chaos because [of] the structure of baseball....[I]t could be...a very chaotic situation."

Drawing upon his own experience of going directly from the college gridiron to the NFL's Detroit Lions, Reynolds pointed out that player development in professional baseball is totally different than in football. He noted that the average baseball player takes 4-5 years to develop into a major league prospect; and that "it requires a higher degree of skill to become a major league baseball player than a professional football player".

The defense then shifted its focus to address the apparent discrepancy between a professional football player's

CHAPTER 17: DAY TEN–WEDNESDAY, JUNE 3, 1970

ability to "play out his option" and become a free agent, and the inability of a professional baseball player to do so. Reynolds testified that such a system for baseball was not only undesirable, but was unworkable. Reynolds cited two San Francisco 49er football players who had "played out their options" and became free agents—R. C. Owens who later signed with the Baltimore Colts, and Dave Parks who later signed with the New Orleans Saints. When R. C. Owens became a free agent, the NFL had no rule that required the "prior" team to receive compensation from the "new" team. However, in the Dave Parks transaction, the 49ers were entitled to compensation under the 1961 NFL rule change. The defense wanted to pursue this line of questioning, but after some lengthy and successful evidentiary objections from Flood's counsel, the defense was forced to make what lawyers and judges refer to as "an offer of proof". [Under the rules of procedure, when a party's evidentiary objection (for example, on hearsay grounds) has *succeeded* in excluding important evidence, counsel for the party offering that evidence may make an offer of proof. The offer serves a number of purposes. First, it may convince the judge to reverse his ruling to exclude the evidence. Second, the offer creates a record so that the reviewing or appellate court will know what the excluded evidence was and be able to determine if the exclusion was improper and, if improperly excluded, whether the trial court's ruling constitutes grounds for reversal].

Defense counsel Hadden recited his client's offer of proof in open court.

"Under Rule 43(c) of the Federal Rules of Civil Procedure, my offer of proof is this:
That if the witness were permitted to answer this question and the succeeding questions, he would testify that he is familiar with the fact that the rules of football were amended in about 1961 or 1962, so that the one-year option clause

carried with it a requirement that compensation be awarded by the Commissioner...to that club from which a player left on playing out his option by the club to which the player went. Further, that the *effect of that amendment,* and as it has been administered by the Commissioner of Football, has been to award generous compensation to the club which the player has left; [and] *that the generosity of that compensation has had the effect of inhibiting players from playing out their options because the clubs of the National Football League are reluctant to contract with players who have done so because of the risk of excessive or generous compensation by the Commissioner of the National Football League."*

When asked about baseball adopting the NFL's "free agent compensation" system, Reynolds testified that the Angels would not "bid" on any player that had "played out his option". He also believed that such a system could never fully or fairly compensate a team for the "loss" of a star player.

"A. As a practical matter, if the player involved, say, with the Angels, who happened to be its shortstop, or in another instance, in a key position, and compensation from another club was in the form of a catcher that we might not want, I just don't know how workable it would be....

Q. What, in your opinion, are the differences between major league football and major league baseball which make the one-year option system, including the compensation feature, inappropriate for baseball?

A. Again, to me, to my judgment, you are talking about a structure that exists in baseball of these minor leagues, bringing them up through the ranks, and I just don't think that they can be compared".

Upon the conclusion of Reynolds' direct examination, Judge Cooper adjourned the trial for the day. Day Ten of the trial had concluded.

CHAPTER 18
DAY ELEVEN—THURSDAY, JUNE 4, 1970

Cross Examination of Robert A. Reynolds

On cross examination, Topkis went directly to the discussion of the NFL rule allowing a player to play out his option and become a free agent, as well as the awarding of compensation to the team who lost the player. In an impressive cross examination, Topkis got Reynolds to admit the following:

1) that prior to 1948, the NFL had the same "reserve system" (exclusive right to players on reserve) that existed in major league baseball;

2) that since 1948, the NFL system allowed a player to play out his option and become a free agent;

3) that in 1961, the NFL system required that compensation be paid to the team losing the free agent; and

4) that despite the ability of a professional football player to play out his option and become a free agent (since 1948), the NFL had grown in popularity and had become more financially successful than at any other time in the history of professional football.

Topkis continued to press Reynolds on the "safeguard" of the Commissioner determining fair compensation in the event the affected teams could not agree on compensation.

"...With the players involved, it is a matter of quality matching quality. I don't know whether it would be fair or not.... It is not a question of whether or not I trust the judgment of the Commissioner or anyone else when it comes to the compensation, of losing one ballplayer for another. The judgment of what that quality might be on an exchange might best rest in the field manager who is going to have to play the ballplayers....To my view, the matter of compensation in baseball would be a difficult procedure...."

Continuing on with the alleged distinctions between baseball and football, Topkis pointed out that a number of professional football players would soon become free agents, including Jim Nance (running back—Boston Patriots); Joe Kapp (quarterback—Minnesota Vikings); Marv Fleming (tight end—Green Bay Packers); and Don Maynard (wide receiver—New York Jets). Having previously testified that the Angels would *not* "bid" on a *baseball* player who may become a free agent, Reynolds testified that as a director of the Los Angeles Rams, he *would* "bid" on one or more of these free agent *football* players. From Plaintiff Curt Flood's perspective, this discrepancy constituted a major inconsistency on the part of the owners; but to the defense, Reynolds' testimony was just another "factor" in furtherance of its position that professional baseball was "unique".

Contrary to the testimony of the other owner witnesses, Topkis got Reynolds to concede a number of points. First, Reynolds acknowledged that if "fair compensation" could be assured, he did not know whether there would be any disadvantageous impact if baseball were "to adopt the football rule". Second, when asked if, as an option, the owners could jointly subsidize the costs of the minor leagues, Reynolds stated that "it might be feasible". Third, Reynolds "just did not know" whether a system which allowed a team to retain a "free agent" player by matching the salary offer

Chapter 18: Day Eleven—Thursday, June 4, 1970

of the "new team" would have a detrimental effect on professional baseball. Finally, when asked about a system of impartial arbitration of salary disputes in which the arbitrator would "choose between the figure suggested by the club and the figure suggested by the player", Reynolds stated that he was "not certain" that such a system of salary arbitration "would be good, but it might work."

Toward the very end of Reynolds' cross examination, the subject of the "secret document" and confidentiality of the owners' financial data presented some controversy. The trial record reveals that in the course of his cross examination of Reynolds, Topkis turned to defense counsel Hughes to discuss what turned out to be Plaintiff's Exhibit 7. There was some brief "off the record" discussion between counsel, an objection by defense counsel and a request to recess the trial for further discussion in the judge's chambers. The record also reveals that only the lawyers, Judge Cooper and Cooper's two law clerks were allowed to be present in chambers for the discussion. Even Plaintiff Curt Flood was excluded.

In chambers, the discussion focused on Plaintiff's Exhibit 7. Page 5 of that document included income and loss statements for the various major league baseball clubs on a club-by-club basis for the years 1965 through 1969 inclusive. This income and loss information was furnished to Flood's lawyers before the commencement of the trial pursuant to an order of the court. This order expressly provided that the individual club identities could be disguised in the form of a code and disclosed only to the Court pending further consideration of the matter at trial. Accordingly, Plaintiff's Exhibit 7 did not identify the individual clubs except by a letter code. During his cross examination of Reynolds, Topkis asked defense counsel to identify which letter of the code identified the California Angels. Relying on the prior court order, defense counsel Hughes declined to identify the appropriate code letter and asked for a meeting in chambers.

Following a lengthy argument in chambers, Judge Cooper announced his ruling:

1) Defense counsel were ordered to disclose the identity of the clubs and the corresponding data contained in Plaintiff's Exhibit 7 to Flood's lawyers.

2) Public disclosure of the club identities and related financial information was prohibited.

3) Judge Cooper *specifically ordered* that *no disclosure be made to the plaintiff himself or to representatives of the Major League Baseball Players' Association.*

4) The club identities and the related figures were available to Flood's lawyers for the sole purpose of their use in preparation for cross examination and rebuttal.

Judge Cooper's decision to keep this financial data from public disclosure was further underscored by the following portion of his order.

"...[*A*]*ny examination*, whether cross or direct, rebuttal or case in chief, *which concerns these figures* and the disclosure of the *identities of the individual clubs will be conducted in chambers* and any record of such examination *will be kept in separate transcript form and not distributed with the public portions of the transcript,* but *distributed only to...counsel for the plaintiff and defendants for their use in connection with this action, and of course, to the Court.*

After Judge Cooper announced his ruling, Topkis stated his objections. Topkis specifically objected to limiting the use and disclosure of this data, and to the prohibition on any such testimony being given in open court. In response to the objections articulated by Topkis, and, amazingly without explanation, Judge Cooper reiterated the Court's conclusion:

"...*It is the Court's desire that there be held inviolate, insofar as the public is concerned*, the material embraced within Plaintiff's Exhibit 7, together with such testimony as is taken *outside of the courtroom.*"

CHAPTER 18: DAY ELEVEN—THURSDAY, JUNE 4, 1970

The Court's insistence upon secrecy was both strange and somewhat alarming. If, as the various club owners testified, investments would not have been made and teams would not be able to compete financially in the absence of baseball's reserve system, the financial data of the clubs was essential.

When the trial resumed in open court, Judge Cooper described the conference as follows:

"I should say...in open court, that there was a conference in the robing room [judge's chambers] lasting possibly 30, 40 minutes, in *which I took up some very, very serious problems, legal problems*, which we resolved and which *would never have been resolved had I not had confidence in counsel*, all counsel, before me, and *I must thank them openly for aiding the Court* and *making the Judge's burden so light.* They are men who are reasonable, who fight as advocates should, *who nevertheless couple all of that with a show of fair play and uprightness, and who have made this trial for me one of the scintillating experiences of my career...*"

Testimony of Ewing M. Kauffman

Ewing M. Kauffman was the founder and president of Marion Laboratories and Pharmaceutical Company based in Kansas City, Missouri. At the time of the trial, Kauffman was 52 years old. In 1945, after serving in the U.S. Navy, Kauffman took a job as a pharmaceutical salesman, and eventually started Marion Laboratories "working out of his basement and garage". In 1968, for a little under $6 million, Kauffman purchased the rights for one of the two American League expansion franchises. The franchise became known as the Kansas City Royals, and began play during the 1969 season.

At the beginning of his direct examination, Kauffman, not surprisingly, reiterated the responses of the other owners establishing his understanding of and reliance upon baseball's reserve system before investing in the Royals franchise. Kauffman testified that he would not have made that financial investment in the absence of a club's exclusive, lifetime rights to a reserved player's services.

Kauffman highlighted the development of the Royals' Baseball Academy.

"In buying the Kansas City baseball team, I wanted to build a winning team as rapidly as possible....The first thing I did was insist upon placing extra coaches down at the rookie level and on through to the Triple A level so that the ball players could get more instruction. The second thing was to hire Tommy Heinrich as a hitting instructor....We hired the best scouts available....But this would still take a long time to build a winning team, and I felt that there might be another source of ballplayers that wasn't being utilized....I hired a doctor of research psychology...to analyze physical attributes necessary to play baseball. He came up with the following four qualifications: speed of foot; fast reaction time...tremendous eyesight; and lateral movement of the body....He then developed tests to measure these attributes among players. He developed special machines to do it, and we have now tested 160-some players, minor and major leaguers, who are in the Kansas City organization...so it is my conclusion that a boy doesn't have to play baseball all his life to learn to be a tremendous major league ballplayer. I feel that if we can take high school graduates who have these four attributes of physical ability—of speed, reaction time, eyesight, lateral movement—that we can place them in a baseball academy and we can teach them baseball. This is my primary purpose....This led to the next step, that a major league baseball player should be able to make public speeches and use English correctly. So we have tied this in with a junior college and...[the players]...receive ten or eleven credits...take baseball in the afternoon and study at night. We will finish in a matter of

CHAPTER 18: DAY ELEVEN—THURSDAY, JUNE 4, 1970

four months a million and a half dollar complex at Sarasota, Florida where this academy will be held...."

Later, Kauffman was even more precise in his description of the ideal ballplayer's physical attributes:

"What we are looking for, *and I am sure that we can find it*...among hundreds of thousands of 17, 18, 19-year old boys...is the speed of Maury Wills, the reaction time of [Carl] Yastrzemski, the eyesight of...Ted Williams, and the body movement of Brooks Robinson. *I know we can find 50 of them* and when we give them the finest in baseball coaching, I am convinced many of them will become major league baseball players...."

The confidence and optimism of Kauffman's vision is striking. After all, how hard could it be to find fifty young players with the skills of these players, three of which were Hall of Famers?

Predictably, Kauffman's direct testimony included his commentary on the various proposals and suggested revisions to baseball's reserve system. When asked his view on revenue sharing among the clubs, Kauffman did not hesitate:

"I think that is as ridiculous as asking Curt Flood to share his hundred thousand dollars a year with the poor fringe players on the St. Louis Cardinals....I believe that if you start that type of program so that you equalize the competition, that you are turning baseball more into an exhibition like ballet, and you know what their attendance is, and I think we both could lose in the long run...."

Additionally, Kauffman was completely opposed to a system whereby the Commissioner, in his sole discretion, would determine and award "just compensation" to a club that had lost a player to free agency. Kauffman believed that a system of binding arbitration for salary disputes would be "harmful to baseball"; that the establishment of minimum salary levels would not be detrimental provided those salary levels were negotiated and agreed to in the collective bargaining process; and that a system whereby a player could play out his option and become a free agent would be beneficial to the upstart Kansas City Royals franchise, but "destructive to baseball overall".

Somewhat surprisingly, Kauffman's testimony provided examples of some aggressive business practices and predictions of success. After acquiring the franchise, Kauffman made public statements that Kansas City fans would have a pennant winner within six years. Prior to the 1969 season, Kauffman contacted Oakland Athletics' owner Charlie Finley and offered to pay Finley $1 million for any one Oakland player of Kauffman's choosing. Similarly, prior to the 1970 season, Kauffman offered Finley $3 million for any four Oakland players of Kauffman's choosing. Neither offer was accepted. Finally, despite his belief that a system in which a player could play out his option would be "destructive to baseball overall", Kauffman emphatically stated that he and the Royals organization would aggressively compete to acquire the contracts of any such free agent players.

Topkis began his cross examination of Kauffman by discussing the concept of an "open market" and by comparing the pharmaceutical business with professional baseball. Kauffman had testified that major league ballplayers are free to sell their services in the open market. The following exchange ensued:

"Q. Where is the open market?

A. Well, the ball players, when they sign their contract, are taught baseball and eventually come on up to the major leagues and they have the opportunity in the negotiations to earn money commensurate with their ability.

Q. Where is the open market?

A. Define the open market for me, sir.

Q. The opportunity to deal with more than one purchaser of one's services would strike me as an appropriate defi-

CHAPTER 18: DAY ELEVEN—THURSDAY, JUNE 4, 1970

nition. Would you agree with it?

A. Possibly, yes, sir.

Q. There is no such open market in organized baseball today, is there, Mr. Kauffman?

A. I don't believe it can exist with it...

Q. You think that there are substantial differences between the drug business and the baseball business, is that it, Mr. Kauffman?

A. Yes, sir, very much so.

Q. Big enough to make it appropriate, those differences, for baseball to establish a system where for any player's services there is only one possible buyer?

A. Yes, sir....

Q. You would much prefer the situation in which you had a number of sources available as a businessman, isn't that right?

A. Yes, sir, as a businessman.

Q. And so far as your customers are concerned, you wouldn't like it very much if you had only one possible purchaser for your goods, would you?

A. We probably wouldn't be in business; they couldn't use enough of it.

Q. You would have to go out of the drug business?

A. Yes, sir.

Q. That would be your alternative?

A. We couldn't sell enough to one person, probably.

Q. Right, so you would have to shut down?

A. Yes, sir.

Q. You wouldn't like that situation where you either had to deal with that one customer or shut down, would you?

A. I wouldn't have started the business, sir, if that had been the case."

Topkis then examined Kauffman on the relative bargaining power between an owner and a player during salary negotiations. In the instance of a "star player", the club had a significant investment in that player that the club was extremely reluctant to lose. According to Kauffman, this club reluctance worked to the benefit of the "star player". Kauffman also stated that the fans asserted public pressure on the club to field a competitive team—another factor which gave leverage to the star player.

Interestingly, Kauffman refused to concede the existence of the all important counterbalance—that a player could not negotiate, offer his services or otherwise deal with *any other club*. After all, the player could either sign and play for "his club", or not play professional baseball at all.

According to Kauffman, it was only with respect to the "fringe" or "marginal" players that the club owners had significantly more leverage and bargaining power. Such players were routinely "sent to the minors for some more training and playing experience". Despite some effective cross examination, Kauffman concluded that "overall, it balances. I think with your stars, the power is on their side, and,...[with]...the fringe players, the power may be on the club's side."

Topkis then attempted to use Kauffman's testimony to establish Curt Flood's value (and consequently, Flood's damages) by asking Kauffman what the Royals would pay for Curt Flood's services. Before drawing an objection from defense counsel as well as the ire of Judge Cooper, Topkis was able to obtain the following from the Royals' owner.

"Q. Tell me something, if you could get him, what would you pay Curt Flood as a salary...

A. Well, I would have to study a little bit. I need to know his age...I would say a hundred twenty-five thousand from what I understand of his ability. If he signed a contract to stay with us for a little longer, I might be willing to pay him more....

Q. If he would sign a five-year contract you would be willing to pay a good bit more per year?

A. Yes. That's the way I could build a good team fast, if I could get a lot of players like that.

Q. How high do you think you might go for a five-year contract?

A. I don't know. You let me choose my players, we'll go pretty high....

Q. With Curt Flood.

A. May I ask some questions about him?...How old is he?

Q. Thirty-two...

A. I would need to know something about his personality, how he gets along with his teammates....You would have to give me a lot more information about him.

Q. What information would you like?...[H]e was co-captain of the Cardinals last year. I suppose that is a —

Judge Cooper: Well Mr. Topkis, really this is interesting, but I wonder whether there is enough basis for any answer he gives with regard to Mr. Flood?

Topkis: Well your Honor, that is perhaps a problem that would be faced by Mr. Flood, but the only way we can prove damages or one of the most effective ways, I should think, would be by eliciting from such fairminded witnesses as Mr. Kauffman what their estimate is of his salary."

Even though this line of questioning was terminated, Topkis accomplished his goal. The remainder of Kauffman's cross examination consisted of rather lengthy and seemingly pointless discussions about the pros and cons of revenue sharing, and the possibility of only the "rich club owners" having the resources to bid on free agents. Although his scientific approach to player development was somewhat unique and at times interesting, his analysis and conclusions (not unlike much of the testimony elicited from prior witnesses) had absolutely nothing to do with the core legal issues presented in Curt Flood's suit.

CHAPTER 19
DAY TWELVE—FRIDAY, JUNE 5, 1970

Testimony of John J. Gaherin

It was Friday, June 5th. At the hour of 10:00 a.m., the defense called its next witness. John Gaherin was a consultant and the chief labor negotiator for the twenty-four club owners. At the time of his testimony in the Curt Flood trial, Gaherin was fifty-four years old, and had been in that job for just under a year. Gaherin had extensive experience as a labor negotiator in the railroad industry. In the summer of 1967, the club owners entered into an exclusive arrangement for Gaherin's services.

Up to this point in the trial, all of the defense witnesses provided testimony supporting the *necessity* of baseball's reserve system, and claimed that the reserve system was *indispensable* to the game of baseball. Gaherin, on the other hand, provided testimony on what ultimately became the most critical issue in the decision rendered by Judge Cooper.

Gaherin's impressive presentation focused on major league baseball's collective bargaining process; the status of the discussions and negotiations between the union and the club owners on proposed modifications to baseball's reserve system; and the jurisdiction of the National Labor

CHAPTER 19: DAY TWELVE—FRIDAY, JUNE 5, 1970

Relations Board (NLRB) over major league baseball.

Gaherin testified that:

1) major league baseball was under the jurisdiction of the NLRB;

2) the Players' Association and the club owners were required by federal law (National Labor Relations Act) to negotiate in good faith;

3) baseball's reserve system was a *mandatory* subject of collective bargaining between the Players' Association and the club owners;

4) the Players' Association and club owners had in fact agreed to negotiate on the reserve system;

5) the Players' Association had previously submitted proposals to modify the reserve system to the club owners for consideration;

6) the Players' Association and club owners had negotiated and agreed to modifications to the Basic Agreement (between the Players' and club owners) in 1968 and again as recently as the spring of 1970; and

7) the Players' Association and club owners were in the process of negotiating further modifications to the reserve system (including free agency) when the Curt Flood suit was filed.

If, under the National Labor Relations Act (NLRA), modifications to the reserve system were a mandatory subject of collective bargaining between the *union* and the *club owners*, and if, in fact, the club owners were refusing to negotiate in good faith (if proven, a violation of the NLRA), why were these issues being presented and argued by Curt Flood in *his* suit against major league baseball? After all, it was Flood's position (both in his written Complaint and his sworn testimony) that baseball's reserve system was illegal and must be abolished. Alternatively, if the union and club owners were required to negotiate, those negotiations are conducted *at the bargaining table.* Gaherin's testimony would point out that Judge Cooper was, in effect, being asked to consider the proposed modifications and choose a "reasonable alternative" to the current reserve system in order to settle a labor negotiation. Why were these parties litigating these issues in federal court at all?

The points adduced during Gaherin's testimony were key to Judge Cooper's decision. It would also represent the basis for the defense's continued assertion that the suit itself, although brought in the name of Curt Flood, was in reality the *union's* case.

In his testimony, Gaherin described his work with the Player Relations Committee which was composed of the American and National League Presidents, and two representatives from each of the Leagues. The Player Relations Committee had the responsibility for conducting negotiations with the Players' Association, the formulation of proposals and communicating with the club owners.

Gaherin testified that he acted as the spokesman and chief negotiator for the club owners; that he was in regular and sometimes daily contact with Marvin Miller and Richard Moss, the Association's General Counsel; and that Miller and Moss were "exceptionally well qualified and extremely able in their present occupation[s]."

Gaherin testified that since August 1, 1967, the Players' Association and the club owners completed three vital negotiations. Gaherin summarized the first such negotiation:

Negotiations Conducted: September 1967—February 1968

Changes In Basic Agreement:
- increase minimum salary from $7,000 to $10,000 per season
- maximum annual salary reduction reduced from 25% to 20%
- increase spring training meal allowance from $8 to $12 per day

CHAPTER 19: DAY TWELVE—FRIDAY, JUNE 5, 1970

- increase in season meal allowance from $12 to $15 per day
- increase spring training miscellaneous allowance from $25 to $40 per week
- changes in the grievance procedure.

Gaherin described the change in the grievance procedure as a "significant improvement".

"...Now, while the players always had access to the Commissioner of Baseball as the final adjudicator of disputes except those involving individual salaries, there was no formal procedure except that promulgated by the Commissioner himself for the conduct of such matters. We negotiated with the Association a formal grievance procedure providing for...a final and binding arbitration by the Commissioner of Baseball."

Gaherin testified that the second "vital negotiation" took place during the latter part of 1968 and early 1969. In this negotiation, the owners and players "updated and agreed upon" improvements in the players' benefit plan—including retirement benefits, disability, life and health insurance. During this negotiation, Miller, as part of bargaining strategy, encouraged the players to withhold signing their playing contracts for the 1969 season. Despite the players' "holdout", an agreement was reached on February 25, 1969.

The third "vital negotiation" was what became known as the 1970 Basic Agreement. The players and owners had just completed this negotiation one month earlier—May, 1970. Gaherin again summarized the specifics:

- increase minimum salary from $10,000 to $12,000 for 1970, to $12,750 for 1971 and to $13,500 for 1972;
- slight increases in meal allowance and miscellaneous weekly allowances for spring training;
- reduction in the maximum salary "cut" from 20% per year to not more than 30% for 2 years;

- players entitled to receive portion of revenues from playoff and World Series games;
- right for a player to be represented by counsel during individual player salary negotiations with club owner.

Gaherin then described "the most important single issue" involved in the 1970 bargaining. Gaherin testified that the union and owners successfully negotiated

"...a grievance procedure which sends to the Commissioner all matters *which involve the integrity of the game or maintenance of public confidence in the game*, and his decision in all such matters is final and binding upon the parties....The second part of the grievance procedure provides for grievances *arising out of the interpretation or the application of the Basic Agreement* being ultimately referred *to a panel of arbitrators*, each of the parties to select an arbitrator and probably those two to try to select upon a third...and the neutral man *will not be the Commissioner in this case*."

Again, Gaherin had just described perhaps the cruelest irony of the entire Curt Flood case and trial. In the spring of 1970, *while Flood v. Kuhn was pending*, the club owners and players' union negotiated an agreement wherein, *for the first time*, certain disputes and grievances would no longer be decided by the Commissioner, but rather, would now be decided by a neutral third party. At this very same time, Curt Flood, with the assistance and support of the players' union, had filed a suit asking the federal courts to hold baseball's reserve system (a system which was embodied in that Basic Agreement) illegal in its entirety. There is little, if any, doubt that without the pressure and potential result of Flood's suit, the club owners would never have agreed to allow certain disputes to be settled in a system of binding arbitration by a neutral third party. Yet, there was Curt Flood sitting in a courtroom in New York City in the summer

CHAPTER 19: DAY TWELVE—FRIDAY, JUNE 5, 1970

of 1970, challenging the legality of baseball's reserve system—unable to avail himself of the neutral third party arbitration system which his very actions, in part, no doubt created. It was this neutral third party arbitration system—negotiated and agreed to in 1970—which would ultimately "strike down" baseball's reserve system and usher in the era of free agency.

Up to this point, Gaherin was not asked about prior negotiations between the union and club owners *specifically on the issue of the reserve system*. Defense counsel Hadden now directed his witness to this most critical issue.

"Q. Turning to the subject of the reserve system, Mr. Gaherin, do the clubs recognize that the reserve system is a mandatory subject of bargaining upon which the clubs are legally obligated to bargain with the Association?

A. Yes."

Judge Cooper immediately grasps the significance of this line of questioning as well as Gaherin's answer. Departing from normal and customary trial procedure, Judge Cooper began posing his own questions to the witness:

"Judge Cooper:...How long has that been so?

Witness: *The National Labor Relations Board, having asserted its jurisdiction over baseball,* and the clubs having acquiesced in that action, we recognized that we had an obligation of bargaining.

Judge Cooper: When was that?

Witness: ...Sometime last year...

Q. And before the beginning of this lawsuit?

A. Yes, before the beginning of this lawsuit.

Q. And did the clubs undertake any negotiations with the Players' Association with reference to the reserve system in the course of the negotiations leading to the first Basic Agreement?

A. Yes sir."

The defense offered into evidence a document entitled

Baseball's Reserve System: The Case and Trial of Curt Flood v. Major League Baseball

Major League Baseball Players' Association's Statement of Policy, dated July 28, 1967. This "policy statement" was delivered to the club owners for consideration on or about August 1, 1967—the day Gaherin began working for the owners. This document stated in pertinent part:

"The present Uniform Player's Contract provision under which a club asserts the right to renew the contract without the player's agreement and to determine unilaterally the salary to be paid (subject only to limitation on the amount of a cut), requires a review.

The impact of this provision is to deprive the player of bonafide bargaining power in his salary "negotiations" with the club. In addition to placing the player in the untenable position of being required to accept the club's proposed salary or leaving organized baseball, *the reserve clause is of doubtful legality.*

The solution to this problem lies neither in a sudden elimination of the reserve clause, whether by judicial decree or otherwise, nor in the preservation of the status quo. We find no validity in calamitous predictions that chaos will result from any change whatsoever. Rather, the solution lies in a reasoned, open minded approach which seeks an accommodation in the interest of fairness for the player in his salary negotiations and of the growth and prosperity of baseball as a whole."

Following receipt of the union's July 28, 1967 policy statement, Gaherin testified that both parties discussed the union's proposal and the parties agreed "to enter into a joint review or joint study of possible alternatives or changes in the reserve system"; and that the parties memorialized that joint study in Article 8 of the 1968 Basic Agreement.

Judge Cooper continued to express his keen interest in the details and chronology of these discussions and negotiations on the reserve system.

" Judge Cooper (to defense counsel Hadden)

Chapter 19: Day Twelve—Friday, June 5, 1970

We will take a short recess. You may not think much of this, but I would like to have more detailed testimony as to dates, action by management with respect to...[the July 28, 1967 document]. In other words, when management was confronted with it, I would like to have more details of how much consideration was given. I take it there was no flat rejection of it. Just approximately what dates, what time, what amount of consideration was given to it."

Still addressing the 1967-68 negotiations (which led to the 1968 Basic Agreement), and even though the NLRB had not yet formally asserted jurisdiction over major league baseball, Gaherin emphasized that the clubs and union did in fact bargain with respect to the reserve system and gave several specific examples.

Gaherin cited the negotiation and agreement to incorporate the Uniform Player's Contract into the 1968 Basic Agreement (Article 2). By doing so, the parties agreed to adopt and comply with all major league rules, agreements and contractual provisions—*thereby adopting the entire reserve system into the 1968 Basic Agreement.*

Also cited by Gaherin was the new language stating that the termination of the *Basic Agreement* did not in any way affect, impair or abrogate the rights and duties of the club owners and players under any *individual player contract.* Gaherin explained that the parties negotiated this language to make clear that the termination or expiration of the 1968 Basic Agreement would in no way affect the rights of a club to renew an individual player's contract under an existing individual (Uniform Player's) contract. Almost parenthetically, Gaherin also recalled that during those 1967-1968 negotiations, Miller and Moss *orally* stated that it was not the *union's* intention during the life of the agreement (1968 Basic Agreement) to test the legality of the reserve system by way of a lawsuit.

Gaherin then testified as to the next series of discussions on the reserve system—the joint study and review. Gaherin described this phase as a series of five or six informal meetings where much "freewheeling and in depth exploration" of all aspects of the reserves system occurred. While this phase of talks produced no resolution, the union, in August 1969, requested that the negotiations be reopened and submitted, in writing, specific proposed modifications to the reserve system—modifications that Gaherin called "very drastic" proposals.

"...Basically they proposed a free agency status for any...player after three years. It provided for a reduction in the number of players that could be reserved by the club. It provided for salary arbitration. It provided for a bar against transfer of contracts without the consent of the person being transferred. It provided for a change in the definition of what is known as veteran status."

Gaherin testified that the negotiations conducted through summer and fall of 1969 included a number of subjects in addition to these specific union proposals to modify the reserve system. According to Gaherin, it was not until the club owners' winter meeting in December 1969 that Marvin Miller and Richard Moss informed the owners that there was a "possibility of a lawsuit" to challenge the legality of the reserve system. Gaherin noted that the commencement of Flood's suit in January 1970 brought the negotiations on the reserve system to a screeching halt. Gaherin summarized the club owners' next communication to the Players' Association.

"...[W]e advised the Association that we were confronted by two efforts *of theirs* which had diametrically opposite goals. We were bargaining...on the assumption that the goal of the Association was to seek to *amend* the existing reserve system. We were confronted in Mr. Flood's action, *joint action*,...to *destroy* it. This made a very difficult atmosphere in which to try to bargain. You were in the position of

CHAPTER 19: DAY TWELVE—FRIDAY, JUNE 5, 1970

trying to ride two horses galloping in opposite directions."

This portion of Gaherin's testimony clearly revealed the club owners' conviction that the *Flood v. Kuhn* litigation was the union's work product and part of the union's calculated strategy.

Ultimately, an agreement was reached between the Players' Association and the club owners to put the reserve system negotiations "in limbo" until the Flood litigation had concluded. This memorandum stated in pertinent part:

"...[T]he parties have differing views as to the legality and as to the merits of such [reserve] system as presently constituted. This agreement shall in no way prejudice the position or the legal rights of the parties or of any player regarding the reserve system. It is agreed that until the final and unappealable adjudication (voluntary discontinuance) of *Flood versus Kuhn, et al*, now pending in the Federal District Court of the Southern District of New York, neither of the parties will resort to any form of concerted action with respect to the issue of the reserve system and there shall be no obligation to negotiate with respect to the reserve system. Upon the final and unappealable adjudication (or voluntary discontinuance) of *Flood versus Kuhn, et al.*, any party shall have the right to reopen negotiation on the issue of the reserve system...."

At the conclusion of his direct testimony, Gaherin told Judge Cooper that the collective bargaining process was "well suited to the resolution of this [reserve system] issue". Perhaps now playing to the Judge, Gaherin elaborated by expressing the club owners' *desire* to resolve the issue *by negotiation.*

"...I don't know if expertise is the proper term, but we certainly have all of the ability in the two sides to sit down and in the free arena of collective bargaining resolve a matter of this nature. *And I may say parenthetically, if I may, Judge, we are quite willing to do so.*

Targeting in on this issue of *negotiation*, Judge Cooper again interjected himself and asked the witness a most illuminating question.

"Judge Cooper: Is it your testimony that nevertheless as you envision it, the possibilities are quite strong that it might be resolved?

Gaherin: "Yes. I think all problems are resolvable....I think the parties...are always the best judges of what they should live with, and how they reach that understanding is quite another matter."

The cross examination of John Gaherin by Topkis was very brief. Essentially, Topkis attempted to make two points. First, Topkis got Gaherin to acknowledge that, despite the discussions between the parties, the club owners *never formally proposed* modifications to the reserve system. Secondly, Topkis established that of the twenty-two player representatives that signed (as the union representative for the players of their respective teams) the 1968 Basic Agreement with the club owners, twelve of those player representatives had been traded. In other words, in a period of just over two years (from February 1968-May 1970), over 50% of those player representatives had been traded to another club. It was clear that Topkis decided not to spend much time attempting to cross exam Gaherin, but rather to counter by calling Marvin Miller as his own rebuttal witness later in the trial.

On the issues of whether and to what extent the Players' Association and the club owners *negotiated* on the reserve system, Gaherin's testimony was detailed, impressive and persuasive. Gaherin's testimony gave Judge Cooper another basis to *not decide* Flood's suit on the merits. This legal analysis was relatively simple. The NLRB had asserted jurisdiction over major league baseball, and the reserve system was a mandatory subject of collective bargaining. Under federal labor law (NLRA), the Players' Association and the

CHAPTER 19: DAY TWELVE—FRIDAY, JUNE 5, 1970

club owners were legally obligated to bargain in good faith (but not legally required to come to an agreement). Based upon the evidence actually presented, the court could conclude that the plaintiff was proposing to *modify, but not abolish,* baseball's reserve system. Accordingly, there was no reason or legal basis for Judge Cooper to assume the position of the NLRB and, in effect, "mediate" a labor dispute. That was the purpose of collective bargaining, and modifying the reserve system was a matter that could and should be settled at the bargaining table. Judge Cooper now had another "out". (Pardon the pun!)

Chapter 20
Day Thirteen—Monday, June 8, 1970

Testimony of John Clark, Jr.

When the trial resumed on Monday, June 8th, the defense called economist John Clark, Jr. as an expert witness. Clark possessed an impressive resume and a number of doctoral degrees from the Harvard Business School. After his military service from 1943-46, Clark taught in the business school at the University of Arkansas until 1953. Soon thereafter, Clark joined the firm of Arthur D. Little, Inc. in Cambridge, Massachusetts. Clark described Arthur D. Little, Inc. as an engineering and economic consulting firm that performed research for a wide variety of institutions, businesses and governmental entities. In that vein, Arthur Little performed economic analyses, antitrust studies, and revenue forecasts. Specifically with respect to baseball, Clark and the Arthur Little firm had previously worked for the National League in relation to the transfer of the Braves' franchise from Milwaukee to Atlanta during the early 1960s.

In preparation for his testimony in the Flood case, Clark compiled and the defense offered into evidence a document entitled, "*Economic Analyses of Certain Aspects of Organized*

CHAPTER 20: DAY THIRTEEN—MONDAY, JUNE 8, 1970

Baseball." Clark described his "assignment" and the content of that document as follows:

"The assignment was essentially to analyze and review the salaries, the benefits, the operating costs of baseball, the financial situation of baseball...under the existing structure...between players, the game, the profitability of clubs and so on.... The report gives the findings on several particular analyses that I conducted. The first is on salaries and benefits. The second is player development and replacement costs. The third was an economic analysis of baseball operations. The fourth was an analysis of the franchise values and earnings. The fifth is relative financial capability of baseball clubs, and the sixth is the attendance as related to the size of the city and performance of [the] club."

Clark concluded that from 1965 to 1969, the average salary for major league baseball players increased 27.9%; and from 1965 to 1970, the average salary increased by 44%. When defense counsel inquired into the detail of his conclusions and analysis, Clark apparently felt compelled to describe the compensation for other "comparable" professions and occupations. Clark droned on about the salaries of these "comparable" occupations such as physicists, linguists, psychologists, economists, computer scientists, attorneys, accountants, draftsmen, public elementary and secondary school teachers!

Clark concluded that the salary increases that the established major league baseball players received between 1965-1969 "far outstrip the increases of any of the professional and paraprofessional groups listed" in the report. Clark continued by comparing the percentage of increases for households in the U.S. This part of Clark's testimony, of course, had absolutely nothing to do with any argument or issue presented by Curt Flood. Flood was not arguing that the reserve system deprived him of his right to negotiate a salary, in whatever amount, to play major league baseball. He was, however, arguing that the reserve system deprived him of *any opportunity* to negotiate a salary and play for the *team of his choice—for the remainder of his life.*

Flood's expert witness, Robert Nathan, previously testified that the reserve system had a "depressing effect" upon a player's salary level. Clark disagreed. According to Clark, the average salary of a major league baseball player had increased "at a reasonable level" and that salary increases were "really quite substantial in absolute terms and in relative terms"; and that an "established player" had substantial bargaining power vis-a-vis the club, but that a "marginal player" had less bargaining power. Clark noted, however, that the bargaining power of the marginal player would not improve and, in fact, "would be hurt by" the elimination of baseball's reserve system.

Clark testified that collective bargaining had a "positive effect on salaries for players and that the current set up was effective"; that major league baseball was "unique" and quite different from any other industry with respect to player development cost; and that the reserve system was effective in maintaining league play and in keeping teams from becoming financially unable to compete.

A good portion of Clark's direct examination consisted of lengthy, tedious and completely irrelevant commentary and statistical data. For example, Clark went into excruciating detail about the amount of pension benefits; the average player development costs; average team operating revenues, including concessions, ticket sales, advertising, stadium costs, depreciation, taxes and "net margins". More specifically, Clark suggested that major league baseball may not be that "profitable". Based upon Clark's analyses:

"...the normal business of baseball declined to a level of 3.7 percent in 1969 and that is a narrow enough margin that

CHAPTER 20: DAY THIRTEEN—MONDAY, JUNE 8, 1970

I would say it is really at the level of whether it is enough or not to be secure in your operations. It is really at a marginal level of operations. Income is exceeding the costs associated with the game by a very narrow margin in the last three years."

Clark's direct examination took most of Day Thirteen. The statistical data and discussion of Flood's potential pension benefits, team revenues, stadium costs, etc., seemed endless—and to a large extent, pointless. After all, Flood was not arguing that his salary or benefits were inadequate or unacceptable. Flood simply had no option or opportunity to play for a club of his choice—*ever*. It was late in the afternoon on Day Thirteen—and now time for Clark's cross examination.

The first subject of cross examination by Topkis was the reliability of the data upon which Clark relied for *all* of his economic analyses and conclusions—*unaudited* figures prepared by the accounting firm of Arthur Andersen.

"Q. Now, you have observed, I take it, that the Arthur Andersen Report is unaudited, have you not?

A. Yes, sir.

Q. That is to say, Arthur Andersen does not certify or otherwise vouch for the accuracy or reliability of any of the figures contained in that report, isn't that right?

A. That's right.

Q. And that means to you, does it not, that the statements made in the Arthur Andersen report could be true and could be a pack of lies and neither Andersen knows and you don't know, is that right?

A. That's right....

Q. I...ask you,...if those figures showed that a club had lost money, you wouldn't have any way whatsoever of knowing whether that loss was the result of the club's doing its best and nonetheless losing money or the loss was generated by the fact that there were 20 relatives of the club owner on the payroll; you wouldn't know one way or the other, would you?

A. No.

Q. And so those portions of your report that we have been talking about could be based on proper business expenses and could be based on having a pack of relatives on the payroll, is that right?

A. Yes, sir."

Next, Topkis very effectively turned the tables on Clark and illustrated the core of Curt Flood's plight:

"Q. You are being paid to testify here?

A. Yes.

Q. Tell me, how would you like to have no choice but to work for Arthur D. Little forever?

A. Well, actually I enjoy it a great deal.

Q. That is why you left for Cresap, McCormick [another employer]?

A. No, I left because I would prefer not to move back to Cambridge.

Q. Oh, that's why you left [Arthur D.] Little?

A. Yes.

Q. Because you didn't want to move to Cambridge?

A. Yes. I like New York.

Q. Ever hear of a man Curt Flood liking St. Louis?

A. Yes.

Q. You sympathize with him then?

A. Yes, I certainly do sympathize with him."

Topkis continued to destroy Clark's conclusions regarding the relative affluence of major league baseball players. Clark was forced to acknowledge that the data he relied upon regarding the level and increases in the salaries of major league baseball players did *not* include any comparison to professional basketball, hockey or football players; nor to motion picture entertainers. Clark had not even inquired as to the availability of such comparative data.

Chapter 20: Day Thirteen—Monday, June 8, 1970

"Q. Doctor, you compared the salary advances of ballplayers with those in the manufacturing trade, industries, lawyers, computer scientists and so on. Did you compare the experience of ballplayers with the experience of basketball players?

A. I did not have any basketball data.

Q. Did you ask for it?

A. No.

Q. Did you compare their experience with the experience of hockey players?

A. No.

Q. Did you ask for it?

A. No.

Q. It has been suggested, I believe, in the press that the median figure of basketball players in the National Basketball League or at least in the New York entry...is over $50,000 a year. Have you ever heard that report?

A. No.

Q. Did you compare the experience of baseball players with that of motion picture stars?

A. No.

Q. Did you compare the experience of...major league baseball players with the experience of any other group which was at the top of its profession?

A. No, there is no statistical breakdown that I know of for that sort of information.

Q. And you didn't ask for any information about motion picture stars or anything like that?

A. I really wouldn't know who to ask."

Finally, an exasperated Topkis asked whether it had occurred to Clark that Clark's data was making "essentially meaningless comparisons"? Clark's responses were pathetically absurd.

"Q. Did it occur to you, Doctor, that you were making essentially meaningless comparisons when you compared major league baseball players with accountants and teachers and computer scientists?

A. No.

Q. You thought it perfectly valid comparison to compare people at the pinnacle of their profession, namely, baseball, major league, baseball players with the average run of wage earners in the manufacturing industries and with the average run of attorneys and accountants and computer scientists?

A. I thought that a number of the occupations used were reasonably alternative occupations *if a person had not gone into ball playing.*"

On that incredulous series of responses, Day Thirteen had come to conclusion.

CHAPTER 21
DAY FOURTEEN—TUESDAY, JUNE 9, 1970

On the morning of Day 14, Topkis resumed his cross examination of John Clark. Unlike the day before, Clark's testimony this day meandered around more meaningless comparisons and club financial data. The overall thrust of Clark's testimony was that most major league baseball players "had it pretty good" and were "reasonably well compensated" compared to the rest of American society. Assuming that this view could be established as fact, why or how was this line of testimony in any way relevant to the issues presented in *Flood v. Kuhn?*

Still attempting to discredit Clark's position, Topkis got Clark to acknowledge that the salaries paid by the club owners to "non players" in the aggregate exceeded the salaries paid to their players; and using the data available for 1969, Clark noted that 109 of the 600 players on the active rosters of the twenty-four clubs (approximately one of every five players) were being paid the *minimum* $10,000 annual salary. Near the very end of his cross, Clark was forced to yield some additional ground and admitted that "as a matter of history, the reserve system has not operated to produce any reasonable level of competition on the field". Later, however, Clark would attempt to qualify that conclusion by stating that the level of competition would be "even more unequal if there were no reserve system at all."

The economic data presented and the "battle of the economists" again demonstrated the lack of preparation and the poor execution of a trial strategy by Flood's counsel. At one point during Clark's cross examination and in response to an objection by counsel, Judge Cooper felt compelled to reiterate the evidentiary dilemma which the lawyers had created. More specifically, Judge Cooper reminded counsel that he accommodated counsel's request for an expedited trial schedule, and further, that he had granted *Flood's* pretrial requests that various financial (and other) data be prepared and provided by the defendants. Cooper pointed out that the production of fully audited financial records for each of the twenty-four clubs would have taken months to prepare and produce — a fact with which Flood's lawyers were fully aware. Consequently, Topkis found himself challenging and rejecting the accuracy (and relevancy) of much of the very financial data which he and Goldberg had requested, and which was produced by the defendants in order to accommodate plaintiff's request for an expedited trial.

In the final analysis, neither Robert Nathan, Flood's economic expert witness, nor John Clark, Jr, the defense's economic expert witness were crucial or overly persuasive. Nathan presented cogent economic theory and conclusions in relation to his understanding of baseball's reserve system, but did not perform or present any study specific to baseball. Clark, on the other hand, presented *unaudited* financial data for the period of 1965-1970 for the twenty-four clubs and major league baseball, none of which financial data were even prepared by him or his company. Most importantly, however, what did this financial data have to do with Curt Flood and his claim that baseball's reserve system illegally deprived him of any opportunity to negotiate a contract and play professional baseball for a team of his choice?

At the conclusion of Clark's testimony, all of the defendants rested their cases. When the trial reconvened in the afternoon, Flood's lawyers had an opportunity to present what is known as "rebuttal evidence". In what would eventually provide more fodder for the defense, plaintiff's lawyers chose not to recall Flood to testify on rebuttal, but rather presented and recalled Marvin Miller to the witness stand.

Rebuttal Testimony of Marvin Miller

Flood's legal team clearly understood the significance of John Gaherin's damaging testimony at the end of Day Twelve. Topkis knew he needed to respond to Gaherin's specific and, up to this point, unrefuted testimony: 1) that major league baseball was under the jurisdiction of the NLRB; 2) that the reserve system was a mandatory subject of collective bargaining; and 3) that the union and the club owners had negotiated changes to the reserve system.

During his rebuttal testimony, Miller did not attempt to explain or clarify a mere misunderstanding, but rather totally *contradicted* Gaherin's testimony on almost every relevant detail. First, Miller denied that the union and club owners had *ever* negotiated on the reserve system, and denied that the union ever "accepted" the reserve system in its current form.

"Q. Mr. Miller, based on your experience, would you say that there has been collective bargaining in baseball as to the continuation of the reserve system?

A. None at all.

Q. When the first basic agreement was signed, that was when, sir?

A. That was in February 1968.

Q. Would you tell us, please, whether in signing that

agreement you accepted the reserve system as it then stood?

A. No, your Honor, we did not."

Miller conceded that the union did sign the Basic Agreement in February 1968 in which the club owners and the union agreed to conduct a joint study on possible alternatives to the reserve system as then constituted, but then testified about his *oral statements* (which were nowhere reflected in the written documents) to the representatives of the club owners.

"...The oral statement was made at either the final or next to final negotiating session in trying to wrap up the agreement as a whole, and it was to the effect that we [union] did not accept the reserve system as legal and that therefore we wanted the Player Relations Committee to know that when we [union] agreed on a clause...that we [union] will do our best efforts to carry out the provisions of the agreement, that they [club owners] should know that we [union] considered the reserve clause illegal and therefore we could, of course, not agree to use our best efforts to carry that out."

Miller recounted that there were a total of four meetings, the first of which took place in April 1969—fourteen months after agreeing to conduct the joint study; and that nothing emerged as a result of this joint study.

"Q. At anytime in the course of those meetings did the representatives of management ever come forward with any proposal for modification of the reserve system in the slightest degree?

A. No.

Q. Were there various proposals submitted by you?

A. Yes....

Q. Did there come a time when the joint study or review ended?

A. Yes.

CHAPTER 21: DAY FOURTEEN—TUESDAY, JUNE 9, 1970

Q. When was that?
A. I believe it was in the late summer of 1969.
Q. Had agreement been reached on anything in the course of this review?
A. Nothing that I can recall.
Q. And that was the end of the review?
A. Yes."

What was not in dispute was that the 1968 Basic Agreement was scheduled to expire December 31, 1969. Concerning these 1969 discussions, Topkis quizzed Miller as to whether modifications to the reserve system were again the subject of discussions and negotiations.

"Q. Some months later, I think in late December 1969, the news became public of a possible lawsuit by the plaintiff here, Mr. Curt Flood?
A. Yes.
Q. And at that time were there any discussions going on between you and representatives of baseball's management with reference to the reserve system?
A. Yes.
Q. In what context were those discussions being carried on?
A. In the context of our joint attempts to negotiate a new basic agreement to replace the first one....
Q. So there were discussions going on into the new basic agreement, is that correct?
A. Yes.
Q. And in those discussions, one of the subjects that you had under consideration was the reserve system?
A. Yes.
Q. Did you make proposals as to possible modification of the reserve system in those discussions?
A. Yes.
Q. Were any of them in the slightest degree accepted by representatives of management?

A. No.

Q. Did representatives of management come forward with any proposal whatsoever for modification of the reserve system in the slightest degree?

A. No."

Topkis then directed Miller to the effects of Flood's lawsuit on the 1969 club owners-union discussions. (Gaherin, it must be noted, testified that the Flood suit brought the negotiations to a "crashing halt".)

"Q. When the news of Mr. Flood's impending suit became available, did that news have any impact upon the discussions which you were having?

A. No.

Q. You were in court when Commissioner Kuhn and Mr. Gaherin testified?

A. I was.

Q. Did you hear them testify that, in effect, the news of Mr. Flood's suit brought discussions of the reserve system to a crashing halt?

A. I heard it.

Q. Does that testimony conform with your recollection?

A. No, it does not, your Honor. *There was no difference whatsoever in the nature of the discussions before it was known that Curt Flood intended to file a suit and after it was made known that Curt Flood intended to file suit.* As a matter of fact, *there was not even any conversation between the parties concerning the news about the suit.*

Further, Miller testified that Flood's suit did not bring an end to the discussions of modifying the reserve system, and that the parties continued discussions until on or about February 19th—one month after Flood filed his suit. Miller's recollection of the February 19, 1970 discussion was quite different than John Gaherin's recollection.

"Q. You said you were here when Mr. Gaherin testified?

A. Yes.

CHAPTER 21: DAY FOURTEEN—TUESDAY, JUNE 9, 1970

Q. Did you hear him say, in substance, that at a meeting you said that if amendments to the reserve system were included in the new agreement irreparable damage would be done to...the action brought by Curt Flood?

A. I heard him say that.

Q. *Was he accurately reporting your statement?*

A. *It was completely inaccurate. It was quite the reverse.*

Q. What did you in point of fact say to him?

A. I said to him *that if we could agree on appropriate amendments, there would be no Curt Flood suit because Curt Flood had said whatever amendments were acceptable to the players as a group he would accept and withdraw his suit.*

Q. Following that conversation or that meeting, were you able to arrive at any amendments to the reserve system?

A. No.

Q. At any time during the entire history of your dealings with the representatives of organized baseball, Mr. Miller, have those representatives proposed the slightest modification of the reserve system?

A. At no time."

What is most revealing is that Miller clearly recalled his representation to Gaherin that Curt Flood would withdraw his pending lawsuit if the owners and union could come to an agreement on modifying the reserve system, and that this conversation took place in February of 1970—more than a month after Flood filed his suit. Why and how is it that Miller—and not Curt Flood's lawyers—could be making any legally binding representation regarding Curt Flood's suit or Flood's legal interests to a representative of the defendants? After all, Miller had testified that it was Curt Flood who had brought *his suit* against major league baseball, and that the Players' Association was not the plaintiff. Miller's representation to Gaherin provided significant support to the defendants' contention that there was direct and calculated collaboration between the union and Flood; and more directly, that the Players' Association was using Flood and Flood's suit in its strategy to negotiate modifications to the reserve system.

Moreover, Miller then proceeded to inform Judge Cooper of the *union's position* that the continuation of the reserve system was not an appropriate subject of collective bargaining.

"A. ...your Honor, it has been the position of the players and the Players' Association that the reserve...system *is illegal and by virtue of that feeling we do not feel that it is in the same category as any other bargainable subject.*"

Miller compared collective bargaining on the reserve system between the Players' Association and the owners to collective bargaining with an employer that refuses to pay the statutory minimum wage.

"A. ...[I]f I may use a parallel to explain—if an employer refuses to pay as much as the statutory minimum wage, we might attempt to bargain with him in order to get him to comply with the law, but the fact that he refuses and *insists on violating the law* puts that issue in a completely different category, in our view. It does so *because it is quite clear in our minds, at least, that no individual and no organization can bargain away somebody's legal rights, a member's legal rights.*"

Upon closer review, Miller's comparison to the employer who intentionally and purposefully refuses to pay its employees the legal minimum wage was totally without merit. The minimum wage is set by statute. In so doing, the legislature has established that failure to comply with that requirement is unlawful. Compliance is easily ascertainable. On the other hand, in the instance of baseball's reserve system, the *legality* of that system was precisely what was being litigated in *Flood v. Kuhn*. Moreover, who was Marvin Miller or the Players' Association to unilaterally declare in the course of a labor negotiation that some provision or aspect of baseball's reserve system was illegal? That is what lawsuits test and that is what courts decide.

On the one hand, Miller stridently justified the union's purported refusal to negotiate modifications to baseball's reserve system on the *union's unilateral determination* of the reserve system's *illegality*. In the very next portion of Miller's testimony, however, he elaborated on several ramifications to the union *if in fact or in the event* the reserve system was *declared illegal*. On this issue, Miller was speaking with forked tongue and out of both sides of his mouth.

"A. ...*If in fact the reserve system...is illegal and if in fact the plaintiff is being damaged by such* illegal restriction, the Players' Association can not possibly accept in a package...the continued existence of such illegal restrictions no matter what else is given in the way of concession...."

Miller further explained that the union could even be liable to someone like Flood.

"A. ...In connection with drawing up the new basic agreement, we explained...to Mr. Gaherin and to his associates that *the primary reason* why we [union] could not have an agreement which incorporated the existing reserve rule system was that *under advice of counsel* in view of all the circumstances, we [union] *would be liable* to be a defendant in a subsequent suit against the reserve rule system."

At this particular juncture, Judge Cooper was perplexed and asked Miller to clarify his testimony. In his explanation to Judge Cooper, Miller testified that the owners believed that by signing a new three-year basic agreement, the owners would be relieved of any obligation during that period to negotiate on the reserve system. Miller was emphatic that the Players' Association did not accept this position, and then explained why and how the union would negotiate on the reserve system.

"Q. Do I understand, Mr. Miller, that your basic problem

with the reserve system as you communicated that problem to the management, is that it has been a system of total or absolute restraint?

A. Yes.

Q. And you were perfectly willing to attempt to negotiate a system of significantly lesser restraints which you said would possibly make the entire system lawful, is that right?

A. Yes, and we made it clear at all times...."

The trial transcript clearly reveals that Judge Cooper took keen interest and gave great weight to the testimony of John Gaherin and Marvin Miller regarding the union-club owners' collective bargaining on baseball's reserve system in relationship to Flood's suit. Judge Cooper then interrupted the proceeding and alerted trial counsel in no uncertain terms.

"...You know I stayed away from interrupting throughout this entire trial, and I am not going to start in now, *but I do hope that all of this will be thoroughly gone into by all the attorneys. I would like this meticulously developed....* I am going to count on you to develop this bit by bit, *because I place a great deal of concern on this phase of the trial.*"

In the late afternoon of Day Fourteen, Miller was again tendered to defense counsel for cross examination. Defense counsel wanted to reestablish that the union's "firm position"—that the reserve system was illegal—had been communicated by Miller to the owners during formal collective bargaining.

"Q. Do you want this court to understand that as a firm position you [union] stated in bargaining...to the clubs that the reserve system was illegal?

A. Absolutely."

When asked about the union-club owners' "joint study" of the reserve system, and the various "proposals" made by the Players' Association, Miller was again backpedaling and splitting hairs. Miller told Judge Cooper that these union "proposals" were only "proposals for study, comment and

CHAPTER 21: DAY FOURTEEN—TUESDAY, JUNE 9, 1970

reaction", and were not, in the legal sense, "offers which were open for acceptance".

Defense counsel Alexander Hadden then focused on Miller's prior testimony that the union was only negotiating with the owners in an attempt to "legalize" the reserve system.

"Q. I want you to be sure you understand my question, Mr. Miller. You stated in your rebuttal testimony that...in the course of recent negotiations you stated to the representative of the clubs that...to sign an agreement incorporating the various features of the present reserve system would expose you to a possibility of suit, correct?

A. Yes....

Q. My question is this, and it is a very precise question. *Did you ever in any bargaining session say to the representatives of management what the minimum changes would be which would remove that objection?...*

A. No."

Miller was asked about his testimony in which he compared the illegality of baseball's reserve system to the illegality of paying less than the minimum wage prescribed by law. When pressed as to why he was so certain that baseball's reserve system was illegal, Miller evasively noted that he had been "so advised by counsel".

When forced to admit that the reserve system had been the subject of dialogue between the Players' Association and the club owners *since 1967*, Miller was compelled to explain the difference between "negotiations" and "discussions".

"Q. So...there were discussions starting in '67 about the reserve system?

A. Certainly there were discussions.

Q. Then you must have a distinction in your mind between discussions and collective bargaining?

A. I certainly do.

Q. Now supposing you tell us what that distinction is.

A. The discussions that took place consisted of the Players' Association putting forth ideas, making suggestions for study, and the owners' representative advising us, in substance, they like what they have, period. The difference between that kind of a discussion and collective bargaining is that collective bargaining is a give-and-take proposition in which you give serious consideration to the other side's suggestions, point of view, are prepared to examine in the greatest detail exactly what it is that is being proposed, and attempt, if possible, to put forward modifications, suggestions of your own, rather than what really amounted to a brick wall in which we were simply getting back, 'We like what we have.' We understand that. That is not collective bargaining.

Q. Your position is that all that ever happened regarding the reserve system in negotiations with the players was that management representatives said, 'We like what we have and that's it"?

A. In substance. Other words were used."

Most incredibly, Miller stated that the agreement between the union and the club owners (in February 1970) to hold the reserve system "discussions" in abeyance had nothing to do with the filing of Flood's suit, but rather because other matters made it "inconvenient".

"A. ...The fact is that on February 19 [1970] we were five days away from the end of negotiations *on any convenient basis*. Starting February 25, [1970] Mr. Moss, counsel to the Players' Association, and I were due in Florida to start a series of meetings, one with the executive board and 24 separate spring training camps in Florida, Arizona and California....

It had nothing to do with the suit by the plaintiff or its timing, nothing at all. It was the fact that *we were running out of time to negotiate a basic agreement.* And on February

CHAPTER 21: DAY FOURTEEN—TUESDAY, JUNE 9, 1970

19, [1970] we said—I said that while it would be preferable for us to negotiate appropriate revisions in the reserve clause system that we could agree to, it appeared that we no longer had time to do this, and that was the reason...."

In total contradiction to the prior testimony of John Gaherin, the sum and substance of Marvin Miller's rebuttal testimony on Day Fourteen was as follows:

1. At *no time* did the union and the club owners *ever negotiate* on modifications to baseball's reserve system. The club owners and the Players' Association only conducted *discussions*.

2. Despite the actual language contained in the 1968 Basic Agreement, the reserve system was never incorporated into the Basic Agreement; and despite *signing* the 1968 Basic Agreement, Miller told the representatives of the club owners *orally* that the union could not agree "to use its best efforts" to carry out the terms of the very agreement the union had just signed.

3. Based upon the advice of its counsel, it was the union's belief and the union's firm bargaining position that baseball's reserve system was *illegal*; and that because of potential liability to the union, the Players' Association could not specify *in writing* their belief that the reserve system was *illegal*.

4. It was the union's desire to *negotiate* changes to the reserve system *in order to make the reserve system legal*. At no time, however, did the union ever communicate to the club owners *what specific modifications* would be necessary to make the reserve system "become legal".

5. The filing of Flood's lawsuit had *no effect* on the reserve system discussions between the owners and the Players' Association.

If, as Miller testified, the club owners *never* negotiated and refused to negotiate on modifications to this *illegal* reserve system, why did the Players' Association continue to honor or acquiesce in the enforcement of the reserve system? Why didn't the union consider a work stoppage or organize a strike? Why didn't the *union,* like Curt Flood, file a suit and ask the court to declare baseball's reserve system unlawful?

At best, Miller's rebuttal testimony sent extremely mixed messages. The union's position was imprecise and consequently provided little, if any, benefit to Plaintiff Curt Flood. At worst, Miller's rebuttal testimony consisted of a series of inconsistencies and contradictions, and as such, was literally incredible.

Day Fourteen of *Flood v. Kuhn* had now concluded. The trial's final day would begin the next morning.

CHAPTER 22
DAY FIFTEEN—WEDNESDAY, JUNE 10, 1970

Testimony of Bill Veeck

On the morning of Day Fifteen, and with the consent of Judge Cooper and all defense counsel, Plaintiff Curt Flood was allowed to present the final witness in his case in chief "out of order". The day before, Topkis presented Marvin Miller in "rebuttal". Under normal trial procedure, Flood would not be allowed to present any "rebuttal" testimony or evidence until *after* the plaintiff had presented its entire case in chief; *and after* the defense had presented its entire case. However, in an effort to accommodate the travel schedule of the witness, Judge Cooper allowed Topkis to present witness Bill Veeck in the plaintiff's case in chief on this, the final day of the trial.

At the time of the trial, Veeck was fifty-six years old, and was generally regarded as having "retired" from baseball. Veeck grew up in Hinsdale, Illinois, and was the son of the sports writer and late President of the Chicago Cubs, William Veeck, Sr. By the age of eleven, the younger Veeck was working as a ballpark vendor, ticket seller and groundskeeper. When Veeck's father died in 1933, Veeck left Kenyon College to work for the Cubs, and ultimately became the Cubs' treasurer. In 1941, prior to his military service during World War II, Veeck bought a minor league franchise in Milwaukee. Later, Veeck became the owner of the Cleveland Indians in 1946 and remained its president during that club's pennant winning season in 1948. Veeck became the owner of the St. Louis Browns in 1951, and subsequently purchased ownership of the Chicago White Sox in 1959.

In 1961, under the advice of his physicians, Veeck stepped down as president of the White Sox. Between 1961 and 1970, Veeck wrote syndicated news columns and several books, appeared on the television show *ABC's Wide World of Sports*; and purchased ownership of Suffolk Downs Race Track in Boston, Massachusetts.

Veeck was also well known, and in some baseball circles despised, for his many innovations and creative marketing ploys. Perhaps Veeck is best remembered for sending a midget, Eddie Gaedel, to bat for his lone appearance for the St. Louis Browns on August 19, 1951. Veeck was the originator of the exploding scoreboard, and the promotional "Bat Day" and "Cap Day" at the ball park. He also managed to irk the owners of the other teams by his "moveable fences" and changing their location when the opposing team was batting. Veeck also broke new ground of another sort by signing Larry Doby in 1947 to be the first black player in the American League, and by signing forty-two year old Satchel Paige in 1948 as the oldest rookie in major league history.

On this day, however, Topkis presented the maverick owner's views on baseball's reserve system and the viability of making financial investment in major league baseball. After establishing the witness's familiarity with the reserve system, Topkis asked Veeck about the possible *elimination* of that system.

"Q. ...[O]n the basis of your experience, Mr. Veeck, do you have an opinion as to whether *elimination* of the

CHAPTER 22: DAY FIFTEEN—WEDNESDAY, JUNE 10, 1970

reserve system would help or hurt baseball?

A. Well the complete *elimination* of the reserve system or the reserve clause in contracts I think *would not be helpful to baseball*. I am afraid that if you suddenly terminated and there was no control of contracts by any club, that *it could...result in some rather chaotic conditions*. I feel, however, that this would not be the case if it were done in an orderly manner."

Again, Judge Cooper interjected and asked Veeck what he would substitute for baseball's reserve system? Veeck identified three alternatives which Veeck believed could be "tailored to fit" major league baseball. First, Veeck suggested the use a "movie contract" which would reserve the club's right to a player for a specific number of years, after which the club may renew, and at which point the player may choose not to renew and become a free agent. Second, Veeck suggested the adoption of a slightly revised "NFL rule" pursuant to which a player could play out his option and become a free agent, but pursuant to which the Commissioner would have no authority to award compensation for the loss of that free agent player. Thirdly, Veeck suggested the creation of a system by which a player's development cost would be ascertained and recouped by the team that had incurred that cost. Veeck further noted that the uniform determination and recoupment of these player development costs would apply throughout major league baseball and would be fair to the club owners. According to Veeck, the "movie contract" and the "revised NFL rule" would benefit both players and the club owners, and would not be detrimental to competition on the field.

Veeck was not shy about expressing his beliefs and views on several other related issues. Specifically, Veeck took aim at the defense's repeated assertion that in the absence of baseball's reserve system, all of the "star" players would gravitate to a few "wealthy teams" and thereby destroy competition among the teams. It was Veeck's opinion that "ballplayers do not play for money, but play for pride", and that even if the reserve system were so modified, "it is my opinion that they would continue to play for pride". In addition, Veeck took issue with the definition of a "wealthy club" and noted that it was no more than a particular owner's personal fortune and investing that personal wealth in the club. By way of illustration, Veeck referenced the concepts of "wealth" and "dominance".

"Let us take, for instance, the case of the Yankees. The Yankees' dominance of the American League is, in my opinion, not because they were the wealthiest club, because they weren't...but they did have in their employment three remarkably good scouts...Joe Devine...Bill Essex, and Paul Kritchell...and they had probably the best administrator in the game in...George Weiss.... [I]n my opinion, it was these three fellows rather than any wealth that controlled and guaranteed the steady flow of talent to the Yankees."

On the restrictive nature of the baseball's reserve system, Veeck was outspoken.

"...I believe that everyone should once in their career have the right to determine their future for themselves, whether one be an attorney—you shouldn't, just because a firm wanted you, to be held by that firm *forever in perpetuity*.

Veeck then addressed the reserve system's impact upon what Jackie Robinson referred to in his testimony as "benchwarmers"; and testified that allowing a player to play out his option and negotiate with another club would help "balance the talent" among the clubs and be beneficial to major league baseball.

"...I do think there are a lot of ballplayers...who would profit by being able at some time to go or to renegotiate a contract in place of leaving. I think there are some ballplayers who are not playing because in this particular club

CHAPTER 22: DAY FIFTEEN—WEDNESDAY, JUNE 10, 1970

there are other athletes who may be just a step better than they, but who could play with many other teams, and I think to some extent this would spread the talent more fairly, and if one could play out their option and then renegotiate with another club, I think this would be beneficial to the game itself, and I think there would be a tendency then to balance the talent."

To Veeck, the reserve system tarnished the game of baseball, which he also called "the greatest team game". While Flood called it "peonage", it was Veeck that referred to the reserve system as "human bondage".

"...Well, I think that it would certainly help the players and the game itself to no longer be one of the few places *in which there is human bondage.* I think it would be to the benefit of the reputation of the game of baseball, and I would like to mention just for the record, I happen to think of baseball as the greatest team game there is. I don't happen to agree with all they do, and often I am very unkind [with] my statements, but I still think it is a game that deserves to be perpetuated and to restore it to the position of honor it once held, and I think this would be a step in that direction. *At least it would be fair.*"

It was Veeck's view that the reserve system was in no way related to player development.

"Q. It has been suggested in testimony here...that the reserve system as it operates today is indispensable in order to protect the clubs' cost of developing players in the minor leagues...and is the only way to secure a flow of new player talent to the major leagues.

A. Well, no, I don't think it is the only way.... *I don't think that the reserve clause has anything to do with the development of playing talent* except in one respect, and that is that theoretically,...if you don't have these subsidized minor leagues, you won't have a flow of players from them; and I offer the fact that you can still subsidize the minor leagues directly and you can still have the advantages *without keeping a fellow perpetually under a reserve clause....*"

Veeck thought that it would be "a splendid idea", and that impartial arbitration of salary disputes would improve the relationship between and benefit both the players and management.

"I think that it [impartial arbitration] would create a little better relationship. Just the right to have an arbitration, the right not to be feeling that you are singly, as an athlete, negotiating against the wealth of a club, I think it would improve relationships. I think on many occasions that the club itself might profit a little bit, that on occasion baseball players have been somewhat unrealistic in their various demands. So I think it would be beneficial from both ways."

In contrast to the testimony of the owner-investor witnesses previously called by the defense, it was Veeck's view that the elimination or modification of baseball's reserve system would in no way deter his willingness to financially invest in major league baseball.

"Q. Mr. Veeck, in your judgement—you have invested in many baseball clubs—would modification of the reserve system along the lines that we have been discussing or adoption of one or another substitute for the reserve system deter investment in baseball?

A. Well, I can only speak for myself. If I were going to invest in a ball club *it would not deter me.*

Q. Your degree of eagerness would not be affected one way or another?

A. *No, not in the slightest.*

Q. And would you expect baseball as a whole to prosper or suffer harm by reason of the adoption of any of these alternatives we have discussed?

A. I think it would prosper."

CHAPTER 22: DAY FIFTEEN—WEDNESDAY, JUNE 10, 1970

During his cross examination, defense counsel attempted to impeach Veeck by introducing various quotes from two books authored by Veeck in the 1960s—*Veeck, As In Wreck* (1962) and *The Hustler's Handbook* (1965). Further, the defense wanted to establish that during his career, Veeck had been ostracized by his fellow club owners, and that as a result, Veeck was biased and had a motive to "get even" with those club owners.

The defense confronted Veeck with the following quotes from *The Hustler's Handbook*:

"More money is bet on baseball, I think, than on any other sport, horse racing included."; and (alluding to the so-called "Black Sox" scandal), "Anyone who thinks the moral climate of the United States today is higher than it was in 1919 hasn't looked out the window lately."

Even after Veeck confirmed that those statements from *The Hustler's Handbook* were correctly attributed to him, it was unclear as to why or for what purpose the defense was offering these passages as evidence.

Later, defense counsel Victor Kramer tried to establish that "trades" were a necessary and beneficial part of professional baseball. Directing the witness and the court's attention to yet another passage from *The Hustler's Handbook*, Kramer wanted Veeck to acknowledge that had Curt Flood not been traded from the Cincinnati Reds to the St. Louis Cardinals in 1958, Flood would never have had the opportunity to display his talents and a successful professional career. Following an objection from Flood's counsel and a lengthy evidentiary colloquy, the following quote from Bill Veeck (found on pages 140-41 of *The Hustler's Handbook*) was read into evidence:

" [Bing] Devine's first great trade at St. Louis, hindsight tells us, was getting Curt Flood from Cincinnati. This is a trade which is interesting because it illustrates an important point. Every major league club scouts every other club's players almost as thoroughly as it scouts its own...Devine knew that Cincinnati had another center-fielder in their system, Vada Pinson, who looked as if he was one of the greatest prospects of all time. Pinson had everything Flood had, plus even more speed and considerably more power. When Cincinnati had Flood fooling around in the infield, that was the signal for Bing to make his move. Gabe Paul (Cincinnati's General Manager) has never been famous for undervaluing his players. In this case, Cincinnati needed some relief pitching badly, and Devine was able to pry the 20-year old Flood away from him for three minor-league relief pitchers of exceedingly limited ability. Flood remained a good fielding, no-hit out-fielder for the Cards for three years before he suddenly developed into a top-league hitter. So the question remains: Just what would the Reds have done with him during those three years?"

The cross examination of Veeck was lengthy, but ineffective. The defense did little to discredit Veeck's views on baseball's reserve system. While the defense's "book reviews" of *The Hustler's Handbook* and *Veeck, As In Wreck* were somewhat entertaining, the passages and quotes cited by the defense were largely irrelevant.

As for Plaintiff Curt Flood's case, Veeck's testimony was clear: if baseball's reserve system was abolished or modified, the sky would not fall and the world would not come to an end; and the business of baseball would continue to prosper. However, on the core issue of Curt Flood's case—that baseball's reserve system was illegal and must be abolished—Bill Veeck hedged. At one point in his testimony, Veeck called it "human bondage", but when asked about the elimination of baseball's reserve system, Veeck testified that the system should be modified, but not abolished.

Veeck was the final witness called by the plaintiff, after which the plaintiff rested his case.

CHAPTER 22: DAY FIFTEEN—WEDNESDAY, JUNE 10, 1970

Following the ususal motions and rulings on the admissibility of certain documents into evidence, the defense called its final witness — John Gaherin.

Testimony of John Gaherin (Surrebuttal)

Gaherin was recalled to the stand to refute Marvin Miller's testimony. With Gaherin on the stand, defense counsel Alexander Hadden read that portion of Miller's testimony in which Miller insisted that the Players' Association had, on several occasions, informed the club owners' representatives that baseball's reserve system was illegal; and that as a result, the union could not "use its best efforts" to carry out the terms of the Basic Agreement.

"Q. You heard that testimony, Mr. Gaherin?
A. Yes.
Q. Is [that testimony] true and correct?
A. No....
Q. In the course of the joint study—and if you would refer in your answer, please, to any writings that changed hands during the study, as well as oral statements—were there any other statements made by the Association which expressly or by implication cast doubt upon the reserve system?
A. No, neither orally nor in the—I guess you would call it a position paper that was given to us during the course of the study, probably some time in June of that year [1968]...
Q. At *any time* during the period of your association with major league baseball until the testimony given by Mr. Miller yesterday, did *any representative* of the [Players'] Association *ever* state to you or, to your knowledge, to any other representative of major league baseball the flat assertion that the reserve system was *illegal?*
A. No, sir."

Recognizing that there was no possibility of reconciling Miller's and Gaherin's testimony on these points, Topkis concluded his questioning of Gaherin on cross as follows:

"Q. Mr. Gaherin, you are aware that on some particulars your testimony this afternoon is different from Mr. Miller's testimony of yesterday, aren't you?

A. Yes.

Q. Do you believe that Mr. Miller was deliberately telling untruths or that your memory is somewhat better than his?

A. Well, I guess my memory is better than his.

Q. You don't represent, on the other hand, that you have a flawless memory, do you?

A. No.

Q. Is it possible that his memory as to some matters might be more accurate than your?

A. Conceivably."

At the end of Gaherin's testimony on Day Fifteen, the evidentiary record in the trial of *Flood v. Kuhn* was now complete. Not surprisingly, Judge Cooper then took center stage and delivered a "closing statement" of his own. In typical fashion, Cooper's prepared address was rife with melodrama.

"Very well. But right out here in the open courtroom, and I ask you to bear with me, and won't you please sit down, I would like to close the case with just a few more words.

As you know, this is school commencement time and presumably some kind words are being spoken. How effectively or with what reception is another matter. That is not what prompts these remarks.

It is your individual efforts, your individual and collective efforts before this Court. We say in utter sincerity that before this trial record is closed it is only fitting and proper that it include the Court's sense of appreciation to all counsel for their unflagging industry, unflinching discharge of

CHAPTER 22: DAY FIFTEEN—WEDNESDAY, JUNE 10, 1970

duty and high order of professional deportment.

In short, a brilliant display of advocacy at its best, and to employ an effective, old-fashioned high compliment, you were fair and square.

Mr. Hughes, distinguished past president of the New York County Lawyers Association, effectively quiet, particularly meticulous and ever watchful, once again you gave clear evidence of what it takes to earn the constant respect of Bench and Bar. Compliments go to each of his keen associates and aides.

We must mention at least Mr. Carroll, Mr. Hadden and Mr. Hoynes.

As for Mr. Kramer, every time he got to his feet we all benefited. We regret his office address is Washington D.C., for that reduces the possibility of having him with us often.

And now on the other side of counsel table, Mr. Justice Goldberg, his leadership, and we use that word advisedly and in its finest sense, was exemplary. He demonstrated it here and it has enthused his aides to strain with all their might and main.

And now we come to Mr. Topkis. Your hair-trigger alertness was remarkable and at times truly fascinating. In all sincerity, it is to be hoped you will be able somehow to concentrate your efforts exclusively in the arena where your talents belong and are needed. What greater achievement is there for a lawyer than to be recognized on the merits as an outstanding trial advocate?

Due also are the compliments of this Court to your silent assistants, always on the alert and seemingly convinced, as all of you are, of the merit of thorough preparation.

As to the case itself, it really is a cause in the truest classical sense. Interwoven with the rights of the litigants named in the caption of this matter is baseball itself. That is enough to compel us to proceed with utmost care. It is saying a great deal that we match your genuine concern, and it goes without saying that we are resolved to call them as we see them as they come across the plate.

One last word, gentlemen. Such is the nature of this cause and the challenge involved that it evokes not just an appeal to reason but takes in total judicial reaction, and calls to mind and makes especially meaningful the words of Judge Frank of our own Circuit Court in a case entitled *In re Linehan*, and I quote it:

'The Law does not require a Judge to anesthetize his emotional reflexes. Only death yields such complete dispassionateness, for dispassion signifies indifference. Much harm is done by the myth that, merely by putting on a black robe and taking the oath of office as a judge, a man ceases to be human and strips himself of all predilections, becomes a passionateless thinking machine.'

That is the effect that this case has had on this Judge. I thank you once again for your courtesy to one another and to me."

While "Preacher Cooper" repeatedly heaped praise upon the lawyers and pontificated about the potential magnitude of this litigation upon the "institution of baseball", nary a word was uttered about the significance and the impact of the case upon Curtis Charles Flood—a man who was asking the federal courts to decide a most fundamentally basic legal principle and who was seeking to continue his career as a professional baseball player.

CHAPTER 23
POST-TRIAL

At the close of the trial, Judge Cooper gave the parties just over three weeks to file what lawyers and judges refer to as "post-trial briefs." The purpose of these documents is to allow the parties to summarize the evidence presented during the trial and to submit legal arguments based upon that evidence. The defense's post-trial brief was submitted on behalf of all of the defendants (except Commissioner Kuhn). Both sides filed their briefs on Tuesday, July 7, 1970. The briefs were superbly written and were of outstanding quality.

Plaintiff's Post-Trial Brief

Flood's post-trial brief summarized the evidence and condensed the legal issues into the following seven arguments.

Plaintiff's Argument I—Under the Sherman Act, Baseball's Reserve System is Illegal *Per Se*

In interpreting the Sherman Act, the federal courts had previously held that various practices were so restrictive that no justification would be considered by the courts;

and no evidence of the asserted reasonableness of those practices and conduct would be received. In other words, the federal courts held these restraints and practices illegal *per se* (in and of themselves). Flood's brief cited three practices which he argued were illegal *per se* under the Sherman Act.

First, Flood argued that the owners' agreement to divide the markets for present and potential professional ballplayers so that each team enjoyed the exclusive right to bargain with its reserved or drafted players was a market division, illegal *per se*. Second, the owners' agreement to offer each player only a single uniform contract is equivalent to a trade association requiring its members to deal with customers only on uniform terms, a practice previously ruled illegal by the federal courts. Finally, Flood maintained that the enforcement mechanism for the reserve system was a group boycott by all professional teams against any player blacklisted under Major League Rule 15. Flood argued that the federal courts had regularly and consistently ruled such concerted refusals to deal *per se* violations of the Sherman Act.

Plaintiff's Argument II—Baseball's Reserve System is an Unreasonable Restraint of Trade

Flood argued that the "total restraint imposed upon players' freedom to choose among employers" branded baseball's reserve system as unreasonable; and that the alleged valid purposes for the reserve system could not redeem it. Flood argued that the goals of the reserve system could be protected without totally restraining players' freedom of contract.

Refuting the position of the defense, Flood's brief maintained that public confidence in baseball would be unaffected by elimination of the reserve system; that equality of competition could be protected without a reserve system; that player development could and would continue without a reserve system; and that major modifications could be made in the reserve system without harm to major league baseball.

Plaintiff's Argument III—The Sherman Act Applies to Organized Baseball and the Court Has Jurisdiction to Grant Relief Under the Sherman Act

Flood argued that in 1922, in *Federal Baseball Club v. National League*, the U. S. Supreme Court held that professional baseball *was not interstate commerce, and therefore not subject to the Sherman Act*. In 1953, in *Toolson v. New York Yankees,* the Supreme Court declined to review that finding on the grounds that past conduct in reliance on *Federal Baseball* should not expose professional baseball to enormous liability; and that remedial action, if needed, was better left to Congress.

Flood argued that these U.S. Supreme Court decisions did not bar the trial court from granting him relief. It was Flood's contention that changes in professional baseball since 1922, and even since 1953, had thrust the game squarely within contemporary concepts of interstate commerce. The "reliance interest" of the team owners presented no barrier in that federal courts had the power, in appropriate circumstances, to frame *prospective* relief in antitrust cases. Finally, Flood maintained that the inaction of Congress since 1953 argued *for, rather than against,* a judicial reexamination of the U. S. Supreme Court's ruling in *Toolson.*

Plaintiff's Argument IV—State Antitrust Statutes Apply to Organized Baseball

In *Federal Baseball Club* (1922), *major league baseball argued* (and the Supreme Court concluded) that baseball games were "purely local affairs", and that "a state is entirely competent to reach and deal with any evil in the field of sport requiring legislative remedy." Thirty years later in *Toolson*, major league baseball again "solemnly intoned the adequacy of state law to deal with any problems."

Flood pointed out that now, in 1970, major league baseball had conveniently changed its position. In *Flood v. Kuhn*, major league baseball was urging the federal court *not* to reconsider baseball's antitrust exemption under *federal* law; and, at the same time, was arguing that no *state* antitrust regulation was appropriate. Whether or not baseball was subject to the Sherman Act (i.e., federal law), it was Flood's position that baseball was subject to *state* antitrust statutes.

Flood argued that baseball's exemption from federal antitrust regulation would extend to state antitrust regulation *only if Federal Baseball Club* held that the club owners should be subject to no regulation. Of course, *Federal Baseball Club* did not so hold. The Supreme Court, *with the urging of major league baseball*, merely held that baseball games were "purely local affairs"—subject to state regulation.

Plaintiff's Argument V—If the Reserve System is Beyond the Reach of Federal and State Statutes, It Must be Judged—and Found Unreasonable—Under Common Law Principles

Flood argued that even in the absence of any federal or state antitrust *statutory* regulation, baseball's reserve system was still subject to the common law (principles established by court decisions). Under the common law, all business practices and agreements must meet a test of "reasonableness". Flood argued that baseball's reserve system "represents *not a voluntary agreement* by a tradesman not to compete with the buyer of his business or by an employee not to compete with his employer, but a *unilateral restraint* imposed upon all baseball players by organized baseball."

Flood concluded that baseball's reserve system, unlimited in time or place, and far exceeding any valid purpose allegedly served, plainly failed the test of "reasonableness".

Plaintiff's Argument VI—The Reserve System Constitutes Involuntary Servitude and Violates the Thirteenth Amendment

The Thirteenth Amendment prohibits "involuntary servitude"—a term which the U.S. Supreme Court had held to be broader than "slavery". Federal legislation enforcing the Thirteenth Amendment similarly prohibited holding any person to "involuntary servitude".[9] It was Flood's position that regardless of whether the trial court had jurisdiction to resolve the *antitrust* issues in this case, it clearly had the authority to grant relief under the Thirteenth Amendment and this federal statute.

While the issue of whether baseball's reserve system violated the Thirteenth Amendment constituted a case of first impression for the federal courts, Flood argued that the "total restraint imposed upon the professional ballplayer amounts to nothing other than servitude." The only distinction between the reserve system and servitude is that the player is always free to leave baseball. Flood maintained that this was a distinction without a difference; and that in order to use his skills as a professional baseball player, the player must accept the conditions of slavery. According to Flood, to tell a professional baseball player "that he can purchase his freedom by abandoning his skill is about as helpful as telling another slave that he can buy freedom by cutting off an arm."

Finally, Flood addressed the question raised by some sports columnists and commentators of the day—how

---

[9] 18 U.S.C. § 1584.

could a professional baseball player being paid a $90,000 annual salary be deemed a "slave"?

"...The fact that some baseball players, including Mr. Flood, may earn high salaries scarcely distinguishes the reserve system from involuntary servitude. *Slavery is by definition a restraint on freedom, not a condition of poverty*...A comfortable living may make servitude more bearable. And the master will doubtless try to justify the system—to himself and to others—by pointing out how well he treats his slaves; he deprives them of nothing but freedom and dignity."

Plaintiff's Argument VII—National Labor Policy Does Not Deprive This Court of Jurisdiction of This Litigation

In *Flood v. Kuhn,* the defense was arguing that the trial court should not and, as a matter of law, could not concern itself with baseball's reserve system *because* collective bargaining between the Players' Association and the club owners could indeed modify the reserve system.

Flood cited a number of federal court cases as precedent for his conclusion that collective bargaining does not extinguish individual rights under law. In other words, even though the Players' Association and the club owners were negotiating and were required by law to negotiate in good faith, Flood argued that neither of these circumstances deprived the federal courts of jurisdiction to grant relief to an *individual* whose rights may be violated—even if that individual is a member of a union participating in that collective bargaining.

Defendants' Post-Trial Brief

The presentation of the defendants' post-trial brief was organized and condensed into six major legal arguments.

CHAPTER 23: POST-TRIAL

Perhaps the most compelling portion of defendants' post-trial brief, however, was its preamble. In it, the defense posed two "fundamental questions"—1) who was the real plaintiff in this lawsuit; and 2) what was the role in the litigation of the Major League Baseball Players' Association?

First, the defense focused on the selection of trial counsel, the financial burden of the suit and the execution of trial strategy.

"...Fundamental questions have been posed by the selection and engagement of the attorneys of record and trial counsel for the plaintiff and by the pervasive participation of the Executive Director of the Major League Baseball Players' Association in this action.... The title of this action indicates that the plaintiff is Mr. Flood...and...we have no doubt that the assignment of Mr. Flood's player contract to Philadelphia...can be said to be the immediate cause of this litigation. But...the financial burdens of this litigation are not being borne by Mr. Flood...and it was apparent throughout the trial that the strategy of the plaintiff...was being directed by persons other than Mr. Flood.... This curious relationship...can...be simply explained. *There are two separate actions combined under the caption <u>Flood v. Kuhn, et al.</u>* One is the action by Mr. Flood...to nullify the assignment...and to become a free agent able to negotiate with every major league club. The other 'action'...is the attempt by the Players' Association to "modify" the baseball reserve system *in a manner irrelevant to Mr. Flood's own needs and desires*. Recognition of this dual nature of the plaintiff's case is essential to an understanding...of the proof presented at trial. If that proof often appeared inconsistent and irrelevant to Mr. Flood's claim...it is because the plaintiff's counsel were simultaneously representing two different 'plaintiffs', Mr. Flood and the Players' Association....

Mr. Flood...pleaded that he be permitted to disregard the

terms of his player contract...and to reject the assignment to Philadelphia or any other assignment. He asked that he be given the license to negotiate and play for any of the twenty-four major league clubs....The defendants do not doubt that the destruction of the whole reserve system is precisely what Mr. Flood wants. He does not seek a system of salary arbitration. He did not testify to any salary dispute either with St. Louis or Philadelphia...Neither does he seek a schedule of progressive minimum salary levels, reduction of the number of players reserved by each club, separation of the two leagues, more equal division of revenues among clubs, or abolition of the baseball free agent draft. *But all of these proposals were made, nominally on his behalf.*

The other 'plaintiff', the Players' Association, has goals quite different from Mr. Flood's, goals which it has pursued in collective bargaining *and which it now pursues under the guise of Mr. Flood's action.* These goals...are to obtain...certain modifications to the reserve system which will maintain many aspects of player control, including the right of the clubs to assign player contracts, but which will alter the reserve system in ways which the *Players' Association* deems beneficial. What these modifications might do for Mr. Flood is quite another matter. In fact, once Mr. Flood left the stand, he was entirely forgotten, while Marvin Miller...testified on three separate occasions and was continuously at the counsel table, a place usually reserved for counsel and litigants....

Even the testimony involving some form of free agency, which in theory could be of assistance to Mr. Flood, indicated the necessity for the accomplishment of change on a gradual basis...in order to avoid the creation of 'chaotic conditions'. Where would Mr. Flood fit into this pattern of gradual modification? No one on the plaintiff's side seems to have been in the least concerned about this question....

The defendants submit that Mr. Flood, either intentionally or unwittingly, is acting as a representative or nominal plain-

tiff for the Players' Association, and that much of the evidence adduced at the trial purportedly on his behalf is irrelevant to his grievance, cannot benefit him and has been presented in the wrong forum by the wrong plaintiff."

Clearly, it was the defense's strategy to muddy the waters by presenting its theory that Flood was being used by and was acting as the "alter ego" of Marvin Miller and the Major League Baseball Players' Association. The defense desperately sought to avoid having the Court frame the issue for decision in terms of Curt Flood, an individual and professional baseball player, who, unlike any other professional athlete (as well as any other citizen in any other profession or occupation), was unable *as a matter of law* to seek employment and negotiate with any club other than the club that "owned" him, *for the remainder of his natural life*. As was evident from the trial record, however, and as the defense quite effectively presented in the preamble of its post-trial brief, it was Flood's legal team and the lack of a clear and coherent trial strategy that provided the defense with that opportunity.

Defendants' Argument I—The U.S. Supreme Court Has Already Held That Baseball's Reserve System Is Not Subject To The Federal Antitrust Laws

As expected, the defense argued that controlling precedent and previous decisions of the U.S. Supreme Court mandated a decision in favor of major league baseball. The defense argued that *Federal Baseball* (1922) and *Toolson* (1953) held that the federal antitrust laws do not apply to professional baseball. The defense also argued that subsequent U. S. Supreme Court decisions made it clear that this federal antitrust exemption continues unless and until changed by the Congress. To the extent that there have been changes to baseball's operations and its structure since these court decisions, these changes support, rather than undermine, the continuance of the exemption. The defense maintained that "Congress has given extensive consideration to baseball's status under the antitrust laws, and has repeatedly declined to disturb it." Finally, the defense noted that professional baseball had grown and developed, "and millions of dollars have been invested in reliance on the exemption."

Defendants' Argument II—The Reserve System Falls Within The Protection of National Labor Policy and Is Therefore Exempt From the Sherman Act.

Defendants cited a number of U.S. Supreme Court cases involving an apparent conflict between antitrust laws and policies on the one hand, and labor laws and policies on the other. The defense argued that "federal labor policy places beyond the reach of federal antitrust regulation matters which are mandatory subjects of bargaining, which the reserve system is recognized by all parties to be." The defense maintained that the defendant club owners negotiated in good faith with the Players' Association on many subjects, and made substantial concessions on many issues and matters, including baseball's reserve system. The defense suggested that collective bargaining was the best and most appropriate means of achieving modifications to baseball's reserve system. Even if, as 'plaintiff' argued, it were clear that the club owners were unwilling to bargain on this subject, the *exclusive* remedy would be by way of an unfair labor practice charge filed with the National Labor Relations Board.

Defendants' Argument III—Baseball's Reserve System is Not Subject to State Regulation

The defendants disputed plaintiff's arguments that baseball's operations must also comply with and were subject to various state laws. First, with respect to state antitrust law, defendants cited the Wisconsin Supreme Court's decision in *Wisconsin v. Milwaukee Braves, Inc.,* (1966). According to the defendants, this Wisconsin Supreme Court decision held major league baseball exempt from state antitrust laws because application of such laws would conflict with national policy and would violate the Commerce Clause of the U.S. Constitution by regulating an interstate activity requiring uniformity. Further, defendants maintained that a contrary ruling would subject professional baseball to diverse and inconsistent treatment under differing systems of state regulation which might well destroy its existence.

Defendants also insisted that the same constitutional principle was equally applicable to the plaintiff's claims under state civil rights laws and under state common law. Finally, the defense submitted that federal labor policy and laws also prohibited state regulation of interstate labor relations of major league baseball.

Defendants' Argument IV—Organized Baseball Is a League Joint Venture and its Reserve System is Reasonable and Necessary to Secure the Legitimate Objectives of That Venture

The defense argued that even if organized baseball were subject to the federal antitrust laws, the reserve system's rules and regulations would not constitute a violation of those laws because they are reasonably necessary to organize the game as a league sport, to preserve the competitive balance among the clubs and to preserve the integrity of the game. Further, the defense maintained that the *per se* violation theories which the plaintiff advanced were entirely inapplicable because of the unique requirements of the baseball business as a team and league sport.

Finally, the defense argued that all other professional team sports had reserve systems and player control practices not essentially different from baseball's; and also emphasized that *none* of the modifications proposed by the plaintiff's witnesses satisfied the legitimate purposes of the reserve system *and* offered relief to Flood.

Defendants' Argument V—Plaintiff Flood is Not In a Condition of Peonage or Involuntary Servitude

The defense argued that Plaintiff Flood failed to present *any* evidence to support his claim of peonage and involuntary servitude. Defendants' acknowledged Flood's testimony that "he had no choice of where to work"; but also recalled Flood's admission that he had never been in debt to the St. Louis club, and that he was presently engaged in a photography and portrait business. Citing *Pollack v. Williams* (1944), *Hodges v. United States* (1906) and *Clyatt v. United States* (1904), the defense argued that the crucial elements necessary to establish peonage are *compulsion* and *prior debt.*

"...It can hardly be argued seriously that an employee who has the right to play or refuse to play baseball—to pursue any of his diverse economic interests in St. Louis or anywhere else—is under any compulsion, and the plaintiff has admitted that he never was indebted to the St. Louis club. The plaintiff not only mistakenly characterizes his employment contract as peonage, but also erroneously characterizes his status as 'involuntary servitude'.... Compulsion...is...a *sine qua non* to prove involuntary servitude. But plaintiff's complaint alleges in substance that the requirement of being able to play for only one club constitutes involuntary servitude. The plaintiff has not suggested that he is in any way *compelled* to do anything. No law or statute compels him to play baseball for Philadelphia or any other club. None of the defendants is insisting that the plaintiff must work, nor is there even any indication that

Chapter 23: Post-Trial

anyone would sue him for damages arising out of his failure to play for the Philadelphia club. He has the undoubted right to retire and to enter a different employment outside of the baseball league venture structure....

Since the plaintiff has not demonstrated that he is being *compelled* to perform any services, since he is not being forced by legal sanctions to work off a debt, and since he is perfectly free to change employments, there is no basis in law to his claim that his contract violates the Thirteenth Amendment and statutes enacted pursuant thereto."

Defendants' Argument VI—Plaintiff is Not Entitled to Money Damages

The defendants argued that Flood had an obligation to mitigate his damages and to take reasonable steps to avoid any financial damages which might result from the defendants' allegedly illegal acts; and that Flood failed to fulfill that obligation.

"...The plaintiff refused to accept the offer of the defendant Philadelphia club to play for it during the 1970 season for $90,000 without prejudice to his right to maintain this action. This offer was made before trial and reiterated to the plaintiff at trial.... He thus rejected an opportunity to mitigate damages and is barred from claiming any such damages."

The case was now in the hands of the trial court. Curt Flood, Commissioner Kuhn, the Players' Association, the twenty-four club owners and the sports world would now wait for Judge Cooper to render his decision.

CHAPTER 24
THE DECISION

On Wednesday, August 12, 1970, Judge Irving Ben Cooper issued his written decision in *Flood v. Kuhn, et al.* Prior to addressing the specific claims and legal arguments of the litigants, Cooper discussed some of the relevant history and specifics of baseball's reserve system.

Baseball and the Reserve System

"Baseball is our national pastime and has been so for well over a century.... Organized baseball consists of the twenty-four major league teams which comprise the American and National Leagues and the various tiers of minor leagues which serve principally as training grounds for aspiring players.... All are governed by either the Major League Rules or the corresponding Professional Baseball Rules (applicable to the minor leagues) and are subject to the broad powers of the Commissioner of Baseball.... At the center of this single, unified but stratified organization of baseball leagues is the reserve system, the essence of which has been in force for nearly one hundred years, almost the entire history of organized professional baseball. All teams in organized baseball agree to be bound by and enforce its structure...It is the heart of plaintiff's complaint....

From the standpoint of the professional baseball player, its effect is to deny him throughout his career freedom to choose his employer....

Regardless of whether his entry into organized baseball is through the player draft or as a free agent, he must sign a Uniform Player's Contract, the only form of contract permitted between player and club, which empowers the signing club unilaterally to renew his contract continuously from year to year should he and the club fail to come to terms on a new contract. Once signed he is thereafter forbidden to negotiate toward prospective baseball employment with any club other than the one to whom he is under contract. Thus, the club has a right to his services for as long as it wishes to renew his contract, subject only to his right to retire from baseball....

If it chooses, a club may assign a player's contract to another club without consulting the player or obtaining his consent....If a player refuses to sign his contract and play, as Flood has, he is placed on a Restricted List whereby the club last holding his contract, in this case Philadelphia, retains the exclusive right to negotiate with the player. Only if released does a player become a free agent; he cannot achieve such status by his own choosing....

Plaintiff's witnesses in the main concede that some form of reserve on players is a necessary element of the organization of baseball as a league sport, but contend that the present all-embracing system is needlessly restrictive and offer various alternatives which in their view might loosen the bonds without sacrifice to the game. Plaintiff points to the present experience of other professional sports such as football, basketball and hockey, each of which survives relatively comfortably with a reserve system or organizational structure whose elements to a varying extent offer more freedom of choice and flexibility to its players....

The defendant clubs and Commissioner of Baseball, on the other hand, contend that the restrictions of the present system are reasonable and necessary to preserve the integrity of the game, maintain balanced competition and fan interest, and encourage continued investment in player development; that none of the alternatives suggested by plaintiff would be workable and still satisfy all three of these criteria; and that, upon comparison, baseball with its player safeguards is hardly more restrictive in its reserve system than are the other professional sports....Defendants point to the instability in the early history of baseball and before institution of the reserve system as evidence of the danger to be anticipated from any modification of its substance."

Judge Cooper's discussion of baseball's reserve system included two curious and foretelling references, neither of which would bode well for Curt Flood. Despite the fact that Judge Cooper was presiding over a significant antitrust case involving a major professional sport, he never described the subject at hand as the "industry" or "business" of baseball, but rather as "our national pastime"—a designation which suggested that "our national pastime" was somehow magically entitled to its continued special treatment under the law.

Next, in summarizing the respective positions of the litigants, Judge Cooper distinguished between the plaintiff and "plaintiff's witnesses". More specifically, Judge Cooper pointed out that it was "plaintiff's witnesses" (and not Curt Flood) that had "conceded" that some form of the reserve system on players was a necessary element of organized baseball. Of course, Curt Flood, the Plaintiff, made no such concession.

Again, prior to addressing the legal issues presented, Judge Cooper continued to editorialize on the Court's "impressions", announced his views regarding the necessity of the reserve system, and concluded that negotiations between the Players' Association and the club owners would result in a reserve system satisfactory to all parties.

"Prior to trial, we gained the impression that there was a view, held by many, that baseball's reserve system had occasioned rampant abuse and that it should be abolished. We were struck by the fact however, that the testimony at trial failed to support that criticism; we find no general or widespread disregard of the extremely important position that the player occupies.... *Clearly, the preponderance of credible proof does not favor elimination of the reserve clause. With the sole exception of plaintiff himself,*[10] *it shows that even plaintiff's witnesses do not contend that it is wholly undesirable; in fact they regard substantial portions meritorious.* It lends support to our view...that arbitration or negotiation would extract such troublesome fault as may exist in the present system and, preserving its necessary features, fashion the reserve clause so as to satisfy all parties."

In this passage, Judge Cooper appeared oblivious to the fact that he was presiding over a major trial and that he was charged with deciding serious and significant questions of law based upon the evidence presented at trial. Rather, Judge Cooper's comments suggested that he was presiding over a referendum on the "desirability" or popularity of baseball's reserve system. Quite simply, the issue was whether baseball's reserve system violated those provisions of federal and state law cited by Plaintiff Curt Flood. What difference did it make that one or more of the witnesses contended that the reserve system was "not wholly

---

[10] In a footnote, Judge Cooper referred to the testimony of Jackie Robinson, Hank Greenberg and Bill Veeck.

undesirable"; or that Judge Cooper's personal view was that arbitration or negotiation could "remove some of the troublesome faults of the reserve system"? Baseball's reserve system was either illegal or it was not.

The Federal Antitrust Claims

In this section of the opinion, Judge Cooper reviewed the prior U.S. Supreme Court decisions—*Federal Baseball* (1922) and *Toolson* (1953)—holding professional baseball exempt from federal antitrust regulation. Cooper then reviewed the subsequent U.S. Supreme Court decisions—all of which occurred between 1955 and 1957—which established that *Toolson* was a narrow holding, applicable only to baseball and to no other industry or professional sport. [*U.S. v. Shubert* (1955); *U.S. v. International Boxing Club* (1955); and *Radovich v. National Football League* (1957)]

Prior to announcing the Court's holding on this issue, Judge Cooper noted the July 13, 1970 decision of the Second Circuit for the U.S. Court of Appeals (the same circuit in which the *Flood v. Kuhn* trial court was situated) in *Salerno v. American League of Professional Baseball Clubs*. In entering the Court's ruling against Curt Flood and in favor of major league baseball, Judge Cooper stated as follows:

"...*Salerno* is unquestionably conclusive, at least at this level, of the federal antitrust issues herein.... *Salerno* mandates that Plaintiff's federal antitrust claims be denied. Since baseball remains exempt from the antitrust laws unless and until the Supreme Court or Congress holds to the contrary, we have no basis for proceeding to the underlying question of whether baseball's reserve system would or would not be deemed reasonable if it were in fact subject to antitrust regulation."

Judge Cooper then proceeded to address the remaining issues.

CHAPTER 24: THE DECISION

Labor Antitrust Exemption

It took little time for Judge Cooper to dispose of this issue.

"Despite our firm belief...that these issues can and should be resolved by negotiations between the players and the club owners, we remain in doubt as to whether this matter (baseball's reserve system) stands exempt from the antitrust laws because it is a mandatory subject of collective bargaining....We need not reach this difficult question in light of our disposition that the Supreme Court alone is privileged to overrule *Toolson* and hold baseball subject to the antitrust laws."

State Law Claims

Flood was arguing that baseball's reserve system violated both state statutory and common law. Flood maintained that the defendants could not have it both ways; that if federal antitrust laws did not apply to professional baseball, then state antitrust statutes, state labor statutes, and state common law were applicable. Judge Cooper disagreed.

"Plaintiff would surely be correct if *Toolson* were...based on a supposed absence of interstate commerce. However,...the ground upon which *Toolson* rested was that Congress had no intention to bring baseball within the antitrust laws, not that baseball's activities did not sufficiently affect interstate commerce....

As interstate commerce, baseball is subject to regulation by Congress.... It is not for this Court to write off *Toolson* as an anomaly. Its rationale must be given effect. We believe it unlikely that the Supreme Court would have held...that 'Congress had no intention of including the business of baseball within the scope of the *federal* antitrust laws,' if it considered baseball vulnerable to *state* regulation. Enforcement of such state laws would appear to produce a result inconsistent with the objective of the federal antitrust laws interpreted by the Supreme Court as excluding the business of baseball....

We do not believe that the operation of baseball and its reserve system is a matter which admits of diversity of treatment.... As we see it, application of various and diverse state laws here would seriously interfere with league play and the operation of organized baseball.... Accordingly, plaintiff's state law claims, common law and statutory alike, must be denied...."

Involuntary Servitude Claims

Flood's fourth cause of action asserted that baseball's reserve system violated the Thirteenth Amendment and its enforcing legislation which similarly prohibited holding any person to "involuntary servitude." After reviewing several U.S. Supreme and Appellate Court cases [*Pollock v. Williams* (1944), *Hodges v. U. S.* (1906) and *Wicks v. Southern Pacific Co.* (1956)], Judge Cooper found that a showing of *compulsion* was a prerequisite to proof of involuntary servitude.

In ruling for the defendants and against Flood on these claims, Judge Cooper concluded as follows:

"...Concededly, plaintiff is not compelled by law or statute to play baseball for Philadelphia. We recognize that, under the existing rules of baseball, by refusing to report to Philadelphia plaintiff is by his own act foreclosing himself from continuing a professional baseball career, a consequence to be deplored. Nevertheless, he has a right to retire and to embark upon a different enterprise outside of organized baseball. The financial loss he might thus sustain may affect his choice, but does not leave him with 'no way to

Chapter 24: The Decision

avoid continued service'.... Accordingly, we find that plaintiff has not satisfied the essential element of this cause of action, a showing of compulsory service."

Having announced the ruling of the Court on each of Flood's claims, Judge Cooper simply could not resist the temptation to once again "preach" his gospel to the congregation. At the outset, Preacher Cooper was desirous of "unburdening himself" and would now convey to his flock several of his deep "convictions". In order to fully appreciate the depth of the Court's insolence and its condescending tone, a close reading of Judge Cooper's concluding remarks is essential. It reads as follows:

"Before concluding this opinion, we wish to unburden ourselves of two strong and related convictions which we took away from this trial. First, despite the opposing positions of plaintiff and the Major League Baseball Players' Association on the one hand, the present management and club owners of organized baseball on the other, we found the witnesses appearing on behalf of both sides in the main credible and of high order; they have a genuine enthusiasm for baseball and with constancy have the best interests of the game at heart.... Second, we are convinced that *the conflicts between the parties are not irreconcilable and that negotiations could produce an accommodation on the reserve system which would be eminently fair and equitable* to all concerned—in essence, what is called for here is continuity with change.

This issue is not unique or complex and *the parties* are not at such loggerheads that negotiations could not succeed.... Trial testimony developed several proposed modifications that could serve as bases from which negotiations might proceed toward an accommodation of the valid interests of both sides.... *Plaintiff's witnesses* expressed a belief that *this matter* was capable of being resolved by good faith bargaining between the parties. Thus, Mr. [Marvin] Miller...recited the various modifications suggested by the players and declared a continuing desire to resolve this dispute.

The Major League Baseball Players' Association, organized in 1954, has proved a particularly effective bargaining representative obtaining since 1966 highly significant benefits for the players in such areas as pensions, life and disability insurance, health care, minimum salary, arbitration of grievances, expense allowances, maximum permissible salary cut, termination pay, representation at individual salary negotiations, negotiation of rule changes affecting player benefits or obligations, due process in player discipline....Both management and the Players' Association recognize the reserve system to be a mandatory subject of collective bargaining. The National Labor Relations Board asserted jurisdiction over organized baseball in December, 1969."

This passage from Judge Cooper's sermon clearly reveals that the defense had succeeded in convincing the Court that there were indeed two separate and distinct 'plaintiffs'—Curt Flood and the Major League Baseball Players' Association; and that the "real party" was the Players' Association, and not Curt Flood. The "issues" and "the conflicts" and "the parties" to which Judge Cooper is here referring, of course, pertain to the negotiations and the proposals to modify baseball's reserve system between *the union* and the *club owners*. Which of the proposed modifications, even if agreed to and adopted, would have resulted in Curt Flood being declared a free agent; and which modifications would have allowed him to negotiate a contract with a team of his choice and play professional baseball in 1970? The answer? None. It was as if Curt Flood, the Plaintiff, was invisible, and that *his* issues were nonexistent.

Judge Cooper continued as follows:

Chapter 24: The Decision

"The history of negotiations to date does not appear to us to establish, as plaintiff appears to contend, that organized baseball refuses to bargain with regard to the reserve system and will accept no modification of its structure unless forced to do so by the courts or by Congress. In the first place, several of the benefits mentioned above are directed at alleviating some of the undesirable side effects of the reserve system. Moreover, serious negotiations aimed at the core of this system are of quite recent origin and the failure to reach a quick accord should not be seen, in our opinion, as indicating intransigence on either or both sides.

While it is true the owners have continued to support the status quo of the reserve system and have been critical of the various proposals by the Players' Association for its elimination or modification, they have not closed the door entirely on various suggestions made during negotiations in the immediate past in efforts to ameliorate the objectionable features of the reserve clause. Indeed, Commissioner Kuhn in his testimony at this trial indicated that, 'changes that could be made are changes that are best bargained out between parties that are involved here....

In such matters as labor relations and family disputes, to name just two, Congress (in the case of collective bargaining) and the courts have determined that such disputes as do arise therein are best resolved by the parties without outside interference and that resort to a court imposed solution should be a matter of last resort. This is almost invariably the case whenever two parties must continue to work together amicably toward a common end after the dispute is settled. This is not to hold that the court should adopt a similar hands-off approach toward this case. Nevertheless, we believe that here, as well, the parties themselves are best able to reach a satisfactory accord, and that all avenues toward such an approach certainly have not yet been fully exhausted.

From the trial record and the sense of fair play demonstrated in the main by the witnesses on both sides, *we are convinced that the reserve clause can be fashioned so as to find acceptance by player and club.*

Far more complicated matters accompanied by an exclusive self-centered concern and by seemingly hostile and irreconcilable attitudes, frequently find their way to amicable adjustment and the abandonment of court claims. Why not here—with the parties positive and reasonable men who are equally watchful over a common objective, the best interests of baseball?...

For the first time in almost fifty years opponents and proponents of the baseball reserve system have had to make their case on the merits and support it with proof in a court of law. As a long line of litigation and congressional inquiry attests, this system has often been a center of controversy and a source of friction between player and club. *Existing and, as we see it, controlling law renders unnecessary any determination as to the fairness or reasonableness of this reserve system. We are bound by the law as we find it and by our obligation to 'call it as we see it'."*

Judge Cooper, like any other trial court judge, had a responsibility to determine the facts, apply the law to those facts, and to determine the rights of the parties under the applicable law. Rather than doing so, Judge Cooper appeared to be delivering a lecture or writing an editorial on the merits and utility of settlement negotiations between the union (a non party to the suit) and the club owners. With respect to Flood's antitrust claims, however, the Court failed to articulate any legal basis for its decision and refused to give any rational explanation as to *how* or *why* professional *baseball* was distinguishable from professional ice hockey, boxing, and football, and how, therefore, baseball's reserve system neither violated nor was subject to

CHAPTER 24: THE DECISION

the same federal antitrust laws. In short, Judge Cooper conveniently held that it was up to Congress to pass a statute, or alternatively, up to the U.S. Supreme Court to overrule *Toolson*.

The plight of Curtis Charles Flood was virtually ignored by the Court. It was as if the Court, in the most pompous and patronizing tone imaginable, told Flood, "Go away, Sonny! Don't bother me."

Chapter 25
The Appeal

To escape the relentless news media following Judge Cooper's ruling, Flood embarked on a plane headed for Copenhagen, a location which he had frequently visited. On August 24, 1970, Flood's lawyers filed his appeal in the U.S. Court of Appeals for the Second Circuit. Just six weeks prior, this same Court of Appeals ruled in *Salerno v. American League* that only the U.S. Supreme Court could reconsider whether federal antitrust laws applied to professional baseball. Barring the occurrence of a miracle, Flood and his lawyers knew the Second Circuit would affirm the decision of Judge Cooper, and that the Court of Appeals would be merely a temporary stop on the way to the U.S. Supreme Court. In addition to the ruling itself, what would be lost, of course, was more valuable time.

While major litigation generally moves slowly and is frequently subject to significant delays (or as the lawyers say, "continuances"), the *Flood v. Kuhn* case, on the other hand, moved through the Appellate Court remarkably quickly. The written briefs were filed in November and December of 1970, and oral arguments were heard by the Appellate Court on January 27, 1971.

CHAPTER 25: THE APPEAL

In November 1970, while the case was pending before the Appellate Court, Bob Short, owner of the Washington Senators, negotiated with and bought Flood's contract from the Phillies. If Flood accepted an offer and played for the Senators, however, it would not be without incurring some significant risks to his lawsuit. By playing professional baseball with the Senators (or any other major league team at that time), Flood would be performing professional services pursuant to and within the very same reserve system that he was simultaneously seeking to have the federal courts declare illegal. In lawyers' jargon, by playing for the Senators under these circumstances, it was conceivable that Flood's case would be declared "moot", or in other words, his dispute with major league baseball may no longer be deemed a real case or controversy and, therefore, unnecessary for the courts to decide.

After some lengthy discussions among Flood's lawyers and the lawyers for all of the defendants, a written agreement was entered into pursuant to which all of the defendants agreed *not* to assert that Flood playing for the Senators would "moot" Flood's case. In his book *A Whole Different Ball Game*, Marvin Miller correctly pointed out that despite this agreement among the parties, Flood's actions remained risky.

"...It worried me a bit because an agreement between parties cannot bind a court—that is, a judge was free to interpret Flood's actions in his own manner. Still, Curt wanted to play—he certainly needed the money by now. He didn't talk about, but I think some of his personal obligations, such as child support payments, were weighing heavily on him."

Despite the risks, Bob Short offered and Flood accepted a contract to play for the Senators in the 1971 season for

$110,000. Flood's comeback in 1971, however, did not include a story book ending. After only thirteen games and a .200 batting average (7 hits for 35 at bats), Curt Flood's professional baseball career finally concluded. At that time, it was reported that Flood was unable to maintain his portrait and photography businesses in St. Louis, and that Flood was in dire financial straits. During his short stint with the Senators, Flood was also the recipient of a letter—delivered to his club house locker—threatening his life. Also, Flood and then Senators' manager, Ted Williams, reportedly clashed on occasion. In an interview, Flood's then teammate and 1968 American League Cy Young Award winner, Denny McClain, claimed that the Senators' manager "never gave Curt the respect he deserved", and that it was the Flood-Williams conflict that was the proverbial straw that broke the camel's back.

Whether it was one or a combination of these and other circumstances, Flood's final telegram to Senators' owner Bob Short read as follows:

"I tried, a year and a half is too much. Very serious problems mounting every day. Thank you for your confidence and understanding."

On April 7, 1971, the Court of Appeals entered its ruling in *Flood v. Kuhn.* It would only take the time to read the first full paragraph of the opinion for Flood and his lawyers to know the outcome.

"...For the reasons stated below, we are compelled to affirm the district court's decision."

Despite the Appellate Court's ruling against Flood, the apologetic tone of Justice Sterry R. Waterman's opinion also included a healthy dose of self criticism and doubt. With respect to Flood's *federal* antitrust claims, the court openly acknowledged a lack of consistency and logic.

"...Although faced with the seemingly inconsistent decisions in *Toolson* and *Radovich* [professional football], our court only last summer refused, in *Salerno v. American League*..., to depart from the Supreme Court's holding in *Toolson*...."

Relying upon and quoting from its own decision in *Salerno*, the Appellate Court attempted to explain the incomprehensible.

"We freely acknowledge our belief that *Federal Baseball* was not one of Mr. Justice Holmes' happiest days, that the rationale of *Toolson* is extremely dubious and that, *to use the Supreme Court's own adjectives, the distinction between baseball and other professional sports is 'unrealistic,' 'inconsistent,' and 'illogical'*....However,...we continue to believe that the Supreme Court should retain the exclusive privilege of overruling its own decisions, save perhaps when opinions already delivered have created a near certainty that only the occasion is needed for pronouncement of the doom. While we should not fall out of chairs with surprise at the news that *Federal Baseball* and *Toolson* had been overruled, we are not at all certain the Court is ready to give them a happy despatch."

Regarding Flood's *state* antitrust and state common law claims, the Appellate Court somehow attempted to blame Flood's "predicament" upon the "vagaries of fate."

"...We readily acknowledge that plaintiff is caught in a most frustrating predicament, a predicament which defendants have zealously seized upon with great perspicacity.

On the one hand, the doctrine of stare decisis[11] *binds the plaintiff because of an initial holding that baseball is not 'interstate commerce' within the Sherman Act, and, on the other hand, after there have been significant changes in the definition of 'interstate commerce,' he is now told that baseball is so uniquely interstate commerce that state regulation cannot apply....*However, in our own defense, we do not consider our decision to be internally inconsistent. In disposing of the Sherman Act count in plaintiff's complaint, we are bound by Supreme Court decision, while in our disposition of the state common law counts, we must of necessity decide this question of first impression by present Commerce Clause standards and not the standards applicable in 1922. *Any apparent inconsistency results not from faulty logic, but from the vagaries of fate and this court's subordinate role to the Supreme Court."*

Finally, the Appellate Court affirmed Judge Cooper's rejection of Flood's "involuntary servitude" claim.

"...Inasmuch as a plaintiff retains the option not to play baseball at all, his Thirteenth Amendment argument is foreclosed by this court's decision in *U.S. v. Schackney*,...a decision which we adhere to as sound."

In contrast to the conciliatory tenor of the Appellate Court's opinion (authored by Justice Waterman), the separate but concurring opinion of Justice Leonard P. Moore is aptly described as yet another tribute to our American "heroes" and "Hall of Famers," to the "majesty" of "our

---

[11] The Latin term *stare decisis* means "to abide by or adhere to decided cases". When a court has laid down a principle of law applicable to a certain set of facts, the courts, under the doctrine of *stare decisis*, will adhere to that principle and apply it to all future cases where the facts are substantially the same.

CHAPTER 25: THE APPEAL

national sport" and to the "kingdom of baseball."

"Baseball for almost a century has been *our country's 'national sport.'* Every decade...has developed outstanding players, *heroes in the hearts and minds of millions of Americans—heroes whose names are enshrined in a baseball 'Hall of Fame.'* In this century alone, the names of such players as Christy Mathewson, Walter Johnson...Ty Cobb, Babe Ruth...Lou Gehrig...Ted Williams and Willie Mays were probably better known to a great number of our populace than many of our statesmen; and their exploits better remembered than the activities of our outstanding public figures....In short, *organized baseball existed almost as an enclave or feudal barony throughout the years*, managing its own affairs as best calculated to preserve the sport and maintaining its own officialdom for self-regulation purposes—and, except for the brief scandal of the so-called Chicago Black Sox of 1919, apparently *has handled its little kingdom and its subjects very well.*"

Incredibly, it was as if Justice Moore was articulating the policy and rationale for a well established and long standing federal antitrust exemption for "enclaves and feudal baronies!"

Justice Moore's insightful commentary did not end there. While the Appellate Court's opinion expressly contemplated the possibility that the U.S. Supreme Court would overrule *Toolson* and *Federal Baseball,* Justice Moore's concurring opinion expressed a distinctly different view. Apparently with the aid of his crystal ball, and with the arrogance rivaled only by that Judge Cooper, Justice Moore announced that there was "no likelihood" that the Supreme Court would overrule *Toolson*, and emphatically and pompously declared that professional baseball must continue to remain beyond the reach of the federal courts!

"...In my opinion *there is no likelihood that such an event will occur.* As I analyze the history of organized professional baseball over the last 50 years, it has shown without Court interference remarkable stability under self-discipline. The Supreme Court in 1922 undoubtedly felt that it should adopt a 'hands off' policy as to this one particular sport *which had attained by then such a national standing that only Congress should have the power to tamper with it.* And properly so. *Baseball's welfare and future should not be for politically insulated interpreters of technical antitrust statutes* but rather should be for the voters through their elected representatives. If baseball is to be damaged by statutory regulation, let the congressman face his constituents the next November and also face the consequences of his baseball voting record.... Therefore, without any reservations or doubts as to the soundness of *Federal Baseball* and *Toolson*, I would affirm the decision below...and would *limit the participation of the courts in the conduct of baseball's affairs* to the throwing out by the Chief Justice (in the absence of the President) of the first ball of the baseball season."

The fate of Curt Flood and his lawsuit now rested with the Supreme Court of the United States.

CHAPTER 26
THE UNITED STATES SUPREME COURT

On October 19, 1971, the U.S. Supreme Court issued its order granting Flood's request that the nation's highest court review his case. Just two days earlier, the Pittsburgh Pirates won the 1971 World Series by defeating the Baltimore Orioles in seven games. Also by that time, Flood remained in his self-imposed exile on the Mediterranean island of Mallorca off the coast of Spain. It was there that Flood painted, operated a café and bar, and drank waiting for news of the Supreme Court's decision.

The legal briefs were filed by the parties in December 1971 and January 1972. The quality of the legal writing and arguments were again outstanding. On March 20, 1972, oral arguments in *Flood v. Kuhn* were presented before the U.S. Supreme Court in Washington, D.C. At the trial two years prior, it was Arthur Goldberg who handled much of trial's early proceedings and who presented Flood and the case's first few witnesses. Thereafter, Goldberg appeared only intermittently during the remainder of the trial. The reason for his sporadic attendance at trial during the spring of 1970 was that Goldberg, despite assurances to the contrary, was running in the Democratic primary for Governor of New York. Goldberg won the Democratic nomination, but lost in the general election in November 1970 to Governor Nelson Rockefeller. Now, nearly two years later, it was Goldberg who would handle the oral argument before the U.S. Supreme Court for and on behalf of Curt Flood.

It is noteworthy that at least two accounts concerning the quality of Goldberg's presentation before the Supreme Court suggest that it was not one of Goldberg's better days. In *The Brethren*, authors Scott Armstrong and Bob Woodward wrote the following:

"Oral arguments failed to clarify the issues. Former Justice Arthur Goldberg, in his first appearance before the Court since resigning in 1965 to become Ambassador to the United Nations, had offered such a poor presentation of Flood's case that his former colleagues were embarrassed."

Almost twenty years later, in *A Whole Different Ball Game,* Marvin Miller recalled it this way:

"More important, whether because of the distraction of a political campaign, or the reaction to a stunning defeat by Governor Rockefeller, or some other reason, Goldberg, according to all qualified observers, performed way below his ability in arguing the Flood case before the Supreme Court. In retrospect, I realize it would have been better if Topkis had argued the case all the way through."

Almost three months later, on June 19, 1972, the U.S. Supreme Court announced its ruling in *Flood v. Kuhn*. Justice Harry Blackmun authored the majority opinion. Blackmun was appointed to the Supreme Court by President Richard Nixon on June 9, 1970—ironically, just one day before the end of the *Flood v. Kuhn* trial. It would be an understatement of colossal proportion to say that Justice

Blackmun was an avid baseball fan. Incredibly similar in tone and substance to Justice Moore's concurring opinion in the Second Circuit, Part I of Blackman's opinion was an "ode" to baseball, invoking the names of no less than eighty baseball greats, as well as a reference to "Casey at the Bat"! (Part I of the Court's opinion provoked such a reaction among the Court that even two of the Justices who voted with the majority—Justice Byron White and Chief Justice Warren Burger—refused to concur in Part I of the decision.)

The following excerpts from Part I reveal the depth of Justice Blackmun's fascination with the "game" of baseball—and our "national pastime".

"I. The Game

It is a century and a quarter since the New York Nine defeated the Knickerbockers 23 to 1 on Hoboken's Elysian Fields June 19, 1846....The Cincinnati Red Stockings came into existence in 1869 upon an outpouring of local pride.... [I]n 1871, the National Association of Professional Baseball Players was founded and the professional league was born....The ensuing colorful days are well known. The ardent follower and the student of baseball know of General Abner Doubleday; the formation of the National League in 1876; the formation of the American League...in the 1880s; the introduction of Sunday baseball; interleague warfare...and player raiding; the development of the reserve 'clause';...the first World Series in 1903...the troublesome and discouraging episode of the 1919 series; the home run ball; the shifting of franchises; the expansion of the leagues; the installation in 1965 of the major league draft of potential new players; and the formation of the Major League Baseball Players' Association in 1966.

Then there are the many names, celebrated for one reason or another, that have sparked the diamond and its environs and that have provided tinder for recaptured thrills, for reminiscence and comparisons, and for conversations and anticipation in-season and off-season: Ty Cobb, Babe Ruth...Walter Johnson...Lou Gehrig...Rogers Hornsby...Jackie Robinson...Satchel Paige...Connie Mack...Cy Young...Roy Campanella...Bill Dickey...George Sisler...Hank Greenberg...Bill Terry, Carl Hubbell...Jimmy Foxx.... The list seems endless.

And one recalls the appropriate reference to the 'World Serious,' attributed to Ring Lardner, Sr.; Ernest L. Thayer's 'Casey at the Bat';...and all the other happenings, habits, and superstitions about and around baseball that made it the 'national pastime'...."

In Part II of the opinion, Justice Blackmun recited in detail the facts of the case and Flood's trade to the Phillies; described baseball's reserve system; and outlined each of Flood's legal arguments and challenges. Part III analyzed the relevant portions of both Judge Cooper's decision as well as the holdings and conclusions of the Appellate Court.

In Part IV, Blackmun discussed at great length the chronology and holdings of each of the 'landmark' federal court decision including *Federal Baseball, Toolson, Radovich, Shubert, International Boxing* and *Salerno.* Finally, Blackmun referenced Congressional action and its consideration of approximately fifty bills since *Toolson* was decided in 1953. Remarkably, Blackmun suggested that because some but not all of these bills *would have expanded* the antitrust exemption to other professional sports, *and because* Congress *failed to pass* any of these 50 bills introduced since *Toolson*, that Congress was thereby expressing its intent to acquiesce in the Supreme Court's holdings in *Toolson* and *Radovich* — and in continuing to restrict the federal antitrust exemption to, and only to, professional baseball.

CHAPTER 26: THE UNITED STATES SUPREME COURT

In a five-to-three decision, the U.S. Supreme Court ruled in favor of professional baseball and against Curt Flood. The Court's majority consisted of Justices Blackmun, Potter Stewart, William Rehnquist, Byron White and Chief Justice Warren Burger. (Due to his ownership in some shares of stock in Anheuser-Busch, the corporate owner of the St. Louis Cardinals, one of the named defendants in the suit, Justice Lewis Powell recused himself and took no part in the Court's consideration of the case).

It was in Part V of the opinion that Blackmun explained the Court's rationale and announced the Court's decision.

"In view of all of this, it seems appropriate now to say that:
1. Professional baseball is a business and it is engaged in interstate commerce.
2. With its reserve system enjoying exemption from the federal antitrust laws, baseball is, in a very distinct sense, an exception and an anomaly. *Federal Baseball* and *Toolson* have become an aberration confined to baseball.
3. Even though others might regard this as 'unrealistic, inconsistent or illogical',...the aberration is an established one, and one that has been recognized not only in *Federal Baseball* and *Toolson,* but in *Shubert, International Boxing* and *Radovich,* as well, a total of five consecutive cases in this Court. It is an aberration that has been with us now for half a century, one heretofore deemed fully entitled to the benefit of stare decisis, and one that has survived the Court's expanding concept of interstate commerce. It rests on a recognition and an acceptance of baseball's unique characteristics and needs.
4. Other professional sports operating interstate—football, boxing, basketball, and, presumably, hockey and golf—are not so exempt.
5. The advent of radio and television, with their consequent increased coverage and additional revenues, has not

occasioned an overruling of *Federal Baseball* and *Toolson*.

6. The Court has emphasized that since 1922, baseball, with full and continuing congressional awareness, has been allowed to develop and to expand unhindered by federal legislative action. Remedial legislation has been introduced repeatedly in Congress but none has ever been enacted. The Court, accordingly, has concluded that Congress as yet has had no intention to subject baseball's reserve system to the reach of the antitrust statutes. This, obviously, has been deemed to be something other than mere congressional silence and passivity....

7. The Court has expressed concern about the confusion and the retroactivity problems that inevitably would result with a judicial overturning of *Federal Baseball*. It has voiced a preference that if any change is to be made, it come by legislative action that, by its nature, is only prospective in operation.

8. The Court noted in *Radovich*...that the slate with respect to baseball is not clean. Indeed, it has not been clean for half a century.

This emphasis and this concern are still with us. We continue to be loath, 50 years after *Federal Baseball* and almost two decades after *Toolson,* to overturn those cases judicially when Congress, by it positive inaction, has allowed those decisions to stand for so long and, far beyond mere inference and implication, has clearly evinced a desire not to disapprove them legislatively.

Accordingly, we adhere once again to *Federal Baseball* and *Toolson* and to their application to professional baseball. We adhere also to *International Boxing* and *Radovich* and to their respective applications to professional boxing and professional football. If there is any inconsistency or illogic in all this, it is an inconsistency and illogic of long standing that is to be remedied by the Congress and not by this Court. If we were to act otherwise, we would be withdrawing from the conclusion as to congressional intent made in *Toolson* and from the concerns as to retrospectivity therein expressed. *Under these circumstances, there is merit in consistency even though some might claim that beneath that consistency is a layer of inconsistency."*

(It is seriously doubtful that Blackmun could have successfully explained the meaning of this last sentence—even to himself!)

Upon closer review of the high Court's rationale, Blackmun conceded the "inconsistent" and "illogical" result of exempting professional baseball (and no other professional sport or the entertainment industry) from federal antitrust regulation. Blackmun's attempt to justify this long standing "aberration" is based upon "a *recognition* and an *acceptance* of baseball's *unique characteristics* and *needs*". *Whose* recognition? *Whose* acceptance? Which *unique characteristics*? What *needs*? On this point, the silence was deafening.

In rejecting Flood's *state* law claims, and in affirming both lower courts, Blackmun opined that:

"...*state antitrust regulation would conflict with federal policy* and [that] *national 'uniformity'* [is required] in any regulation of baseball and its reserve system.... As the burden on interstate commerce outweighs the states' interests in regulating baseball's reserve system, the Commerce Clause [of the U.S. Constitution] precludes the application here of state antitrust law.... As applied to organized baseball...these statements adequately dispose of the state law claims...."

In sidestepping the issue of whether the reserve system was, under federal law, a mandatory subject of collective bargaining, Blackmun wrote:

"The conclusion we reached *makes it unnecessary for us to consider* the [defendant's]...argument that the reserve system is a mandatory subject of collective bargaining and that federal labor policy therefore exempts the reserve system from...federal antitrust laws."

Blackmun's final paragraph and summation of the case continued to lay this "aberration" and "anomaly" at the doorstep of Congress. Quoting from *Federal Baseball* and specifically relying upon *Toolson*, Blackmun concluded as follows:

"Without re-examination of the underlying issues, the [judgment] below [is] affirmed on the authority of *Federal Baseball*...so far as that decision determines that *Congress had no intention of including the business of baseball within the scope of the federal antitrust laws*. And what the Court said in *Federal Baseball* in 1922 and what it said in *Toolson* in 1953, we say again here in 1972; *the remedy, if any is indicated, is for congressional, and not judicial, action.*

The judgment of the Court of Appeals is Affirmed."

Chief Justice Warren Burger voted with the majority of the Court, and filed a brief concurring opinion.

"I...like Mr. Justice Douglas,...have grave reservations as to the correctness of *Toolson*.... The error, if such it be, is one on which the affairs of a great many people have rested for a long time. *Courts are not the forum* in which this tangled web ought to be unsnarled. I agree with Mr. Justice Douglas that *Congressional inaction* is not a solid base, but the least undesirable course now is to let the matter rest with Congress; it is time *the Congress acted* to solve this problem."

(Clearly in the category of useless trivia, it should be noted that, perhaps coincidentally, the Chief Justice's concurring opinion included the use of three baseball terms: "error," "web" and "base.")

While the Supreme Court's majority did not and could

not cite a rational policy basis for reaffirming *Toolson* and *Federal Baseball*, and despite the fact that it was the Supreme Court (and not Congress) that created what Burger called "the problem," the Court's majority concluded that it nevertheless was up to Congress (and not the Supreme Court) to "solve the problem." Not only was the Supreme Court *not* going to decide Curt Flood's case on the merits of his claims; and not only was the Supreme Court *not* going to provide any remedy; the Court's majority effectively told Flood that after almost three years of litigation, he was not even in the right forum to seek relief, and that Flood needed to seek redress, if any, before the Congress of the United States!

The Dissent

Justice William O. Douglas and Justice Thurgood Marshall filed separate dissenting opinions. Justice William J. Brennan concurred in both of those opinions. By 1972, Justice Douglas had been a thirty-three-year member of the Supreme Court having been appointed to the Court in 1939 by President Franklin Roosevelt. Douglas was a member of the Supreme Court when *Toolson* was decided in 1953. At the outset of his dissenting opinion, Douglas noted that while he had joined in the Court's opinion in *Toolson*, he had "lived to regret it"; and "would now correct what I believe to be its fundamental error."

Douglas's dissent was clear and concise. The first subjects of his discourse were *Federal Baseball* and the legal concept of "commerce".

"This Court's decision in *Federal Baseball*..., made in 1922, is a derelict in the stream of the law that we, its creator, should remove.... In 1922, the Court had a narrow, parochial view of commerce.... Under modern decisions..., the power of Congress was recognized as broad enough to reach all phases of the vast operations of our national industrial system. An industry so dependent on radio and television as is baseball and gleaning vast interstate revenues would be hard put today to say with the Court in...*Federal Baseball*...that baseball was only a local exhibition, not trade or commerce. Baseball is today big business that is packaged with beer, with broadcasting, and with other industries...."

Douglas then addressed what he called "predatory practices" and the "victims of the reserve clause."

"The owners, whose record many say reveal a proclivity for predatory practices, do not come to us with equities. The equities are with the victims of the reserve clause. I use the word "victims" in the Sherman Act sense, *since a contract which forbids anyone to practice his calling is commonly called an unreasonable restraint of trade.*"

Finally, Douglas challenged the majority's conclusion that "by its positive inaction" and allowing *Federal Baseball* and *Toolson* to stand for so long, Congress was clearly evincing a desire and its intent *not to disapprove* of those decisions by legislation.

"If Congressional *inaction* is our guide, we should rely upon the fact that Congress has *refused* to enact bills broadly *exempting professional sports from antitrust regulation*.... The only statutory exemption granted by Congress to professional sports concerns broadcasting rights,...I would not ascribe a broader exemption *through inaction* than Congress *has seen fit to grant explicitly.*

There can be no doubt that *were we considering the question of baseball for the first time* upon a clean slate, *we would hold it to be subject to federal antitrust regulation*....The

CHAPTER 26: THE UNITED STATES SUPREME COURT

unbroken silence of Congress should not prevent us from correcting our own mistakes."

The dissenting opinion authored by Justice Thurgood Marshall also challenged the majority's reasoning and conclusions. Justice Marshall was the first black American in U.S. history to serve on the Supreme Court. Just five years earlier, Marshall was appointed to the nation's highest court by President Lyndon B. Johnson. Prior to his appointment to the Supreme Court, Marshall's distinguished career included his service as Chief Counsel for the NAACP; the successful challenge of racially restrictive covenants in real estate in the landmark case of *Shelley v. Kramer* (1948); and the successful challenge to racially segregated schools in another landmark decision, *Brown v. Board of Education* (1954).

After summarizing the essential facts and claims in *Flood v. Kuhn*, Marshall described the restrictions of baseball's reserve system in the context of the Thirteenth Amendment.

"...After receiving formal notification of the trade, [Flood] wrote to the Commissioner...protesting that he was not 'a piece of property to be bought and sold irrespective of my wishes' and urging that he had the right to consider offers from teams other than the Phillies....His request was denied,...and...[Flood] was informed that he had no choice but to play for Philadelphia or not to play at all.

To non-athletes, it might appear that petitioner was virtually enslaved by the owners of major league baseball clubs who bartered among themselves for his services. But, athletes know that it was not servitude that bound petitioner to the club owners; it was the reserve system. The essence of that system is that a player is bound to the club with which he first signs a contract for the rest of his playing days. He cannot escape from the club except by retiring, and he cannot prevent the club from assigning his contract to any other club...."

It was in a footnote on the first page of his dissent that Marshall succinctly announced "his ruling" in *Flood v. Kuhn*.

"Petitioner...alleged, among other things, that the reserve system was an unreasonable restraint of trade in violation of federal antitrust laws.... Petitioner also alleged a violation of state antitrust laws, state civil rights laws, and of common law, and claimed that he was forced into peonage and involuntary servitude in violation of the Thirteenth Amendment to the United States Constitution. *Because I believe that federal antitrust laws govern baseball, I find that state law has been preempted in this area. Like the lower courts, I do not believe that there has been a violation of the Thirteenth Amendment.*"

(It was argued by the defense that Flood had failed to assert the "involuntary servitude" claim in its brief filed with the Supreme Court, and that accordingly, Flood had "waived" or "abandoned" that particular claim. It is interesting to note that Blackmun's opinion for the Court's majority failed to specifically *rule upon* Flood's "involuntary servitude" claims.)

Marshall's opinion then addressed the doctrine of *stare decisis*, the issue of interstate commerce and the Supreme Court's prior decisions regarding the applicability of federal antitrust regulation to professional sports and entertainment.

"...This is a difficult case because we are torn between the principle of *stare decisis* and the knowledge that the decisions in *Federal Baseball*...and *Toolson*... are totally at odds with more recent and better reasoned cases....

Much...time has passed since *Toolson* and Congress has not acted. We must now decide whether to adhere to the reasoning of *Toolson*—i.e., to refuse to reexamine the underlying bases of *Federal Baseball*—or to proceed with a re-examination and let the chips fall where they may.

In his answer to [Flood's] complaint, the *Commissioner of Baseball 'admits that under present concepts of interstate commerce defendants are engaged therein.'*...There can be no doubt that the admission is warranted by today's reality. *Since baseball is interstate commerce,* if we re-examine baseball's antitrust exemption, *the Court's decisions in Shubert...International Boxing...and Radovich...require that we bring baseball within the coverage of the antitrust laws."*

Marshall then expanded upon the direct linkage between the enforcement of antitrust laws and the protection of our fundamental personal freedoms. More specifically, Marshall opined that the antitrust laws were as important to professional baseball players as they were to all other professional athletes and entertainers—and that the Court's prior decisions had "isolated" professional baseball players and "made them impotent". Marshall quoted from another 1972 Supreme Court antitrust decision, *U.S. v. Topco Associates, Inc.*:

"Antitrust laws in general, and the Sherman Act in particular, are the Magna Carta of free enterprise. They are as important to the preservation of economic freedom and our free-enterprise system as the Bill of Rights is to the protection of our fundamental personal freedoms.... Implicit in such freedom is the notion that it cannot be foreclosed with respect to one sector of the economy because certain private citizens or groups believe that such foreclosure might promote greater competition in a more important sector of the economy....

The importance of the antitrust laws to every citizen must not be minimized. They are as important to baseball players as they are to football players, lawyers, doctors, or members of any other class of workers. *Baseball players cannot be denied the benefits of competition merely because club owners view other economic interests as being more important,* unless Congress says so."

Marshall had just described the case's fundamental issue from the player's perspective, and in terms of the individual player's *personal* freedom and *economic* freedom. Morever, and not unwittingly, Marshall had just framed one of Flood's core arguments as akin to an "equal protection" issue.

Generally, in the event the law "classifies" or "discriminates" between groups of individuals, the equal protection doctrine requires a showing that the distinction made by the law bears some rational relationship to a legitimate governmental purpose. As it related to Curt Flood, Marshall pointed out that under the federal antitrust laws (and in particular, the Sherman Act), there were two classes: 1) professional baseball players, and 2) all other professional athletes and other classes of workers. Therefore, applying Marshall's analysis, because the members of the second class enjoyed the protection of the federal antitrust laws, and because Curt Flood, a professional baseball player and a member of the first class was denied the protection of those same federal antitrust laws, Flood was arguably denied equal protection under the law.

Marshall's view was that the existing anomaly denied Flood the right to compete freely and effectively, a right guaranteed by the federal antitrust laws.

"...We do not lightly overrule our prior constructions of federal statutes, *but when our errors deny substantial federal rights, like the right to compete freely and effectively* to the best of one's ability as *guaranteed by the antitrust laws, we must admit our error* and correct it. We have done so before and we should do so again here...."

Marshall, like Douglas, was equally critical of the majority's conclusion that Congress, by its failure to pass "corrective legislation", had acquiesced in the Supreme Court's decisions in *Federal Baseball* and *Toolson*.

"Had Congress acquiesced in our decisions in *Federal Baseball* and *Toolson*? I think not. Had the *Court* been consistent and treated *all sports* in the same way baseball was treated, Congress might have become concerned enough to take action. But the *Court* was *inconsistent*, and baseball was isolated and distinguished from all other sports. In *Toolson*, the Court refused to act because Congress had been silent. *But the Court may have read too much into this legislative inaction.*

Americans love baseball as they love all sports. Perhaps we become so enamored with athletics that *we assume that they are foremost in the minds of legislators* as well as fans.

We must not forget, however, that there are only some 600 major league baseball players.

Whatever muscle they might have been able to muster by combining forces with other athletes has been greatly impaired by the manner in which the Court has isolated them. *It is this Court that has made them impotent, and this Court should correct its error."*

Marshall also addressed the so-called "reliance" issue. At trial, a parade of club owners testified that they were entitled to and specifically "relied" upon the *Toolson* decision when they invested in their respective professional baseball teams. It was grotesquely audacious for a group of baseball club owners to claim that *Toolson* was somehow sacrosanct, and that professional baseball was entitled to rely upon that holding *in perpetuity*. In fact, two of the baseball club owners—Francis Dale and Robert Reynolds—testified that they had simultaneously made large financial investments in professional *football* teams, and that they knew professional football enjoyed no such antitrust immunity. To Marshall, this "problem" of reliance was not insurmountable.

"To the extent that there is concern over any reliance interests that club owners may assert, they can be satisfied *by making our decision prospective only*. Baseball should be covered by the antitrust laws *beginning with this case* and henceforth, unless Congress decides otherwise."

In the final portion of his dissent, Marshall correctly pointed out that even if *Toolson* and *Federal Baseball* were overruled and, consequently, professional baseball were subject to federal antitrust regulation, Flood would *not automatically* win the case and would *not automatically* become a free agent. Marshall accurately noted that the lower courts had decided that professional baseball was *exempt* from federal antitrust regulation; and that therefore, the lower courts never reached the question and never decided *whether* the facts presented in *Flood v. Kuhn* constituted a federal antitrust violation.

"...Accordingly, I would overrule *Federal Baseball*...and *Toolson* and reverse the decision of the Court of Appeals. This does not mean that petitioner [Flood] would necessarily prevail, however. Lurking in the background is a hurdle of recent vintage that petitioner still must overcome.... Respondents [club owners] argue that the reserve system is now part and parcel of the collective bargaining agreement and that because it is a mandatory subject of bargaining, the federal labor statutes are applicable, not the federal antitrust laws. The lower courts did not rule on this

CHAPTER 26: THE UNITED STATES SUPREME COURT

argument, *having decided the case solely on the basis of the antitrust exemption*....In light of these circumstances, I would remand this case to the District Court for consideration of *whether petitioner* [Flood] can state a claim under the antitrust laws despite the collective bargaining agreement, *and, if so,* for a determination of *whether there has been an antitrust violation* in this case."

The United States Supreme Court had spoken—and professional baseball remained exempt from federal antitrust regulation. Professional baseball had won, but its victory would be short lived.

Chapter 27
The Aftermath of Flood v. Kuhn and the Era of Free Agency

In the inevitable analysis of "winners and losers", Curt Flood had lost and major league baseball had indeed won a victory. For Flood, his stance cost him the remainder of his professional baseball career; he was financially ruined; his personal life was in shambles; and he was banished from baseball. To the baseball establishment, he was an ingrate and a traitor.

Major league baseball, on the other hand, had won a victory in the courts. As a result, a professional baseball player was still bound to the team that he originally signed with for the remainder of his playing career. The player could still be traded or sold without his consent. Unless unconditionally released by his club, a player could never become a free agent. But things were about to change. Three year later, by 1975, the era of free agency in baseball would emerge and would rock professional baseball—a result that would not have occurred but for Curt Flood and his "loss" in *Flood v. Kuhn*. Amazingly, the era of free agency in professional baseball would come about *without the Supreme Court reversing Toolson* and *Federal Baseball; and without* Congress passing a law sub-

Chapter 27: The Aftermath of Flood v. Kuhn and the Era of Free Agency

jecting baseball to federal antitrust regulation—or legislation of any kind.

The 1970 Basic Agreement

In the chain of events that led to free agency in professional baseball, the single most important development was the concession obtained in collective bargaining by the Players Association in 1970—impartial grievance arbitration. This change was obtained during the negotiations between the club owners and the Players' Association and became a part of the 1970 Basic Agreement. These particular negotiations were concluded after Flood had filed his suit but before the trial began in May 1970. If the Commissioner of Baseball, a paid employee of the club owners, had the right and the power to decide the meaning of a provision of the collective bargaining agreement, it would be difficult if not impossible for the owners to maintain in court that professional baseball was governed impartially. With the pressure of Flood's pending suit, and a keen awareness and appreciation of what was at stake, the owners had to concede that any disagreement regarding or any interpretation of the collective bargaining agreement between the Players' Association and the club owners would be resolved by impartial, binding arbitration.

In other words, for the first time in the history of professional baseball, there was now a set of issues and grievances which would no longer be decided (and only decided) by the Commissioner of Baseball. These grievances would now be decided by someone other than the Commissioner, and the decision of this impartial arbitrator was *binding* on both the owners and the players. While the lawyers for the club owners and Commissioner Kuhn fully understood the potential significance of impartial, binding arbitration in 1970, it would be several years before the owners would fully experience its impact. Professional baseball's "victory" two years later in *Flood v. Kuhn* (1972) would merely provide the owners with a false sense of security.

The First Free Agent—Jim "Catfish" Hunter

In the late 1960s and early 1970s, Jim "Catfish" Hunter was a star pitcher for the Oakland A's. The A's had an outstanding team and won three consecutive World Championships, beating the Reds in 1972, the Mets in 1973 and the Dodgers in 1974. Following the 1973 season, Hunter negotiated a contract for the 1974 season with the A's owner, Charles Finley. Hunter's contract for the 1974 season called for a salary of $100,000, half of which was to be paid as salary, and the other $50,000 was for the purchase of a tax deferred annuity from a life insurance company designated by Hunter. This financial arrangement would allow Hunter to reduce his taxable income while he was an active player.

Sometime during the 1974 season, Hunter learned that Finley had not purchased the annuity as agreed to in his contract for the 1974 playing season. Hunter was advised that Finley's failure to purchase the annuity was a clear breach of the contract; and that unless Finley cured the breach in a timely manner, Hunter had the right to file a grievance, to terminate his contract with the A's and become a free agent.

Section 7(a) of the Uniform Player's Contract provided as follows:

"The *Player may terminate* this contract, upon written notice to the Club, *if the Club shall default in the payments to the Player* provided for in paragraph 2 hereof [payment for the Player's services] *or shall fail to perform any other obligation agreed to be performed by the Club* hereunder and if the Club shall fail to remedy such default within ten (10) days after the receipt by the Club of written notice of such default...."

CHAPTER 27: THE AFTERMATH OF FLOOD V. KUHN AND THE ERA OF FREE AGENCY

The provision in question preexisted the creation of the Players' Association and had been a part of the Uniform Player's Contract for many years.

With the assistance of the Players' Association, Hunter notified Finley in writing of the contract breach and demanded that Finley remedy the Club's default within ten days of the notice. For whatever reason, Finley never responded to this notice. On October 4, 1970, Dick Moss, counsel for the Players' Association, again wrote Finley, this time advising Finley that the contract was terminated due to the Club's default in making the deferred annuity payments in accordance with Hunter's contract for the 1974 playing season.

Upon receiving this written notice of termination, Finley purportedly tried to deliver a check for $50,000 later that same day to Hunter. By that time, the damage was done. The Players' Association filed a grievance for and on behalf of Hunter and against Finley and Major League Baseball demanding that Hunter be declared a free agent.

What was critically important, of course, was that prior to the 1970 Basic Agreement, Hunter would have had no place to go in order to seek a remedy or to file a grievance, except to the Commissioner of Baseball. Now, for the first, Hunter could pursue a formal grievance procedure, have the dispute decided by an impartial arbitrator, and have that decision be binding on the club and all of major league baseball. Obviously, it was a new day. The Major League Baseball Players' Association was organized and its strength relative to the club owners was growing. This particular grievance proceeding would have significant consequences.

Approximately ten weeks later, and after an extensive hearing and presentations by the parties, Arbitrator Peter Seitz rendered his decision on December 13, 1974. Seitz ruled that Finley's failure to make the deferred annuity payments was a material breach of the contract, and that

313

based upon the facts of the case, Hunter had a legally sufficient basis to terminate the contract. More importantly, Seitz ruled that Finley was obligated to pay Hunter the "deferred" $50,000 in the manner specified in the contract; that the contract between the A's and Hunter was terminated; *and that Hunter was thereby a free agent* and could negotiate a contract to play professional baseball with any major league team.

Hunter thereby became the first free agent in professional baseball. He was able to attain that status because an arbitrator had decided that the A's organization had breached its agreement and the remedy was that Hunter be deemed a free agent. Hunter did not attain that status as a result of an attack on the so called "reserve clause" or the purported right of the club owners to unilaterally renew a player's contract in perpetuity. That issue would be the subject matter of yet another arbitration—and soon.

The Cases of Andy Messersmith and Dave McNally

Other events in 1974 and 1975 provided the Major League Baseball Players' Association another opportunity to challenge the heart of baseball's reserve system, and set the stage for perhaps the single most important arbitration decision in the history of professional baseball. Paragraph 10(a) of the Uniform Player's Contract was the provision which allowed the club to *unilaterally* renew the contract of an unsigned player on that club. To the Players' Association, however, the issue which remained unresolved was whether the club's right to renew an unsigned player's contract was a right *for one year* and only one year; or whether the club owner retained the right to renew a player's contract *for the remainder of the player's baseball career.*

In 1974, thirty-year old Dodger pitcher, Andy Messersmith, signed a contract for $90,000 for that playing season.

CHAPTER 27: THE AFTERMATH OF FLOOD V. KUHN AND THE ERA OF FREE AGENCY

During the 1974 season, Messersmith had a record of 20 wins and 6 losses and led the Dodgers to the National League pennant. In his negotiations for the 1975 season, Messersmith and the Dodgers could not agree on a salary. In addition, Messersmith was seeking a provision pursuant to which he could "veto" his trade to another club. Dodger's owner, Walter O'Malley, refused to agree to the "trade veto" provision, and the Dodgers, pursuant to Paragraph 10(a), renewed Messersmith's contract for the 1975 season. Messersmith did not sign. During the 1975 season, Messersmith won 19 games and had an earned run average of 2.29.

Also, after the 1974 season, Dave McNally, a thirteen-year veteran Baltimore Oriole star pitcher, was traded to the Montreal Expos. McNally was unhappy with the Expos' offer for the 1975 season and he refused to sign his contract. After suffering an injury to his wrist and struggling with a 3-6 record, McNally, only two months into the season, decided to walked away from approximately $85,000 remaining in his contract for the 1975 season. Even though McNally was on "inactive status," (and not being paid), he was still "owned" by the Expos and could not take a job, for example, as a coach or manager for any other club without the consent of the Expos.

Although their circumstances were quite different, and Messersmith and McNally were at very different stages of their baseball careers, the Players' Association filed a grievance on the final day of the 1975 playing season. The grievance would seek to have the meaning of Paragraph 10(a) decided by an arbitrator. Obviously much was at stake. The owners immediately filed a suit in federal court seeking to enjoin the arbitration from going forward on the grounds that the contract renewal provision was not part of the basic agreement, and therefore, not subject to arbitration. The federal district court disagreed and denied the owners' injunction request.

Finally, the arbitration commenced. After three days of hearings and almost nine hundred pages of transcript, arbitrator Peter Seitz rendered his decision on December 23, 1975. Seitz's sixty-one page decision concluded that nothing in Paragraph 10(a) authorized the Uniform Player's Contract to be renewed for more than one year; and because Messersmith and McNally had already played out the club's option year, both players were free to negotiate a contract and play for any team in the league. In explaining his decision, Seitz, among other things, made reference to and distinguished the case of Curt Flood.

"It deserves emphasis that this decision strikes no blow emancipating players from claimed serfdom or involuntary servitude as alleged in the *Flood* case. It does not condemn the Reserve System presently in force on constitutional or moral grounds. It does not counsel or require that the System be changed to suit the predilections or preferences of an arbitrator acting as a Philosopher-King intent on imposing his own personal brand of industrial justice on the parties. It does no more than seek to interpret and apply provisions that are in the agreements of the parties. To go beyond this would be an act of quasi-judicial arrogance!"

Again, the owners immediately filed suit in the U.S. Federal District Court arguing that the decision was beyond the authority of the arbitrator. The owners lost this suit and lost on appeal to the U.S. Court of Appeals. When the club owners decided not to seek an appeal to the U.S. Supreme Court, Messersmith and McNally had officially and legally attained "free agent" status by challenging and defeating the very "reserve clause" that had been the reserve system's "choke hold" on professional baseball players for almost a century.

CHAPTER 27: THE AFTERMATH OF FLOOD V. KUHN AND THE ERA OF FREE AGENCY

With baseball's reserve system now effectively abolished, the 1976 season got off to a bumpy start with the owners "locking out" the players. Eventually, cooler heads prevailed and the club owners and the Players' Association ultimately negotiated a four year agreement which included and set forth the terms and conditions pursuant to which a player, if so desired, could become a free agent and offer his services to another club.

In the end, a system of free agency was adopted and implemented not as a result of a Supreme Court decision nor an Act of Congress, but rather by an agreement negotiated at the collective bargaining table.

The Curt Flood Act of 1998

In the years following the U.S. Supreme Court's 1972 decision in *Flood v. Kuhn*, and despite the fact that free agency had since been negotiated and was now incorporated into baseball's collective bargaining agreement, the *scope* of baseball's antitrust exemption continued to confront the federal courts. More precisely, the issue which lingered was whether the federal antitrust exemption applied to the entire business of professional baseball, or whether the federal antitrust exemption was limited to baseball's reserve system.

During the 1990s, various federal courts came to different conclusions with respect to this issue. The 1990s also saw the proliferation of baseball labor strife, including the strike of 1994 and the cancellation of the 1994 season and World Series. On January 20, 1997, after a long battle with throat cancer, Curt Flood died at the age of fifty-nine. On the very next day, legislation was introduced in the United States Senate—legislation which on October 27, 1998 was signed into law by President Clinton and became known as the Curt Flood Act of 1998. (Public Law #105-297)

As set forth in Section 2 of that Act:

"...[T]he purpose of this legislation [is] to state that *major league baseball players* are covered under the antitrust laws...." (emphasis added)

However, what the legislation also makes clear is that the federal antitrust laws do not apply to many other agreements and practices impacting major league baseball. For example, the Curt Flood Act of 1998 specifically exempts from antitrust regulation labor issues affecting umpires and minor league players; agreements and practices between the major leagues and minor leagues; professional baseball broadcasting rights; franchise ownership, expansion and relocation; and the relationship between the Commissioner of Baseball and the club owners.

It may well be argued that the Curt Flood Act of 1998 is limited in scope, narrow in its application and largely symbolic. What cannot be denied, however, is that nearly thirty years after Curt Flood was traded to the Philadelphia Phillies, the following declaration now appears in the laws of the United States:

"[M]ajor league baseball players will have the same rights under the antitrust laws as do other professional athletes...."

If you listen carefully, you can almost hear Curt Flood whispering "Thank you. That's all I was trying to say."

CHAPTER 28
CONCLUSIONS AND OBSERVATIONS

It is now nearly thirty-five years since the conclusion of the trial of *Flood v. Kuhn*. Some may deem my criticism and assessments of certain individuals involved in the Flood case as unfair or unduly harsh. Others may deem my commentary on the evidence, trial preparation and the arguments presented (or not presented) at trial as classic "armchair" and "Monday morning quarterbacking." If so, fair enough. That being said, I hereby submit the following questions and observations for future analysis, comment and evaluation.

1. Perhaps one of the most intriguing ironies in *Flood v. Kuhn* involves the lack of support by the major league baseball players for Curt Flood and his challenge to major league baseball. While Flood had the support of the union's executive committee members, and the union provided financial support and helped Flood pay his legal fees, not a single active player showed up in person at any one of the fifteen days of trial in New York City during May and June of 1970. In a telephone conversation with Marvin Miller in June 2003, Miller told me that he did not have any personal knowledge of any owner who may have threatened or intimidated players to refrain from showing support for Flood.

However, Miller was also quick to point out that the players knew that showing up at the trial to show solidarity and support for Flood "would not have been a good career move." Many former players have subsequently admitted that they knew Flood's stance would get him "blacklisted" by the owners, and that they simply did not have the courage stand up and support their colleague.

2. Marvin Miller spent a great deal of time and effort to get Arthur Goldberg to be Flood's trial counsel. Goldberg presented Flood as the case's very first witness, but was conspicuously absent from much of the remainder of the trial. The reason? Goldberg became the Democratic Party's nominee for Governor of New York in the 1970 election. Goldberg won the primary, but lost the general election. In his book, *A Whole Different Ball Game*, Miller noted that he would not have asked Goldberg to handle the Flood case had he known that Goldberg was going to run for Governor. Moreover, Miller wrote that he specifically asked Goldberg about his political aspirations and that Goldberg assured Miller that he had no intention to run for Governor. Did Goldberg's circumstances and his absences from the trial impact the outcome of the Flood case? While the answer to that inquiry will never be resolved, it was certainly another basis for Flood to feel like he had been "abandoned" by those who had previously committed their support.

3. In retrospect, I cannot help but wonder whether the presentation of the arguments or the result of the legal challenge to baseball's reserve system in the early 1970s would have been different if the plaintiff had not been Curt Flood, but rather the plaintiff was one of the white "superstars" of the same era such as Johnny Bench, Carl Yastrzemski, Sandy Koufax, Mickey Mantle, Brooks Robinson, Warren Spahn, Pete Rose, Jim Palmer, Roger Maris, Eddie Mathews,

CHAPTER 28: CONCLUSIONS AND OBSERVATIONS

Harmon Killebrew—just to mention a few. Conversely, would the result have been the same if the plaintiff had not been Curt Flood, but one of the many "non white" superstars of the day such as Willie Mays, Roberto Clemente, Elston Howard, Willie McCovey, Juan Marichal, Ernie Banks, Bob Gibson, Lou Brock, Hank Aaron, Frank Robinson, Willie Stargell, again, just to name a few?

Similarly, I wonder about the affect (both legal and practical) Curt Flood's "comeback" in 1971 with the Washington Senators may have had on his case. When Flood agreed to be traded to the Senators, the trial was over and his case was on appeal, but not yet decided by the Appellate Court. Although it could be argued that his legal case and position had not changed, the court certainly was aware that Flood had agreed to be traded within the very same reserve system that he was challenging in court; that by returning to play professional baseball and agreeing to be paid, Flood's "damages" had thereby been significantly reduced; and that when Flood subsequently "quit" the Senators in April 1971, Flood had indeed "retired himself." In other words, as a practical matter (not necessarily a legal one), there was no longer any "real case or controversy" and there was no longer any genuine urgency for the courts to decide the case of a player in the prime of his career allegedly being denied his livelihood. Rather, the case may have been perceived (unofficially) by the courts as a suit brought by a former (now retired) player challenging the legality of a system which now only affected him indirectly.

Flood's comeback may have also made it easier for the courts and the press to characterize his lawsuit as the complaint of a single "disgruntled" former player who was irritated at being "mistreated" and unappreciated by his former team. In light of this single player's complaint, why should the court feel compelled to throw out a system that had been in existence and served major league baseball for nearly a hundred years? The perception that this was a "single disgruntled player's suit" may have even been reinforced by the absence of any active player testifying at trial or even attending the trial.

4. As he discusses in *Hardball: The Education of a Baseball Commissioner*, Commissioner Bowie Kuhn's "view of the world" was that Marvin Miller "used" Curt Flood to further the interests of the Players' Association. Kuhn also suggested that Miller urged the Players' Association to support Flood in litigation that the Association, by law, could not undertake. It was Kuhn's assessment that the union, in 1970, was not yet strong enough to strike. According to Kuhn, modification of the reserve system was a mandatory subject of collective bargaining between the union and the club owners. If, as Kuhn surmised, Flood, *as an individual*, challenged baseball's reserve system, then Miller and the Players' Association would get "two bites at the apple"—first, the Flood litigation, and second, the collective bargaining process. According to Kuhn, Flood's litigation was a "godsend" to Marvin Miller and the union.

Like Bowie Kuhn, Phillies' General Manager John Quinn believed that Marvin Miller "talked Flood out of signing" with the Phillies, and instead convinced Flood to file the suit challenging baseball's reserve system. For what it's worth, Flood, in *The Way It Is*, directly and completely refuted those assertions, and specifically stated that Quinn's criticism of Miller on this point was both inaccurate and unfair.

5. In a suit of the magnitude and significance of *Flood v. Kuhn*, the choice of forum (or in which court to file the action) should have been no small consideration in trial strategy. Why was the suit filed in New York? Was it filed in New York simply as a convenience to Arthur Goldberg and his firm; or as a convenience to Marvin Miller and the Asso-

CHAPTER 28: CONCLUSIONS AND OBSERVATIONS

ciation? After all, Flood, a citizen of Missouri, could have filed the suit in any number of federal courts throughout the country. Was any consideration given to New York as the venue in contemplation of Goldberg running for Governor in 1970?

Another trial strategy issue which remains a mystery is the decision to waive Flood's right to a jury trial. Was it the potential length of the case that triggered that decision? Did Flood's lawyers believe that the case would be heard and decided in a shorter period of time if it were decided without a jury? After all, Flood had hopes of playing in the 1970 season. Whatever the reason or basis for the decision, it is not inconceivable that a jury may have been more sympathetic to Flood's circumstances, and the fact that professional baseball players were subject to a very different and far more restrictive set of rules than those which applied to every other major professional sport and athlete. Conversely, it is possible that a jury may not have been sympathetic at all to a professional baseball player making $90,000 annually.

6. Much to his credit, and nearly twenty years after *Flood v. Kuhn*, Marvin Miller criticized himself and identified what he described as mistakes—his mistakes. In *A Whole Different Ball Game*, Miller blamed himself for the lack of visible support for Flood by the players, and discussed his feelings surrounding Goldberg's "betrayal."

"...For one thing, the players themselves could have taken a more visible and active part in the trial. This may seem like a small point, but it was foolish to overlook the media appeal of big-name athletes. They could have been seen attending the trial, going in and out of the courthouse. That, I think, would have given the Players' Association more of a human look to the public and shown that ballplayers were capable of demonstrating courage and solidarity off the field as well as on.

Why didn't I encourage it? Well, for one thing the trial was held during the season, and I was reluctant to urge players to do anything that would distract them from their jobs. For another, it was in the back of my mind that a great many marginal players might be targets of owner revenge if Flood lost....To my knowledge, not one of them [players] attended a single session of the trial. This was as much my fault as the players....To be honest, I wasn't as certain of the unity and solidarity of the Association then as I became a few years later. By the time *Flood v. Kuhn* came to trial in 1970, I had been executive director only four years, and we had not been tested by our first strike.... Still, if I had to do it again, I'd do more to get players to show up in support of Flood. That was undoubtedly a failure of leadership—my leadership.... It was also true that many players didn't care. They may have wanted Flood to win, but they felt that they had their careers to be concerned with, and that was that.... Nevertheless, the fact that not one player showed up at the trial to demonstrate his support highlighted the "me-first" attitude that, regrettably, has always been a part of the game and perhaps a major element in our society as well."

Miller was equally as hard on himself with regard to his selection of trial counsel.

"...There's something else I should mention under the category of mistakes, and it, too, is traceable to me. Before retaining him, I had asked Arthur Goldberg point-blank if he intended to run for governor against Rockefeller, and he answered no. If he had said yes or equivocated, I would have sought a different counsel. I accepted what he said about not running and made no back-up plan in case he changed his mind. When he did change his mind, I should have retained someone else as lead counsel. For as the trial went on, he spent more and more time campaigning and less on *Flood v. Kuhn*. I can't say this crippled us; Jay Topkis became, for all intents and purposes, the lead attorney of the case, and he is a brilliant lawyer. But I can't say the distraction of our chief counsel helped all that much, either.

Later, after he lost the election, Goldberg went back to Washington and established his own firm, eventually deciding to argue *Flood v. Kuhn* for us before the Supreme Court. Though I never told Arthur so, I felt he had betrayed us by deciding to run for governor—or more to the point, by not telling us he might change his mind and run—but I didn't feel we were in any position to turn down a lawyer of his stature when the case went before the Supreme Court. I guess I underestimated the allure of political office even to a man like Goldberg."

Regarding his "failure" to get the players to attend the trial and show support for Flood, Miller's assessment of blame was genuine and his self criticism was admirable. However, the fact of the matter was that in 1970, most of the players did not truly understand the magnitude of Flood's case, nor was the union's membership as unified as it would later become in its labor fights with the owners. In that sense, Miller's harsh self criticism is not completely justified.

Finally, Miller's discussion of Arthur Goldberg and the "betrayal" also highlights a view maintained by many. Throughout the discussion, Miller repeatedly refers to *his* decision to retain Goldberg; the effect of Goldberg's decision to run for governor on *our* suit; and Goldberg's betrayal of *us*. To some, Miller's observations—made twenty years after *Flood v. Kuhn*—only reinforce the conclusion that *Flood v. Kuhn*, whether intentionally or inadvertently, was the union's case and not that of Curt Flood.

7. Some commentators have concluded that the Major League Baseball Players' Association did everything in its

power to help Curt Flood in *his* challenge to major league baseball's reserve system. The reality is that the union's participation in the case, the manner and substance of Marvin Miller's testimony, and the presentation of the *union's* proposed modifications to the reserve system *during the presentation of the evidence in Flood's case* merely blurred the issues—all to the detriment of Curt Flood.

Flood's theory of the case was that baseball's reserve system was illegal in its totality. Yet all of the witnesses called in Flood's case testified that the reserve system needed to be modified, not abolished. None of the modifications to the reserve system identified and proposed by the union during the trial of *Flood v. Kuhn* would have or could have resulted in Flood being declared a free agent and available to play professional baseball in the 1970 season.

What Flood needed was someone to advocate *his* interests, and the execution of a trial strategy that presented *his* issues and *his* arguments—not those of the Players' Association. What Flood could have (and perhaps should have) argued was that the reserve system was part of the overall operating agreement between the owners and the Players' Association, and that its terms and conditions were being enforced by *both* sides against Curt Flood. As a result, the union and the owners were co-conspirators, and that the actions of these co-conspirators in furtherance of and in the implementation of baseball's reserve system were illegal and violated Curt Flood's rights under federal law. No agreement, irrespective of whether that agreement is the product or result of collective bargaining, may operate to deprive Curt Flood of his rights under law nor shall any such agreement be exempt from federal antitrust enforcement. What happened at trial, of course, was a very different story. Perhaps without malice, Flood's case was "hijacked" by the union's interests to his detriment. What was actually presented by Flood's lawyers were two competing and irrecon-

CHAPTER 28: CONCLUSIONS AND OBSERVATIONS

cilable positions. The blurred trial record and the simultaneous presentation of inconsistent arguments by Flood's lawyers provided the federal courts another basis to arrive at a conclusion to "leave professional baseball alone" and to "avoid deciding" the merits of Flood's case. While it is conceivable that the federal courts may have still ruled against Curt Flood and in favor of major league baseball, the presentation of Flood's case was botched.

8. The Supreme Court's rationale and its decision in *Flood v. Kuhn* certainly did not represent one of the Court's finest hours. On the merits, the Court did not and could not state a legal distinction between professional baseball and any other professional sport; expressly admitted that the distinction was illogical and inconsistent; and in the end, ruled that it was up to Congress to "right" the "wrong" created by the Court itself. It was a classic "non-decision," and not a candidate for a new chapter in "Profiles in Courage". Some have boldly suggested that the Supreme Court simply decided to "duck" this tough and controversial issue.

Strangely, and by way of contrast, it should be noted that the membership of the Supreme Court that decided *Flood v. Kuhn* was the same as when the Supreme Court decided some of the most controversial and important cases of the era. Perhaps most notably, *Flood v. Kuhn* was argued during the same term of the Supreme Court as was the 1973 landmark abortion rights case of *Roe v. Wade*. Moreover, this was the same membership that decided (unanimously) against the President of the United States in the Watergate tapes case of *Nixon v. United States*—resulting in the resignation of a sitting President. Indeed, this was a group of individuals that was capable of rendering important decisions in "tough cases", and had not shied away from doing so. Its decision in *Flood v. Kuhn*, however, was a notable exception.

REFERENCES AND SOURCES

Legal Bases: Baseball and the Law, Roger I. Abrams
    Temple University Press, 1998

The Business of Major League Baseball, George W. Scully
    The University of Chicago Press, 1989

The Way It Is, Curt Flood with Richard Carter
    Trident Press, New York, 1970

A Whole Different Ball Game, Marvin Miller
    Simon & Schuster, 1991

Hardball: The Education of a Baseball Commissioner, Bowie Kuhn
    University of Nebraska Press, 1987

Memoirs of Bing Devine; Stealing Lou Brock & Other Winning Moves by a Master G.M., Bing Devine with Tom Wheatley
    Sports Publishing, Inc., 2004

The Brethren, Scott Armstrong and Bob Woodward
    Simon and Schuster, 1979

Baseball and Billions, Andrew Zimbalist
    Basic Books, 1992

Trial transcript of <u>Flood v. Kuhn</u>, et al.
    (May 19, 1970—June 10, 1970)

Transcript of oral arguments in <u>Flood v. Kuhn</u> before the U.S. Supreme Court, March 20, 1972

CASES

Federal Baseball Club of Baltimore, Inc. v. National League of Professional Baseball Clubs (Federal Baseball) 259 U.S. 200 (1922).

Gardella v. Chandler, 172 F.2d 402 (1949).

Toolson v. New York Yankees, Inc., 346 U.S. 356 (1953).

United States v. International Boxing Club, 348 U.S. 236 (1955).

United States v. Shubert, 348 U.S. 222 (1955).

Radovich v. National Football League, 352 U.S. 445 (1957).

Salerno v. American League of Professional Baseball Clubs, 429 F.2d 1003 (1970); cert denied 400 U.S. 1001 (1971).

Haywood v. National Basketball Association, 401 U.S. 1204 (1971).

Flood v. Kuhn, 316 F.Supp. 271 (1970); 443 F.2d (1971); 407 U.S. 258 (1972).

BASEBALL'S RESERVE SYSTEM: THE CASE AND TRIAL OF CURT FLOOD V. MAJOR LEAGUE BASEBALL

ANSWERS TO TRIVIA QUESTIONS

1. Page 8—   Ray Sadecki

2. Page 12—   Joe Torre

3. Page 113—   Super Bowl I—January 15, 1967
               Green Bay 35—Kansas City 10

               Super Bowl II—January 14, 1968
               Green Bay 33—Oakland 14

               Super Bowl III—January 12, 1969
               New York Jets 16—Baltimore 7

               Super Bowl IV—January 11, 1970
               Kansas City 23—Minnesota 7

4. Page 126—   St. Louis Blues   Minnesota North Stars
               Philadelphia Flyers California Golden Seals
               Pittsburgh Penguins Los Angeles Kings

5. Page 165—   Giants, Dodgers, Cardinals, Yankees

AUTHOR

Neil Flynn was born and raised in St. Louis, Missouri. He attended St. Philip Neri grade school; attended McBride High School and graduated from St. Louis University High School in 1972; graduated from Western Illinois University in 1975 and from the St. Louis University School of Law in 1980. The 52 year-old author lives and practices law in Springfield, Illinois.

AUTHOR

Jeff Ryan was born and raised in St. Louis, Missouri. He attended St. Philip Neri grade school, Little Flower, and Kenrick High School and graduated from St. Louis University Law School in 1971, graduated from St. Louis University in 1973 and both the St. Louis University School of Law in 1984. He is 52 years old attorney now and practices law in Springfield, Illinois.